Authoritarianism and Polarization in American Politics

Although politics at the elite level has been polarized for some time, a scholarly controversy has raged over whether ordinary Americans are polarized. This book argues that they are and that the reason is growing polarization of worldviews – what guides people's view of right and wrong and good and evil. These differences in worldview are rooted in what Marc J. Hetherington and Jonathan D. Weiler describe as authoritarianism. They show that differences of opinion concerning the most provocative issues on the contemporary issue agenda – about race, gay marriage, illegal immigration, and the use of force to resolve security problems – reflect differences in individuals' levels of authoritarianism. This makes authoritarianism an especially compelling explanation of contemporary American politics. Events and strategic political decisions have conspired to make all these considerations more salient. The authors demonstrate that the left and the right have coalesced around these opposing worldviews, which has provided politics with more incandescent hues than before.

Marc J. Hetherington is currently professor of political science at Vanderbilt University. In 2004 he was awarded the ~~Emerging~~ Scholar Award from the Public Opinion, Elections, and Voting Behavior Section of the American Political Science Association for his scholarly contribution within his first ten years in the profession. He is also the author of *Why Trust Matters: Declining Political Trust and the Demise of American Liberalism* and numerous articles that have appeared in *American Political Science Review, American Journal of Political Science, Journal of Politics, British Journal of Political Science,* and *Public Opinion Quarterly*.

Jonathan D. Weiler is currently director of undergraduate studies and adjunct assistant professor of international and area studies at the University of North Carolina at Chapel Hill. His previous book, *Human Right in Russia: A Darker Side of Reform*, was published in 2004. He blogs daily about politics and sports at www.jonathanweiler.com.

Authoritarianism and Polarization in American Politics

MARC J. HETHERINGTON
Vanderbilt University

JONATHAN D.WEILER
University of North Carolina

CAMBRIDGE
UNIVERSITY PRESS

CAMBRIDGE UNIVERSITY PRESS
Cambridge, New York, Melbourne, Madrid, Cape Town, Singapore,
São Paulo, Delhi, Dubai, Tokyo

Cambridge University Press
32 Avenue of the Americas, New York, NY 10013-2473, USA

www.cambridge.org
Information on this title: www.cambridge.org/9780521711241

First published 2009
Reprinted 2010

Printed in the United States of America

A catalog record for this publication is available from the British Library.

Library of Congress Cataloging in Publication data
Hetherington, Marc J., 1968–
    Authoritarianism and polarization in American politics /
    Marc J. Hetherington, Jonathan D. Weiler.
        p.   cm.
    Includes index.
    ISBN 978-0-521-88433-4 (hardback) – ISBN 978-0-521-71124-1 (pbk.)
    1. Authoritarianism – United States. 2. United States – Politics and government – 2001–
    3. Right and left (Political science) – Case studies. 4. Polarization (Social sciences) – Case
    studies. I. Weiler, Jonathan Daniel, 1965– II. Title.
    E902.H48 2009
    303.3´6–dc22   2009004019

ISBN 978-0-521-88433-4 Hardback
ISBN 978-0-521-71124-1 Paperback

To Mom, Dad, Suzanne, Ben, and Sammy, with all my love.

MH

*To the memory of my father, Lawrence Weiler (1919–1973),
as humane and decent a man as I have ever known.*

JW

Contents

Acknowledgments

This work is both conventional, in its focus on polarization, and unconventional, in its focus on authoritarianism. We hope that in some way it hearkens to an earlier period when scholars attempted to appeal to a wide audience and drew on a range of different scholarly approaches. Our shared time at Bowdoin College, a small liberal arts college with an incredibly talented and broadly interested faculty, informs this hope. In various ways, Eric Chown (Computer Science), Matt Lassiter (History), Joe Bandy (Sociology), Joe Lane (Government and Legal Studies, our old home department), and Pete Coviello (English) all took an interest in this work and shaped our thinking.

We owe an especially large debt of gratitude to Jim Stimson. His scholarly work on issue evolution, co-authored with Ted Carmines, served as an important guide. Jim was also generous with his time, meeting with Jonathan in the early stages of our work. These conversations helped orient us and also helped give us confidence that we were pursuing something worthwhile. Jim also championed our project, bringing us together with the tremendous group of people at Cambridge University Press, notably Eric Crahan and Emily Spangler. In that sense, Jim both helped get us started and helped us finish.

Hetherington has an army of people to thank. Bob Luskin trained him to be a political scientist and continues to push him to be better. Many people in the Department of Political Science at Vanderbilt University read parts of the book and offered helpful feedback, including Bruce Oppenheimer, John Geer, Brooke Ackerly, Christian Grose, Pam Corley, Florence Faucher-King, Stefanie Lindquist, Neal Tate, Carol Swain, Brett Benson, Michaela Mattes, Cindy Kam, and Liz Zechmeister. James Booth, in particular, worked hard to help with the normative elements of this delicate work. Mitch Seligson was also particularly generous in his inclusion of a number of survey items that allowed us to write Chapter 9. Vanderbilt also provided the funding for a semester's leave, which helped get the project moving.

People from outside the Vanderbilt community were also helpful. Paul Sniderman introduced us to the concept of authoritarianism. Jon Hurwitz was central in encouraging us to think about authoritarianism in terms of cognition rather than emotion. Mike Nelson provided a painstaking reading of the manuscript, giving helpful suggestions on style and substance. Chapter 2 of this book is a much revised version of a review article on polarization that Larry Bartels and Fred Greenstein encouraged Hetherington to write. Without this encouragement, it is unclear whether we would have even pursued this book-length project. The article was ultimately published in the *British Journal of Political Science*; thanks to Cambridge Journals for its permission to use it. Larry's and Fred's interest and mentorship has always meant so much personally and been such a benefit professionally. Hetherington would also like to thank John Zaller, Mo Fiorina, Marty Gilens, Geoff Layman, Alan Abramowitz, Stanley Feldman, Howard Lavine, Mark Peffley, Harold Stanley, Markus Prior, Sunshine Hillygus, Nolan McCarty, Paul Goren, David Barker, Steve Finkel, Jane Junn, Cas Mudde, Adam Berinsky, Lynn Vavreck, Jeff Stonecash, Bill Bishop, Joe Smith, John Nugent, Jasmine Farrier, and John Cogan, all of whom provided help along the way.

Hetherington would also like to thank the institutions that invited him for talks and conferences, which provided invaluable feedback. This process started in 2006 with a visit to his alma mater, the University of Pittsburgh, and continued later that fall at the University of Texas at Austin, where he earned his Ph.D. This list also includes the University of North Carolina–Chapel Hill, the Hoover Institute at Stanford University, the Center for the Study of Democratic Politics at Princeton University, and the Ash Institute at Harvard University's Kennedy School of Government. Mike MacKuen at North Carolina was particularly generous with his time and helpful with his comments, as was David King at Harvard.

Hetherington also thanks Linda Wirth, Pete Swarr, Kimberly Bergeron, Pat Goetz, Fleeta Holt, Valerie Holzer, and Dee Moore for all their help. Terrific research assistance was provided by Jeremiah Garretson, Jason Husser, John Hudak, Grace Radcliff, Sarah Hinde, Corey Bike, Jennifer Anderson, and Matt Simpson across the many years that this project has been under way.

As always, Hetherington owes the greatest debt to his family. His mom and dad have always been his greatest supporters. These two remarkable and determined people have been an inspiration, especially when the going has gotten tough. His wife, Suzanne Globetti, did everything imaginable to make this project a success. She has always been willing to make the sacrifices that have allowed him to write his books and articles. Moreover, she always has taken the time to make his work better. This second book project has been more challenging than the first, but Suzanne, as always, managed to smooth out the bumps in the road. Finally, Ben and Sammy – the two most special little boys in the world – were always patient with their old man when he was writing. Better yet, they helped him to smile all the way through it.

Weiler has a handful of additional people to add to the list. Jay Barth provided valuable help and insight, particularly in his comments on Chapter 4. He also generously invited Jonathan to speak about the project at Hendrix

College. Dr. Robert Jenkins, director of the Center for Slavic, Eurasian and East European Studies at UNC Chapel Hill, generously provided Weiler with conference travel funds in 2005 to co-present an early version of the current work. Anne Menkens, the best ex-wife anyone could hope to have, provided valuable editorial assistance and has always been an unwavering supporter. His mom, Alexandra, is the source of whatever moral compass and compassion he has, and his sister, Nina, has been a faithful ally in a shared worldview. And last, and always most, to his daughter, Lillian, the light of his life.

Spanking or Time Out: A Clash of Worldviews?

In September 2004, National Public Radio's late afternoon news show, *All Things Considered*, visited West Virginia to interview potential voters. The state had gone to George W. Bush in 2000, marking a departure from its typical voting pattern. Between 1932 and 1996, Republicans won West Virginia only three times (1956, 1972, and 1984), and each victory was part of an overwhelming Republican landslide. Even in 1980, when Democrat Jimmy Carter carried a mere six states, one of them was West Virginia. Democrats have dominated the state's congressional delegation for decades. In 2000, both U.S. Senators, Robert Byrd and Jay Rockefeller were Democrats, and two of the state's three congressional districts were represented by longtime Democratic incumbents. Bush's victory, moreover, was substantively important. Had West Virginia voted Democratic as was typical, Al Gore would have been elected president with 271 electoral votes.

One of reporter Brian Naylor's interviews on NPR was with a truck driver named Mark Methany. With the September 11 terrorist attacks only three years in the past, the candidates' relative ability to deal with foreign threats and terrorism was, not surprisingly, on Methany's mind. The way he talked about the issue, however, was a bit surprising. In sizing up the contest between Bush and Democratic Senator John Kerry of Massachusetts, Methany said, "I really think that [George Bush] is the man for the job to face down our enemy. He won't just give [Osama bin Laden] a time out. He'll smack him in the mouth."[1]

Bush as tough and Kerry as wimp were familiar campaign personas in 2004. Such personas fit into larger themes of the parties and their respective "manliness." MSNBC's Chris Matthews, host of the popular political talk show, *Hardball*, has dubbed the Democratic Party the "Mommy Party" and the Republican Party the "Daddy Party." Arnold Schwarzenegger, the

---

[1] "Democrats Seek to Return West Virginia to the Fold," *All Things Considered*, September 21, 2004.

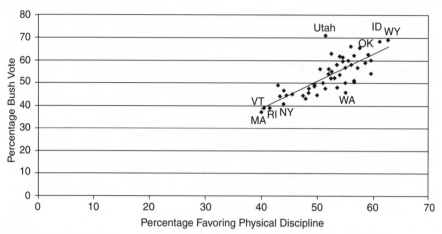

FIGURE 1.1. Bush Vote as a Function of Willingness to Physically Discipline Children, by State

Republican governor of California, referred to his Democratic opponents in the state legislature as "girlie men" who needed to be "terminated." In a similar vein, Ann Coulter, the combative conservative commentator, told Bill O'Reilly, host of Fox News' highly rated talk show *The O'Reilly Factor*, that she "[is] more of a man than any liberal."[2] These labels suggest, of course, that Democrats are softer, providing the public things like compassion and affection, while Republicans are harder, providing things like toughness, protection, and discipline.

In Figure 1.1, we present more systematic evidence that the parental allusions of Methany, the West Virginia truck driver, and Matthews, the television pundit, have taken root in the American electorate. In the months before the 2004 election, Survey USA, a national survey firm, asked random samples of people from all fifty states whether they approved or disapproved of various forms of physical discipline for children, such as spanking them or washing out their mouths with soap.[3] In the figure, the percentage of people from each state favoring these forms of physical discipline is plotted on the *x*-axis and the percentage of people in that state who voted for George W. Bush is plotted on the *y*-axis.

The correlation between traditional parenting practices – the "spare the rod, spoil the child" approach – and voting for President Bush in 2004 is remarkably strong. Massachusetts is home to both the lowest percentage of people who endorse using physical means to discipline children and the lowest percentage of the vote for Bush. People in other states that voted strongly for Kerry, such as Vermont, Rhode Island, and New York, are also among the least likely to

---

[2] Coulter appeared on the *O'Reilly Factor* on June 28, 2007.
[3] These surveys were conducted August 12–14, 2005.

endorse spanking children and washing out their mouths with soap. In contrast, a higher percentage of people in states like Idaho, Wyoming, and Oklahoma both advocate a traditional approach to disciplining children and voted more heavily for Bush. Indeed, each of the top nine corporal punishment states is a Republican presidential stronghold in early twenty-first-century America. These states cluster, for the most part, in the Rocky Mountains (Wyoming, Idaho, and Montana), the South (Arkansas, Alabama, and Tennessee), and the Great Plains (Oklahoma and Kansas), with one state (Indiana) in the Midwest.[4]

Of course, we do not argue that preferences for disciplining children are *causally* related to individuals' vote choice. It is absurd to think that spanking children led people to vote Republican in 2004. Indeed, if favoring corporal punishment actually caused people to vote for the more conservative candidate, liberals never would have been elected president. It is only very recently that alternatives to spanking children have been widely employed. Instead, support for spanking likely emanates from a particular worldview that has a range of ramifications, including political ones.[5]

By worldview, we mean a set of connected beliefs animated by some fundamental, underlying value orientation that is itself connected to a visceral sense of right and wrong. Politics cleaved by a worldview has the potential for fiery disagreements because considerations about the correct way to lead a good life lie in the balance. Specifically, we demonstrate that American public opinion is increasingly divided along a cleavage that things like parenting styles and "manliness" map onto. We will call that cleavage authoritarianism.

WHAT IS AUTHORITARIANISM?

The scholarly literature on authoritarianism is vast, but we focus on a relatively small handful of considerations often associated with it, which are particularly germane to understanding political conflict in contemporary American politics. Those who score high in authoritarianism tend to have a different cognitive style than those who score low. The former tend to view the world in more concrete, black and white terms (Altemeyer 1996; Stenner 2005). This is probably because they have a greater than average need for order. In contrast, those who score lower in authoritarianism have more comfort with ambiguous shades of gray, which allow for more nuanced judgments.

---

[4] The one noteworthy outlier in the figure is Utah. No state voted more loyally for Bush, but it is in the middle of the pack as far as the percentage of residents favoring physically disciplining children. This may be because the Mormon Church, a dominant force in the state, is quite conservative politically but makes it clear to members that they should not employ corporal punishment. Indeed, if we eliminate Utah from the analysis because of the influence of Mormon teachings, the correlation between preference for physical punishment and Bush vote in 2004 jumps from .79 to .83, a very strong relationship.

[5] It is also worth noting that the level of measurement is problematic. These data are measured at the state level, but individuals, not states, cast votes. Indeed, African Americans are among the most likely to endorse corporal punishment and among the least likely to vote Republican.

Perhaps because of these cognitive differences, people who are more authoritarian make stronger than average distinctions between in-groups – the groups they identify with – and out-groups – groups that they perceive challenge them. Such a tendency has the effect of imposing order and minimizing ambiguity. In addition, those who are more authoritarian embrace and work to protect existing social norms (Feldman 2003). These conventions are time-tested in their ability to maintain order. Altering norms could result in unpredictable changes with undesirable consequences.

Since the more authoritarian view the social order as fragile and under attack (Altemeyer 1996), they tend to feel negatively about, behave aggressively toward, and be intolerant of those whom they perceive violate time-honored norms or fail to adhere to established social conventions (Stenner 2005). Specifically, scholars have shown a strong relationship between authoritarianism and negative affect toward many minority groups. Over the past fifty years, these groups have included Jews (Adorno et al. 1950; but see Raden 1999), African Americans (Sniderman and Piazza 1993), gays (Barker and Tinnick 2006), and Arabs after September 11 (Huddy et al. 2005).[6]

Authoritarianism is a particularly attractive explanation for changes in contemporary American politics because it structures opinions about both domestic and foreign policy issues. In addition to having concerns about racial difference and social change, those who are more authoritarian tend to prefer more muscular responses to threats than those who are less. A proverbial punch to the mouth of an adversary results in a less ambiguous outcome than, say, negotiation or diplomacy. Not surprisingly, scholars have consistently drawn links between authoritarianism and a hawkish attitude toward foreign policy and resolution of conflict (Lipset 1959; Eckhardt and Newcombe 1969; Altemeyer 1996; Perrin 2005). Those scoring high in authoritarianism were also more likely than those scoring low to support military action after the September 11 terrorist attacks (Huddy et al. 2005). Viewed as a whole, research on authoritarianism suggests that the same disposition that might dispose people to be anti-black or anti-gay might also dispose them to favor military conflict over diplomacy and protecting security over preserving civil liberties. A preference for order and a need to minimize ambiguity connects both impulses.

The events from another time in history provide suggestive evidence that the same disposition motivates both. Particularly in the early 1950s, Senator Joseph McCarthy set his sights not only on rooting communist elements out of the State Department and other government agencies. He also focused his

---

[6] Though some studies argue that there is an identifiable authoritarian personality type on the left as well as the right (Shils 1954; Rokeach 1960), most of the literature identifies authoritarianism as a conservative or right-wing phenomenon, as is clear from Jost et al.'s (2003) exhaustive review on conservatism as "motivated social cognition." Altemeyer (1996) argues, in fact, that there is no left-wing authoritarian phenomenon to speak of in contemporary North America comparable to right-wing authoritarianism.

attention, for a time, on purging homosexuals. McCarthy pointed to supposed links between communism and homosexuality, and his speeches often made passing reference to "Communists and queers" (Johnson 2004). Other conservative senators, including Styles Bridges, Kenneth Wherry, and Clyde Hoey, pressed the issue of homosexuality along with communism during the Red Scare as well.

All this suggests that preferences about many of the new issues on the American political agenda, such as gay rights, the war in Iraq, the proper response to terrorism, and immigration are likely structured by authoritarianism. These are all potentially divisive topics, characterized by deeply held, gut-level views. Although contemporary American politics is perhaps not polarized in a strict definitional sense, insofar as preferences are not clustering near the poles (Fiorina, Abrams, and Pope 2004), it undeniably *feels* different than it has for decades. We argue that this is because preferences about an increasing number of salient issues are structured by a deeply felt worldview, specifically authoritarianism. And the colliding conceptions of right and wrong embedded in the opposite ends of this continuum make it difficult for one side of the political debate to understand (perhaps, in the extreme, even respect) how the other side thinks and feels.

THE TERM "AUTHORITARIANISM"

The term *authoritarianism* certainly sounds pejorative and has often been used pejoratively. At a minimum, it conjures negative images, and research into it is often (rightly) criticized as hopelessly value-laden. When we asked our students to identify a person who was an authoritarian, they typically named leaders of authoritarian political regimes, past and present, such as Saddam Hussein, Kim Jong-Il, and Fidel Castro. One even identified Darth Vader. The scholarly literature tends to focus on followers rather than leaders, mostly painting an unflattering picture of authoritarians as angry people suffering from some cognitive defect, which causes them to blindly follow a Hussein, a Castro, or a Vader.

The term has, at times, been co-opted for political purposes. To cite one particularly high-profile recent example, John Dean (2006), former White House counsel under Richard Nixon and now a vocal critic of the Bush administration, penned a *New York Times* bestselling polemic, provocatively titled "Conservatives Without Conscience." It characterized George W. Bush as an authoritarian leader of weak-minded lemmings, a view that we do not share.[7] Indeed, it is not possible for scholars to know with any certainty how

---

[7] Although some of Bush's decisions are consistent with an authoritarian disposition, they have, by and large, centered in the foreign policy realm. This focus obscures areas where Bush's worldview seems nonauthoritarian. His position on immigration and affect toward Latinos departs from accepted understandings of authoritarianism. The same is true of his calls for tolerance toward Muslims in the United States in the aftermath of 9/11.

authoritarian political elites are because no data have been collected to measure it. In any event, it is likely that these dark, normative undertones have undermined authoritarianism's scholarly impact and have made it nearly impossible to discuss it in nonscholarly circles.

Given our concerns about the term, some may question why we continue to use it. First, it is not as though *all* the scholarly literature on the topic is problematic; much is carefully done and conceptually and methodologically rigorous. Indeed, many of the giants among professional political scientists and political historians, including Robert Lane, Seymour Martin Lipset, Herbert McClosky, and Richard Hoffstadter, employed this term at one time or another in their research. Second, our work makes use of and builds upon existing research that specifically uses the term *authoritarianism*. We found our efforts to substitute a less polarizing term, while retaining much of the conceptual framework, disorienting.[8] Had we found a suitable alternative, we would have gladly used it. Unfortunately, we did not.

Since the term authoritarianism carries unwanted baggage, we want to make clear from the outset that we are not arguing that all Republicans are authoritarians and all Democrats are not. That is far from true. Authoritarianism runs deep among some racial minorities, not to mention lower education and lower income whites – all traditional Democratic constituencies, though, importantly, decreasingly so, for lower education whites. In fact, we provide evidence in Chapter 9 that, among non-African Americans, a preference for Hillary Clinton or Barack Obama in the 2008 Democratic nomination struggle was in large part a function of authoritarianism. At first blush, this result might seem inconsistent with our argument that authoritarianism now structures interparty conflict, with Democrats now the nonauthoritarian party. On closer inspection, however, the importance of authoritarianism should come as no great shock, given the presence of a black candidate and the fact that the white working class, a disproportionately authoritarian group (see, e.g., Lipset 1959), figured prominently in the Clinton coalition. It should also remind us that party sorting on any issue or attitude is never likely to be complete.

As for differences in authoritarianism between Republicans and Democrats, the average distance is significant and increasing to be sure, but it is important not to exaggerate the magnitude of such attitudinal differences between mass partisans (Fiorina et al. 2004). Moreover, we show that the authoritarian divide we identify as having crystallized soon after the turn of the twenty-first century results from a sorting process in which both the average Democratic identifier is

---

[8] It is also worth noting that we explored the possibility of using negatively valenced terms to describe those scoring low in authoritarianism to balance the negative valence of the term *authoritarian*. One term we considered was *relativist*. Ultimately we decided that relativism might be a "characteristic" of someone scoring low in authoritarianism, but it was conceptually distinct from it. Conceptually, anarchist fits the bill better than relativist but the opposite end of our measure of authoritarianism, which we discuss in Chapter 3, does not tap anarchism.

becoming significantly less authoritarian and the average Republican identifier is becoming somewhat more so.

In that sense, our treatment of authoritarianism departs fundamentally from most others. Unlike most scholars, we do not focus on the supposed pathologies of "the authoritarian personality" or, to use a more up-to-date term, *authoritarian disposition*. Oftentimes, the real stars of our show are the less authoritarian (those scoring in the middle of the distribution) and the nonauthoritarian (those scoring toward the bottom of the distribution), whose preferences, we demonstrate, change under identifiable conditions such that they actually mirror those of authoritarians. Perceived threat, which supplies these identifiable conditions, plays a critical supporting role, but in a way that challenges the scholarly conventional wisdom. Using mostly experimental methods, scholars have often demonstrated that threat "activates" authoritarianism, causing those scoring high in authoritarianism to become less tolerant and more aggressive than usual. Conversely, threat supposedly causes nonauthoritarians to become more tolerant and principled. We challenge this reasoning. Such findings likely result from the fact that scholars have generally provided experimental subjects stimuli that are more threatening to those scoring high than low in authoritarianism (see Oxley et al. 2008). While these studies tell us a lot about who is more sensitive to threat, they tell us less about what happens when threat is perceived by people who score in different parts of the authoritarianism distribution.

When those scoring lower in authoritarianism do perceive significant threat, we find that they are not heroic, small "d," democrats. In fact, under such conditions, their preferences on issues become indistinguishable from those who score high in authoritarianism. Hence, when threat is perceived symmetrically across the distribution of authoritarianism, as seems to have occurred after the September 11 terrorist attacks, opinions converge on issues in which preferences are structured by authoritarianism. Real world manifestations of such convergences include the relatively high percentage of Americans willing to trade off civil liberties for security in late 2001 and 2002 and George W. Bush's stratospheric approval ratings during the same period.

Those scoring low in authoritarianism do not perceive much threat from groups such as gays and lesbians, blacks, or immigrants. When threat is perceived asymmetrically across the distribution of authoritarianism, as is the case with matters involving these relatively unpopular political minorities, a polarization of opinion results.[9] Our results in Chapter 7 reveal that as authoritarianism has become an important determinant of party identification in the early twenty-first century, it has produced a *partisan* polarization or sorting of preferences on a range of issues for which preferences are structured by authoritarianism. Provided threat continues to be perceived more by those scoring high in authoritarianism than those scoring low, this sorting process ought to deepen in the future. Although partisans were more divided on traditional

---

[9] As a matter of frequency, this ought to be the case much of the time because those scoring high in authoritarianism tend to feel threatened constantly (Altemeyer 1996).

New Deal issues than cultural issues in the late 1990s and early 2000s (Layman and Carsey 2002; Bartels 2006), it might not be the case forever. As sorting progresses along these lines, we expect that divisions on preferences structured by authoritarianism ought to continue to gain on those along the traditional New Deal cleavage.[10]

This interaction between perceived threat and authoritarianism also helps us understand recent dynamics in party competition. Our results suggest that those who score in the middle of the authoritarianism distribution (the less authoritarian) are particularly politically relevant in election campaigns. If they come to perceive significant threat from things like changing societal norms or the specter of world terrorism, their preferences on related issues move to the right, which ought to make them more sympathetic to Republican candidates. When they perceive less threat, their preferences swing toward the left, which ought to make them more sympathetic to Democratic candidates. In that sense, Barack Obama was probably correct in his assessment that the 2008 presidential election was a competition between hope and fear.

Importantly, our theory and results square with recent party fortunes. Since feelings of threat from terrorism were basically symmetric right after 9/11 (personal communication with Stanley Feldman), our theory would predict a convergence of preference on national security matters that would benefit Republicans. Of course, Republicans dominated the 2002 elections and fared quite well in 2004. As September 11 has become a more distant memory, however, those who score lower in authoritarianism have come to feel less threat from terrorism faster than those who score high. As a result, we have seen a surge in the Democrats' fortunes, not to mention at least a gradual increase in partisan polarization (Fiorina and Levundusky 2006; Abramowitz and Saunders 2008).

So, while some might hope to caricature our effort as an exercise in name-calling, such an attack would be unjustified. Our goal is not to deride one side of the political divide and, as a consequence, elevate the other. Rather, our goal is to demonstrate that many political choices are now, in part, structured by a potentially polarizing worldview, while they were not before. It is not authoritarians, per se, who are interesting, but rather it is the *concept* of authoritarianism that most merits close scrutiny.

AUTHORITARIANISM AND WORLDVIEW EVOLUTION

In situating authoritarianism near the center of the contemporary partisan divide, we borrow heavily from Carmines and Stimson's (1989) theory of issue evolution. An issue evolution occurs when a new issue potent enough to stir

---

[10] The financial crisis during the 2008 general election campaign surely had some impact on voting behavior and, as we note in Chapter 10, it is possible that a major financial upheaval could set in motion a newly evolved set of cleavages. We take up these issues in greater depth in the Epilogue.

passions cuts across the existing line of cleavage. The parties take distinct and opposing views on such issues, prompting ordinary Americans to follow suit. For example, race in the 1960s was the catalyst to an issue evolution which split the Democratic Party of the time into roughly northern and southern factions and prompted a reconfiguration of partisan battle lines – to the benefit of the Republican Party (GOP).

In this book, we document the rise of a number of sometimes diverse issues which, taken together, form a tapestry of reinforcing themes. Each issue, in its own way, threatens to unsettle the established way of life in America. As such, each issue threatens to upset how Americans view their country and themselves – in short, their *worldview*. This worldview taps into Americans' tolerance for difference, ambiguity, and order and is thus animated by authoritarianism. We therefore characterize American politics as undergoing a *worldview evolution* in which politics is increasingly contested over issues for which preferences are structured by authoritarianism. Rather than one dominant, critical issue dividing Republicans and Democrats as has traditionally been the case throughout American history (Sundquist 1983; Burnham 1970), we have a cluster of related issues for which authoritarianism provides the connective tissue.

The issues we have in mind start with race and the civil rights movement in the 1960s. As previously discussed, the issue of race proved sufficiently powerful that it evolved a new party system (Carmines and Stimson 1989). Although race initially worked to the Democrats' advantage in 1964, it became a Republican advantage in subsequent elections, with the GOP dominating the White House and later Congress in the decades that followed. Some scholars have charitably suggested that the white backlash against African Americans resulted from the belief that blacks violate time-honored norms of hard work and individual achievement (Kinder and Sears 1981; Huckfeldt and Kohfeld 1989; Kinder and Sanders 1996). Other scholars have more bluntly asserted a direct link between racial policy preferences and authoritarianism (Sniderman and Piazza 1993). Based on our understanding of authoritarianism, racial resentment justified in terms of norm violation is authoritarian in nature (see also Kinder and Sanders 1996, Chapter 9).

Similar to race, the battle over women's rights evokes notions of the proper societal order and threats to it. Increasingly women moved from their roles as housewives and protectors of the home fires into the workplace, causing a sea change in American life that directly affected a broad swath of Americans. More recently, gay rights have become centrally important in the 2000s. Again, whether or not people endorse gay marriage has much to do with their notions of time-honored traditions and norms in American life.

Race, women's issues, and gay issues are similar in nature, so it may seem logical that they cluster together on an authoritarian dimension. But there are other issues, which subsequently rose to national prominence, that may seem unrelated to these social issues but which are likely structured by authoritarianism as well. For example, the string of liberal decisions handed down by the

Warren Court in the 1950s and 1960s, particularly those involving criminal rights, have aroused great passions since Richard Nixon's presidency. Whether it is more important to protect the safety of citizens or the rights of the accused has divided Americans ever since. Patriotism and its symbols became central concerns in the 1984 presidential election campaign after Timothy Johnson burned an American flag outside the Republican National Convention. And, in 1988, whether or not school children should be required to say the Pledge of Allegiance played an important role. More recently, the war on terrorism has become an increasingly important part of the political landscape. Importantly, preferences for how best to deal with terrorist threats, whether forcefully or diplomatically, and what kinds of civil liberties citizens are willing to forgo to protect their safety are powerfully a function of authoritarianism, too.

To precipitate a worldview evolution, the major parties had to, over time, take distinct and opposing positions on these issues. Indeed, they have. The Democratic Party, formerly the main vehicle for segregation, is now the party of inclusion, both in terms of race (Carmines and Stimson 1989) and, more reluctantly, sexual orientation (Lindaman and Haider-Markel 2002). Republicans, over the last several decades, have evolved from the "party of Lincoln" on racial matters to the "states' rights" party. Most Republicans supported President Bush's endorsement of a constitutional amendment to ban gay marriage as well. On feminism, Republicans, starting in the 1980s, articulated a preference for more traditional norms, starting with their opposition to the Equal Rights Amendment in 1980 (Wolbrecht 2000). Democrats, in contrast, have championed a less traditional role for women. Despite the Democrats' best efforts, they have been tagged as the party that protects civil liberties while the Republicans are seen as the party that protects Americans' physical safety.

Although both parties adopted a tough, multilateral stance to confront the Soviet Union during the Cold War, the parties have more recently adopted different philosophies on foreign policy. Nowhere is this clearer than in their divergent approaches to a post-September 11 world. Republicans have shown a preference for the concreteness of armed conflict over the subtleties of diplomacy. Especially as the situation in Iraq began to deteriorate in mid to late 2004, Democrats articulated a more multilateral, diplomacy-heavy position with a firm emphasis on ending the U.S. commitment as soon as possible. It is telling that there were no doves among the leading Republicans, and there were no hawks among the leading Democrats in the quest for the 2008 presidential nomination.[11]

This authoritarianism-based worldview evolution apparently results more from campaign strategies adopted by conservative elites than liberal ones, a process we elaborate in Chapter 4. Although liberals complain bitterly about

---

[11] It is also noteworthy that Hillary Clinton was criticized in Democratic circles for her unwillingness to admit her vote to authorize war in Iraq was a mistake while the major Republican hopefuls calculated that admitting mistakes in this realm would be viewed by their constituency as damaging.

conservatives' use of these types of issues in campaigns, politics ain't beanbag. In general, issues emerge because one set of political elites think the issues will help them win elections, and these issues have often helped Republicans win elections since the 1960s because a substantial percentage of self-identified Democrats, particularly from the working class, do not share their party's position on them (Hillygus and Shields, 2008). In general, strategic considerations drive the behavior of political operatives.

Republicans came to realize that race had the potential to peel off a substantial number of conservative Democrats. This belief was embodied in Richard Nixon's "Southern Strategy"; Ronald Reagan's decision to kick off his 1980 presidential campaign in Philadelphia, Mississippi, the site of the murder of three young civil rights workers in 1964; and George H.W. Bush's use of Willie Horton to paint his opponent in 1988, Michael Dukakis, as soft on crime (Jamieson 1992). Campaign professionals are paid to win elections, so it is not surprising that they would search for issues that had a similar effect. In gay rights and maintaining security in a post-9/11 world, Republican operatives have found several. Indeed, we believe the reason they have all "worked" in a similar fashion is because they are all structured by the same worldview.

In the end, understanding what divides us and what worldview organizes many of these divisions provides a potentially powerful explanation for why American politics seems so polarized even if the difference between the average Republican and average Democrat on many issues of the day are simply not that large (Fiorina et al. 2004). Differences in policy preferences on some of the key issues go far beyond disagreements over policy choices and even ideology, to conflict about core self-understandings of what it means to be a good person and to the basis of a good society. We believe that the differences between the more and less authoritarian explain an important piece of that conflict which, in turn, has become central to the nature of political conflict more generally in American politics today.

THE PLAN OF THE BOOK

We will demonstrate that the rise of an authoritarian cleavage sheds light on several fundamentally important features of contemporary American politics. First, it helps explain why politics today seems so much more acrimonious than before, even as people have remained fairly moderate, albeit better sorted by party, in their preferences on the issues (Fiorina et al. 2004).[12] The key point here is that Americans are now divided over things that conjure more visceral reactions. Second, it helps explain why increasing polarization in Washington

---

[12] By sorted, we mean that people are aligning their policy preferences better with their party identification. For example, although opinions on abortion are not becoming more extreme, there is more distance between the average Republican and average Democrat because pro-lifers are increasingly identifying as Republicans and pro-choicers are increasingly identifying as Democrats.

coupled with relatively stable and moderate preferences in the electorate have not led to the alienation of moderates but rather to increased participation (e.g., Hetherington 2008). When a worldview structures political disagreements, it puts a premium on being involved, even if the public's issue preferences are not neatly matched to choices available at the elite level. Third, it helps explain the ebb and flow of party fortunes over recent years. We provide evidence for why Republicans do well in times of perceived moral and physical/existential crisis while Democrats do better otherwise. When they perceive physical or existential threat, those who are less authoritarian are more inclined to adopt more conservative preferences, a boon to the GOP. When the threat fades relative to other concerns – like economic ones – this group adopts more liberal preferences. And, finally, it helps explain why people who have long identified with one of the parties might feel like their party has changed. Some Republicans complain that their party has lost its small government, libertarian focus. Some Democrats express dismay that their leaders lack toughness and resolve. The increased role of authoritarianism in separating Republicans from Democrats helps explain these puzzles.

In Chapter 2, we put the question of mass level polarization in perspective. By most definitions of polarization, the American electorate is in no way, shape, or form polarized. It is, however, much better sorted. The most important lesson to take away from this chapter is that the electorate is now better sorted on several "high heat" dimensions – those that people feel passionately about. One of those dimensions is authoritarianism. As this sorting deepens, the way we judge political leaders and interpret political stimuli will reflect these considerations, causing people to feel more strongly about their choices.

In Chapter 3 we tailor a relatively narrow understanding of authoritarianism that speaks to the recent developments in American politics. The literature on authoritarianism is sprawling, full of assertions and charges that are, in many cases, impossible for empirical data to substantiate. We are, however, able to use empirical data to substantiate the claims that we make about the interplay between authoritarianism and the predicted response caused by the changing shape of the contemporary issue agenda. In this chapter, we also articulate specific features of a nonauthoritarian worldview alongside the much more familiar attributes of an authoritarian one. In Chapter 4, we provide a narrative account of worldview evolution. We focus on the rise of issues over the last forty years, from race to civil liberties to feminism to the projection of American force on the world stage, that all map onto the authoritarian dimension. Each has deepened and widened the original racial cleavage wrought in the 1960s.

In Chapter 5, we demonstrate that preferences on a range of different issues are, in fact, structured by authoritarianism. For example, we demonstrate that preferences for gay rights and feelings about groups like Christian fundamentalists who are central to the debate about gay rights are, in part, explained by how authoritarian a person is. But we go beyond demonstrating these well-understood relationships. In addition, we demonstrate that support or opposition to a number of matters involving the tradeoffs between security and civil liberties and the use of force versus diplomacy – all of which have been fundamentally important in a post-September 11 political world – are also a function of authoritarianism.

In Chapter 6, we explore the relationship between threat and authoritarianism, a source of much interest in the scholarly literature. We do this to show that it is the changing behavior of the less authoritarian, not the highly authoritarian, that is important to track in understanding the ebb and flow of public opinion on issues in which preferences are a function of authoritarianism. Specifically, since the more authoritarian tend to perceive external and internal threat from all manner of things much of the time, their behavior is less inclined to change much when objective levels of threat increase. Instead, we show that nonauthoritarians begin to mirror the behavior and opinions of authoritarians under such circumstances. This means that authoritarians and nonauthoritarians will differ least in threatening times, which suggests that the effect of authoritarianism will actually be at its minimum. When the threat abates, however, the effect of authoritarianism will increase, provided that issues that are structured by authoritarianism remain near the top of the political agenda.

In Chapter 7, we demonstrate that worldview evolution is progressing and apparently deepening. As a precursor to worldview evolution, we show that authoritarianism began to structure presidential vote choice in the early 1990s and congressional voting some years later. Changes in voting behavior, of course, often presage changes in the party system (Carmines and Stimson 1989). We demonstrate that authoritarianism began to structure party identification, the most important variable in the study of political behavior, in 2004. Moreover, we present data to suggest that this relationship has deepened since then.

In Chapter 8, we detail the emergence of immigration as a challenge to the major parties, particularly the Republicans. Republican political operatives who take a long view of the party's fortunes, such as Karl Rove, realize the importance of Latinos in building a majority coalition. In 2004, the party's efforts to attract Latinos were, in fact, successful. The worldview evolution that has crystallized, however, has created a Republican base that is not particularly warm toward immigrants. As was the case in California in the 1990s, this part of the party has constrained national efforts to attract a more diverse voting coalition. This issue also provides challenges to Democratic constituencies as the party has to balance minority group interests with those of the white working class, which they are terrified to lose.

In Chapter 9, we examine the turns in the 2008 Democratic primary fight through the lens of authoritarianism, demonstrating that no other variable has a larger impact on preferences between Barack Obama and Hillary Clinton, two ideologically indistinguishable candidates. Given that this race came to be viewed by pundits as polarized, even though Clinton and Obama could hardly be more ideologically similar, it calls into question whether explanations of polarization that focus solely on issues and ideology are adequate. We suspect that something more deeply held than issue preferences and more instinctively understood than ideology is at play in understanding the strong feelings produced by recent interparty battles.

We conclude the book by suggesting that this "something that is more deeply held" is inherent in the cognitive styles of the more and less authoritarian. Those who score high in authoritarianism tend toward concrete, black and white understandings of problems, while those who score low tend toward more nuanced, potentially ambiguous understandings of problems. As the parties have become sorted along these lines, it has become increasingly difficult for one side of the political divide to understand the other's positions on a set of hot-button issues. This, to us, is the key source of what feels like polarization in contemporary American politics.

Finally, in the Epilogue, we briefly consider in the context of our larger theory the 2008 general election campaign and Obama's decisive victory. John McCain's choice of Sarah Palin was attractive to the base of the Republican Party, and the behavior of the crowds at her rallies at certain points suggested that her appeal was particularly strong to those scoring high in authoritarianism. It also seems clear that Barack Obama was perhaps even more attractive to those scoring low in authoritarianism than Palin was to those scoring high. Highly educated and high income voters, both disproportionately low authoritarianism groups, both favored Obama much more than they have Democratic candidates in the past. Indeed, the continued politicization of nonauthoritarians that we develop throughout the book is critical in understanding the shape and nature of Obama's victory.

2

Putting Polarization in Perspective

In mid-2003, Rep. Bill Thomas (R-Calif.), chairman of the House Ways and Means Committee, attempted to rush a ninety-page pension reform bill through his committee. Not having had an opportunity to read the bill, the Democratic members fled the committee room to review the legislation in an adjacent library. An irate Thomas called for an immediate vote and passed the bill with only one Democrat, Representative Pete Stark (D-Calif.), still in the room. When Stark objected to Thomas's tactics, Representative Scott McInnis (R-Col.), a majority party committee member and Thomas ally, told Stark to "shut up." The seventy-one-year-old Stark challenged McInnis, twenty-one years his junior, to "make him" shut up and then repeatedly called him a "little fruitcake." Chairman Thomas took the unusual step of calling the Capitol Police to subdue Stark and eject the Democrats from the library. Although such a move was not unprecedented in the modern era, it was, to say the least, highly irregular. This is emblematic of the intense polarization that characterizes contemporary American politics.

There are many indications that American politics is now more sharply divided and more intensely conflicted than has typically been the case. A distinctly conservative Supreme Court decided the 2000 presidential election in favor of the conservative candidate who was the popular vote loser, causing Democrats much consternation and Republicans much exhilaration. Income inequality has reached its highest point since the United States started keeping such data in the 1940s (McCarty, Poole, and Rosenthal 2006), and class-based voting has become the most pronounced it has been in at least the last fifty years (Stonecash 2000; Bartels 2006). New policy disputes about issues with the potential to evoke strong feelings, such as the legality of gay marriage and the future of abortion rights, occupy more space on the issue agenda (Hunter 1991, 1994; Hunter and Wolfe 2006). Religion has once again become a potent political force, creating a deep new partisan cleavage between the faithful and the secular (e.g., Legee et al. 2002; Layman 2001; Green, Rozell, and Wilcox 2006; Wilcox and Larson 2006). And the war in Iraq has caused the political left to accuse the president of lying and the political right to accuse the left of undermining the war. Little wonder that 85 percent of Americans said they cared "a great deal" who won the 2004 presidential election, a higher percentage by far than any time since the survey question was first asked in 1952.

At the elite level, many studies show that Congress is increasingly polarized, with party members clustering toward the ideological poles and the middle a vast wasteland (e.g., Rohde 1991; McCarty, Poole, and Rosenthal 2006). Evidence that ordinary citizens are truly polarized, however, is less clear. We certainly do not hear many stories about fights breaking out in polling stations or the public square like the one between Congressmen Stark and McInnis. In fact, Morris Fiorina (Fiorina et al. 2004), in his compelling book *Culture War? The Myth of a Polarized America,* argues that voters only *appear* polarized because the political arena offers mainly polarized choices. He argues that voter preferences remain moderate, have generally not moved farther apart over time even on hot-button social issues, and are increasingly tolerant of difference.

Not all scholars of public opinion share Fiorina's view. Jacobson (2007) sees polarization in the unprecedented partisan differences in evaluations of George W. Bush, a larger partisan split on the war in Iraq than any previous war, and the mental gymnastics that mass partisans apparently engage in now to buttress their opinions even when they are demonstrably false. Importantly, however, most of Jacobson's evidence of polarization hinges on direct evaluations of President Bush or evaluations of policies that he is closely identified with. Although Abramowitz and Saunders (2008) see polarization in the increased consistency in liberal and conservative views in the mass public, their measure of polarization is geared to tap consistency of responses rather than their extremity from a midpoint, which is how most others in this debate are evaluating polarization claims.

Assessing the extent and pattern of polarization is an important endeavor. Elite polarization without mass polarization has the potential to alienate a moderate public. Ideologues might be invigorated but the middle might participate less. In addition, the policy outcomes produced by polarized political elites may not reflect those of a moderate mass public. Specifically, party leaders in Congress may adopt strategies that make it more likely for outputs to correspond to the median party position than the median chamber position, which would be at odds with the preferences of the median voter (Aldrich and Rohde 2000). Whether polarization consistently leads to nonmedian policy outputs is another matter (Krehbiel 1998; Oppenheimer and Hetherington 2006), but this probability is certainly higher than when elites are not polarized.

We begin this chapter by reviewing the scholarly debate about mass level polarization, finding that much of the disagreement can be understood as a question of definition. Moreover, the definition that has become the metric for assessing polarization claims seems rather narrow, focusing on whether preferences are clustering at the ideological extremes. When it comes to the mass public, such a standard is probably impossible to meet. Hence, when scholars talk about specific issue stances, the word that best describes what has happened over the last twenty years is probably *sorting*, meaning that Republican and Democratic voters are doing a better job aligning their preferences with their respective parties. Their preferences, however, are not getting more extreme.

Throughout the book, we adopt a somewhat broader understanding of polarization that centers more on the heat that politics seems to generate and the ability of political adversaries to understand the other's perspective. We present evidence that suggests important changes have occurred in the American electorate that might justify the use of the term *polarization*. Namely, the public is now better sorted by party on things like racial attitudes, how to keep the nation safe and secure, and morally charged issues like gay rights than they have been in recent memory. All represent deeply felt preferences and, although they might not seem on the surface to be related in any way, are all structured by authoritarianism, which has emerged as a new line of cleavage between the parties. In succeeding chapters we demonstrate the implications of these changes, which, although not bound up in issue preferences clustering near the poles, might explain why politics feels different now than before.

MASS POLARIZATION?

Elites are prone to polarization because they know and care about politics. As a consequence, they understand the issues and are more inclined to invest themselves in one side or another. In contrast, most ordinary Americans care little about politics and are, instead, consumed with their work, family, and other nonpolitical pursuits (e.g., Campbell et al. 1960). Despite all the talk about red states versus blue states, it is not clear that regular people are polarized today.

A number of factors militate against the emergence of mass level polarization. Most central, the issue agenda is often not conducive to it. Political disagreements differ in their divisiveness from era to era. Some enduring divisions were born of events rather than ideas, which is important because polarization implies deep philosophical differences. The New Deal party system was forged by a problem - the Great Depression - and the Republicans' inability to solve it. Although the New Deal was akin to the second French Revolution for some conservatives, the Democrats' more government-oriented philosophy was, for most, less important in 1932 than the fact that the Democrats were not the Republicans. Certainly the specific policy prescriptions offered by Roosevelt were of secondary import to non-ideologues. Although his policies moved further to the left as the economic crisis deepened, it seemed to have little effect on his popularity.

Polarization suggests an intensity that draws on attitudes that people hold deeply. People come to perceive that their views of right and wrong and good and bad are diametrically opposed to those of their opponents, making it difficult to understand (or perhaps even respect) the worldview that makes those preferences possible. Importantly, people tend to feel most intensely about issues that are understood on the gut level. Carmines and Stimson (1980) refer to these as "easy" issues. An easy issue – race –forged a new party system in the 1960s (and the 1860s for that matter).

Easy issues are at the heart of what sociologist James Davison Hunter (1991) forecast as the emerging polarization of American politics. In *Culture Wars: The Struggle to Define America*, which is often cited as the impetus for Pat Buchanan's fiery speech at the 1992 Republican National Convention and the dawn of polarized politics, he suggests that the emergence of new social issues, such as abortion, the death penalty, and gay rights, make polarization inevitable. According to Hunter, such issues have scant middle ground. People either think life begins at conception or not; they believe people are gay by choice or by genetic predisposition; they believe moral values are constant or they believe they are mutable to a changing world.[1] Whether or not these are true dichotomies, the important point remains that such issues require people to use their core values to make political judgments, uniquely dividing Americans into what Hunter described as "orthodox" and "progressive" camps.

Much recent scholarship, however, questions whether "values issues" even represent the dominant cleavage in contemporary American politics. The traditional New Deal cleavage has proven remarkably durable. As evidence, class now plays a much more important role in structuring party identification and vote choice than it did in decades past (Stonecash 2000). While the import of social issues today is greater than it was in the 1980s and 1990s, attitudes about the traditional left-right economic dimension remain much more important (Bartels 2006; see also Ansolabehere, Rodden, and Snyder 2006).

Although these micro-level treatments suggest the continued preeminence of the New Deal cleavage, it is hard to square with recent presidential outcomes and an increasingly regionally distinct congressional map. Miller and Schofield (2003) use the state as the unit of analysis to argue for the primacy of the social dimension in contemporary American politics. They demonstrate that the states won by Kennedy in 1960, a New Deal election, bore little resemblance to those won by Gore in 2000 (and, by extension, Kerry in 2004). The states won by (Republican) McKinley in 1896 when the social dimension was ascendant and those won by (Democrat) Gore in 2000, however, were highly correlated. They conclude that the social dimension has reawakened and switched parties such that the Republican Party is the more conservative one and the Democratic Party the more liberal. If so, it would help to explain why politics today seems more acrimonious than it did during the New Deal party system, when economic issues reigned supreme.

If anything, the issue environment has recently become increasingly conducive to a culture war, with gay rights, in particular, playing a central role

---

[1] In reality, these issues can have middle ground. For example, people can prefer that abortion remain legal but with certain restrictions. Similarly, people can prefer civil unions to either gay marriage or not recognizing monogamous gay relationships. Such middle ground is significantly less sexy than seems to be preferred by interest groups on both sides of the issue not to mention the news media, which is driven by conflict.

in 2004. Indeed, fully eleven states offered anti-gay marriage ballot initiatives in 2004, with another eight following in 2006. But a definition of polarization that merely centers on the issues on the political agenda does not allow scholars to evaluate polarization claims. The presence of hot-button issues is a necessary condition, but these issues must be more than present. Unfortunately, scholars have not agreed on what serves as evidence of polarization, which has led to very different conclusions drawn from the same data sources.

LITTLE EVIDENCE OF POPULAR POLARIZATION

Operational definitions of polarization are numerous, which helps explain why some top-notch scholars argue passionately that it does not exist in the American electorate while other top-notch scholars argue, with equal passion, that it does. DiMaggio, Evans, and Bryson (1996) provide a straightforward definition of polarization, which Fiorina adopts. Although they use the generic term *polarization*, it relates to what Fiorina refers to as *popular* polarization, which is simply movement in the preferences of individuals toward the poles of a distribution (see also DiMaggio, Evans, and Bryson 1996; Fiorina and Levendusky 2006). It is characterized by wide dispersion of preference between groups and, eventually, bimodality, or a clustering of preferences near the poles. In statistical terms, this rendering requires (1) a large difference of means (or proportions) between two groups and (2) large and increasing standard deviations in distributions of interest.

Based on the DiMaggio, Evans, and Bryson definition, there is not much evidence of popular polarization. Extending DiMaggio, Evans, and Bryson's work (which covered the period from the early 1970s through 1996) into the 2000s, Fiorina quite convincingly shows that Americans' issue preferences have been and remain generally moderate (see also Evans 2003). A key piece of his evidence is the National Election Study's (NES) ideological self-placement question. When people are asked to place themselves on a 7-point scale from extremely liberal at one end to extremely conservative at the other with moderate, middle of the road at the midpoint, about 50 percent of Americans either characterize themselves as moderate or are unable to place themselves on the scale.

Figure 2.1 shows the responses to the ideological self-placement question in 2004 broken down by party. The modal response among Democrats is "moderate" or "haven't thought enough about it." Less than 40 percent of Democrats are even willing to label themselves as liberals of any sort. Although Republicans embrace the conservative label more easily than Democrats do the liberal label, nearly 30 percent of Republicans think of themselves as moderate or say they haven't thought enough about it. Fiorina, moreover, shows similarly overlapping, moderate preferences for a litany of issues. While it is true that there is much less overlap today than there was decades ago (Abramowitz and Saunders 2008), ideological sorting by party is far from complete.

Such an operational definition of polarization has both advantages and limitations. Its main advantage is its face validity. The hostility and venom that is

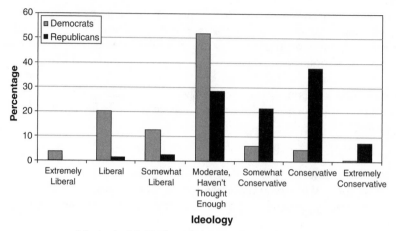

FIGURE 2.1. Ideological Self-Placement by Party Identification, Leaners Not Treated as Partisans, 2004

implied by polarization seems to require significant distance between groups. Moreover, since polarization has the word "pole" as its root, examining whether groups are moving toward and clustering at the poles certainly makes sense.

However, perhaps this is not a fair test of polarization in the electorate. Given what scholars have known for decades about the nature of public opinion and the survey instrument itself, such a definition may be too limited because the conditions imposed by it are perhaps impossible to meet. Surveys tend to depress dispersion because respondents, especially the ill-informed, tend to choose the midpoint of survey items regardless of their true preferences (if such preferences can be gleaned at all). If the most esteemed theories of the survey response are correct, a relatively small percentage of Americans will have the cognitive ability and/or the political certainty to cluster toward the poles of a distribution (e.g., Converse 1964; Zaller 1992). Even in the case of elite polarization in Congress, moreover, members today are not clustering together at the ideological poles. DW-NOMINATE scores, which are measures of congresspeople's ideology derived through the analysis of each member's voting record on all non-unanimous floor votes each session, show the clustering of members is occurring around −0.5 and 0.5, not at the −1 and 1, which are roughly the poles of the measure. That means that even though party leaders in Congress do not allow members to consider the most extreme alternatives, most members' measured preferences generally do not approach the ideological poles. Although scales of elite and mass opinion are not directly comparable, we should expect that mass preferences will tend to bunch much closer to the middle than those of elites because of the massive differences in ideological sophistication.

If ordinary people are unlikely to cluster at the poles, how far apart do they need to be for them to be polarized? The DiMaggio, Evans, and Bryson definition suffers from the fact that there is no agreed-upon amount of distance between groups necessary for popular polarization to exist. Do their preferences, on a scale from 0 to 100, need to cluster around 90 and 10, 70 and 30, or something else? Can groups be polarized if they are far apart but are on the same side of the midpoint?

In comparing residents of red and blue states, Fiorina often dismisses differences of 10 and 15 percentage points as not representing polarization, which seems appropriate. It is theoretically possible for these groups to be 100 percentage points apart. Of course, differences of this magnitude are really a Never Never Land possibility. After all, you can always find some Red Sox fans in a city as big as New York, and perhaps a few more, even braver Yankees fans in Boston. Even during the Civil War, probably the most polarized time in the nation's history, significant numbers of southerners sympathized with the North and vice versa, making it unlikely that northerners and southerners would have differed by anything approaching 100 points on slavery. Indeed, 94 percent of blacks were effectively barred from voting in the North as well as the South, and even less than a year before secession, "abolitionist" was not in the vernacular of ordinary citizens (Dahl 1976, 423). To the extent that group differences approached 100 percent, surveys would have struggled to reflect it.

Some context might be helpful. Although the survey era has generally been characterized by muted differences, the struggle over civil rights provides an exception. Prior to the time that the courts extended civil rights protections to nonsouthern blacks in the late 1960s and early 1970s, southern and nonsouthern whites are portrayed as having fundamentally different preferences about segregation. Fortunately, survey data are available to test how different their preferences were, which might provide a sense of how far apart groups might be for polarization to exist.

In 1964, the year the Civil Rights Act was enacted, the NES asked people their positions on whether the federal government should work to ensure school integration, their preferred degree of segregation, and support for housing segregation. The results appear in Table 2.1. The differences between white southerners and white nonsoutherners were substantial: nonsoutherners were 22.7 percentage points more likely to support a federal role in school integration, 22 points more likely to support desegregation rather than segregation or something in between, and 25.5 points more likely to believe that African Americans should be able to live wherever they could afford. Fiorina often dismisses large differences in the contemporary context if both groups are on the same side of the midpoint, indicating that the two sides agree on substance but differ only in degree. But regarding civil rights in 1964, less than a majority of southern and nonsouthern whites supported both a federal role in school integration (41.9 percent nonsouthern vs. 19.2 percent southern) and the notion of full desegregation more generally (31.5 percent to 9.5 percent). Perhaps northerners and southerners were not polarized on civil rights, but if not on this issue at this point in time, it is not clear where to look for it.

TABLE 2.1. *Whites' Opinions about Blacks' Civil Rights, 1964*

	Non-South	South	Difference
School Integration			
Federal Government Should See to It	41.9	19.2	22.7
Depends	8.2	5.3	
Federal Government Should Stay Out	36.4	64.3	27.9
Failed to Answer	13.5	11.3	
Degree of Segregation			
Desegregation	31.5	9.5	22.0
In Between	49.0	42.2	
Segregation	19.5	48.3	28.8
Housing Integration			
Whites Have Right to Keep Blacks Out	23.7	51.5	27.8
Blacks Have Right to Live Where They Can Afford	54.8	29.3	25.5
Failed to Answer	17.9	19.2	

Source: American National Election Study, 1964

It is worth noting that the gulf between nonblack Democrats and Republicans on gay rights is roughly the same today as was the difference between southerners and nonsoutherners on civil rights in the mid-1960s. In fact, opinions today on gay rights are, in some cases, even more divergent.[2] Table 2.2 displays the results. On both support for gay marriage and gay adoption, Democrats are more than 30 percentage points more tolerant than are Republicans. The differences are somewhat smaller, but still substantial, for protecting gays from job discrimination and supporting gays in the military.

This example highlights another problem with the DiMaggio, Evans, and Bryson definition. Measures like standard deviations and differences of means do not capture salience. By salience, we mean the degree to which an issue is important to people. Partisans will tend not to differ much on issues that are not on the issue agenda because party elites will not have provided them clear cues about where they should stand. For example, Republicans and Democrats did not differ in their preferences about immigration in the 1990s (Citrin et al. 1997), likely because the issue received little attention outside of California and the desert Southwest. We demonstrate in Chapter 8, however, that party

---

[2] We confine this analysis to nonblacks because blacks do not identify with the Democratic Party because of its positions on social issues. Indeed, African Americans are, on average, quite conservative on most social issues, while the Democratic Party is increasingly liberal. Since blacks have remained the party's most stalwart supporters, it appears that this group is not inclined to leave the party based on the party's socially liberal positions.

TABLE 2.2. *Nonblacks Opinions about Gay Rights, by Party, 2004*

	Democrats	Republicans	Difference
Gay Marriage			
Should Be Allowed	52.4	17.3	35.1
Should Not Be Allowed but Civil Unions Should (VOL)	3.9	3.6	
Should Not Be Allowed	43.7	79.1	35.4
Gay Adoption			
Favor	65.9	34.8	31.1
Oppose	34.1	65.2	
Gays in the Military			
Favor	90.1	71.9	18.2
Oppose	9.9	28.1	
Protect Gays from Job Discrimination			
Favor	86.5	63.7	22.8
Oppose	13.5	36.3	

Source: American National Election Study, 2004

differences in the electorate began to emerge around 2004 as party elites began to talk about the issue and take positions, making the issue more salient (see also Carmines and Stimson, 1989, on race).

Salience helps to determine the weight that opinions carry. Indeed, accounting for salience explains why the politics of race in the 1960s was much more polarized than the politics of gay rights in the 2000s, despite the fact that preferences are somewhat more dispersed now than they were then. In 1964, the percentage of Americans who responded "civil rights" to Gallup's most important problem question was generally greater than 30 percent. The percentage of Americans who think gay rights is most important today is typically in the low single digits. Gay rights and other social issues are more important than they were ten years ago, but they do not define politics as race did in the 1960s.

Excluding salience from our understanding of polarization, however, can also be used to argue that there is *more* polarization today than working from the DiMaggio, Evans, and Bryson definition would suggest. Salience can make issues seem more polarizing even if the distance between groups remains relatively small. Consider public opinion about homosexuals, a hot-button issue with the potential to polarize. Since the 1980s, the average distance between how Republicans and Democrats feel about gays and lesbians on the NES's feeling thermometer – which asks people to rate groups on a scale ranging from 0 to 100 based on how warmly they feel toward them – has actually decreased from about 12 to about 10 degrees. Tolerance among both has increased, but since Republicans started from a lower baseline, their average score has increased faster. From this, the DiMaggio, Evans, and Bryson definition would conclude that no polarization exists because the two sides are moving closer.

Such a conclusion, however, misses an important change. Although the distance between partisans is now smaller, it is substantively more important because gay rights have become more salient, as Republican elites have used it to good effect to pry Democratic identifiers away from their party (Hillygus and Shields, 2008). In fact, the very reason that gay rights has become more salient is because opinion has become so much more moderate. Gays and lesbians were so unpopular in the 1980s (average feeling thermometer 28.50 degrees in 1988 – seven degrees cooler than for the ever popular "illegal aliens") – that neither the political left nor right could be closely associated with them. In 2004, however, tolerance for gays and lesbians had increased markedly (average feeling thermometer in 2004 was 48.52 degrees), making discussion of gay rights possible.

Perhaps, then, another way to consider the relative degree of polarization caused by an issue is as the product of the distance between groups and the salience of the issue. Considered this way, gay rights can still be a source of at least relative polarization even as the distance between groups has shrunk. Consider the homosexuality example. The distance, in this case, was 12 in the 1980s, but, since the issue was not salient, its weight was 0. Polarization could be calculated as $12 * 0 = 0$. Even though the distance has dropped to 10 more recently, its salience has increased dramatically. Let's say it carries a weight equal to 10. Polarization in this rendering would be calculated as $10 * 10 = 100$. Even if the difference in means or proportions remains constant or even shrinks a little over time, relatively higher levels of polarization can result if the weight attached to that issue is increasing.

Finally, the emergence of new issues challenges the DiMaggio, Evans, and Bryson definition. The definition of polarization used by most scholars often focuses on the amount of change that has occurred over time. The proper response to terrorism defies the use of time. Prior to 1993, the salience of terrorism in the United States approached 0, with few Americans living in fear of a terrorist attack. Now the percentage of Americans identifying it as an important problem is consistently in the double digits and has approached 50 percent at times. To the extent that people perceive meaningful party differences on this issue today – and survey evidence suggests that they do (Beinart 2008) – its marked increase in salience will affect how polarized the political environment feels. Since personal and national security are at stake, there is little doubt that whatever feelings people express, those feelings are intense.

The key point here is that the definition most often used by scholars to test for polarization is apparently impossible to meet. Given the place that politics occupies in the life of most people, their preferences are unlikely ever to cluster at ideological poles. To the extent that we use the term *polarization*, we must carve out a different understanding of it. To us, the essence of polarization is when hot-button issues become salient concerns for a large percentage of people. People feel intensely about these issues because they tap into something deep inside them. It might be the case that people's preferences are not that different from those of their opponents, but they do not see it that way. When it becomes difficult for people to understand how their adversaries come to have the preferences they do, the political system feels polarized. Even if middle ground is available, people fail to perceive it.

STRONG INDICATION OF PARTISAN POLARIZATION (OR SORTING)

Those who argue that polarization exists on the mass level are, for the most part, conceptualizing polarization differently from Fiorina. They most often highlight increasing distances between the average Republican and Democrat in the electorate irrespective of whether those opinions are clustering near the ideological poles.[3] In statistical terms, differences in means and, when appropriate, proportions are the only measures of concern. With the poles out of the picture, Fiorina and Levendusky (2006) question the use of the term *polarization* to describe the phenomenon. Instead, they favor the term *party sorting*. By sorting, they mean that mass partisans are following what are now clearer elite cues to sort themselves into the "correct" party, which decreases intraparty heterogeneity and increases the difference between party adherents.

With sorting, differences in means or proportions can increase, even as the dispersion of opinions in the population remains relatively constant. For example, the distribution of opinion on abortion might not have become more extreme over time, but the average Democrat and Republican could be farther apart if formerly Democratic pro-lifers changed their party affiliation, realizing their old party was not an appropriate home (and vice versa). Democratic partisans will have become more homogenously liberal and Republican partisans more homogenously conservative, with the average distance between them larger as a result.

This is an important part of our story because without party differences, there is no basis for disagreement. Significant ideological sorting has indisputably occurred. For example, the distance between ideological self-placement of the average Democrat and Republican using NES data has increased dramatically, and, accounting for the entire range of these variables, so, too has the correlation between partisanship and ideology. In 1972, a mere 0.66 points separated mass partisans on the 7-point scale, with a correlation between the two variables of .28. By 2004, the mean distance had more than doubled to 1.62 points, and the correlation increased to .57. These results, however, do not reveal how many people are better sorted. Fiorina agrees with his critics that political activists are well sorted ideologically. In fact, they are probably even polarized (Aldrich 1995; Layman and Carsey 1998; Fiorina et al. 2004). On a whole range of issues, the most involved segments of the electorate differ by a

---

[3] Abramowitz also demonstrates that people have become more consistently liberal and more consistently conservative in their preferences over time, which seems more a measure of preference constraint than polarization. See Abramowitz and Saunders, "Is Polarization a Myth?"

lot. This is true of abortion (Adams 1997), women's issues (Wolbrecht 2000; Sanbonmatsu 2006), the environment and gay rights issues (Lindaman and Haider-Markel 2002), and most recently, the war in Iraq (Jacobson 2007).

Less clear is how far below the activist level that sorting penetrates. Fiorina argues, not much. Jacobson (2006) as well as Abramowitz (2006) argue, however, that the increase in the correlation between party and ideology is too large to be confined to hard-core activists. In addition, Abramowitz (2006) believes that not only is the "politically active" segment of the population larger than Fiorina allows but that it has recently increased markedly in size.

One way to assess the percentage of people who are showing obvious signs of sorting is to segment the electorate by political acuity. Although many people say they are interested in politics, that they vote, and that they participate in other ways, they say so because it is the socially desirable response. People who *really* do these things, however, ought to know more about politics than those who do not. Those who are most politically sophisticated should reflect the elite polarization in the information environment better than those who know less about politics. As a consequence, they will be more likely to have sorted their ideological predispositions with their partisan predispositions. Zaller (1992) suggests that factual political knowledge is the best measure of political acuity, so we create a measure of political knowledge by summing the number of correct answers that respondents provide to questions such as which party holds the majority in the House of Representatives and what jobs or offices do political figures like Dick Cheney, Tony Blair, and William Rehnquist hold. Since 2004 shows a large jump in the correlation between ideology and partisanship, we focus on these data.

The results appear in Table 2.3. Since we have mapped ideology onto a 0 to 1 interval, the differences can be interpreted as the percentage difference between the mean Republican and mean Democrat. The second column shows that the average distance is very large among those with the most political information – better than 45 percentage points among the 7.8 percent of people who answered all six questions correctly. The 35 and 40 percentage point differences among those who answered four of five questions correctly are nearly as large.

The correlations allow us to account for the entire range of the variables. Those who work with survey data will find their size to be extraordinary. Because of the measurement error inherent in surveys, analysts are often quite pleased to find correlations of .2 or above. An association of .3 is considered very strong. The fact that the correlation between party and ideology among people who answered all six factual questions correctly approaches .8 is remarkable. Political animals like these are rare in the population, but the correlation for those who answered four or five questions correctly, which accounts for another 35 percent of the population, is about .7, still a very close fit. This analysis suggests that more than 40 percent of Americans show evidence of deep party sorting, and another 35 percent (those who answer two or three questions correctly) do not appear to be completely in the dark either.

TABLE 2.3. *Mean Distance in Ideology between Partisans and Bivariate Correlation (Pearson r) between Partisanship and Ideological Self-Placement by Political Knowledge, 2004*

Political Knowledge	Mean Distance Between Partisans	$r_{(pid,ideology)}$	Percentage of Cases
0	.098	.27	9.2
1	.055	.08	13.0
2	.186	.41	17.5
3	.252	.51	18.1
4	.353	.69	19
5	.401	.73	15.6
6	.457	.78	7.8
			100

Source: American National Election Study, 2004.

These data do not allow us to assess whether the electorate is better informed now than before. Delli Carpini and Keeter (1996) show that Americans did not come to know appreciably more about politics between the 1960s and 1990s, but their data stop before the 2000s. Unfortunately, the battery of factual items we use here is not conducive to over-time comparison because their difficulty differs depending on context. Although Americans say they are more involved and interested, these responses may simply be a function of increased efforts by parties and interest groups to mobilize an evenly divided electorate, not because Americans are more polarized themselves (Hetherington 2007).

THE THINGS THAT DIVIDE AMERICANS TODAY RUN TO THEIR CORE

There is no doubt at all that Americans are polarized in their voting behavior and evaluations of George W. Bush. In the 2004 election, over 90 percent of partisans voted for their party's candidate, which is a high point since the dawning of the survey era. In addition, the partisan gap in President Bush's approval rating is higher than for any president in the survey era. Jacobson (2007) notes that the partisan gap in approval ratings measured from President Eisenhower, when Gallup introduced the presidential approval measure, through President Clinton *never* exceeded 70 percentage points. In the twelve polls leading up to the 2004 election, however, the partisan gap for Bush never fell below 70 percent. Similarly, support for Bush's signature issue, the war in Iraq, is polarized by historical standards. Partisan differences on Vietnam averaged about 5 percentage points, and for Korea, Kosovo, and Afghanistan, they ran about 12 percentage points. But by the fourth quarter of 2004 with the Iraq war about a year and a half old, Republicans and Democrats differed on the war by an average of 63 percentage points, more than twice the maximum partisan difference achieved during the first Gulf War (Jacobson 2007).

The polarization in voter behavior and evaluations of partisan players is hard to square with the lack of polarization on issues. We argue that the key to solving this puzzle is accounting for the things that divide ordinary Americans today. In our view, the issue is less one of distance than it is the salience, intensity, and nature of issues. To that end, it is worth noting that we find evidence of increasingly deep sorting on several hot-button, gut-level considerations. When people are divided along lines such as these, it becomes much harder for them to view the other political party as an acceptable alternative to theirs, a position that will yield increasingly favorable evaluations of politicians whom people perceive share their beliefs and increasingly negative evaluations of politicians whom they perceive do not.

Since 1986, the NES – the largest and most esteemed academic political survey available – has asked a battery of questions about what is termed *moral traditionalism*. Respondents are asked their agreement with a set of statements, including "the newer lifestyles are contributing to the breakdown of our society," "the country would have many fewer problems if there were more emphasis on traditional family ties," and "the world is always changing and we should adjust our view of moral behavior to those changes." Those who score high in moral traditionalism are what Hunter terms *orthodox*, people who view morals as unchanging. Those who score low are consistent with Hunter's "progressives" who believe that morals must change with an evolving society.

Figure 2.2 tracks the difference among nonblacks between self-identified Democrats and Republicans over time. Since we have mapped these items onto a zero to one interval, the difference represents the percentage difference between party identifiers. In 1986, the average difference between Republicans and Democrats was only 4 percentage points. Ten years later, it had increased

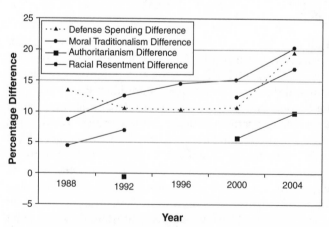

FIGURE 2.2. Changes in the Differences between Mass Partisans on Race, Morality, Defense, and Authoritarianism, 1988–2004, Nonblack Respondents

to 15 percentage points, and by 2004, it had increased further to more than 20 points. Taking the full range of both party identification and moral traditionalism into account, the correlations between them increased from .09 in 1986 when the items debuted to .45 in 2004.

Figure 2.2 shows that the parties are better sorted on racial resentment as well. This concept was developed by Kinder and Sears (1981) and extended by Kinder and Sanders (1996) to tap symbolic racism, which has in their view replaced the overt racism of years past. Rather than arguing that whites see blacks as biologically inferior, they argue that whites now see blacks as violating time-honored norms of hard work. On this measure of anti-black affect, the difference between Republicans and Democrats increased gradually between 1988 and 2000, then surged between 2000 and 2004. This pattern of change is curious in that race has recently come to play a less central role in electoral politics as Americans have become more accepting of African Americans. But given that race is unique in its power to divide ordinary Americans (e.g., Carmines and Stimson 1989), it is potentially a change of great import. We should note that the development of this cleavage is not simply the result of racially resentful southern Democrats becoming southern Republicans over time (see Green, Palmquist, and Schickler 2002). Instead both southerners and nonsoutherners evince this pattern.

Although not as deeply held as a value, we also show here that the distance between partisans on defense spending has increased markedly as well, particularly recently. This is not an ideal measure of hawkishness, but it is the only even somewhat appropriate item asked across a sufficiently long time series. In the 1980s, differences between Republicans and Democrats hovered just below 15 percentage points. After the Cold War came to an end, however, those differences dropped to about 10 percentage points through the 1990s and into 2000. In 2004, however, the difference between the average Republican and average Democrat in their preference for defense spending nearly doubled to 19.5 percentage points with the onset of the war on terrorism and the war in Iraq.

The underlying orientation that structures all these things – race, morals, and hawkishness – is authoritarianism. It provides the connective tissue between these seemingly disparate opinions. Importantly, Figure 2.2 shows that partisans are also now sorted by authoritarianism. Whereas there was no difference between partisans in the early 1990s, there is a marked difference today. Here we tap authoritarianism using a four-item battery of questions asking people to choose between desirable qualities in children, which we will detail in the next chapter. Specifically, the survey asks people to choose whether they would value children more who were "independent" or who "respected their elders" and whether they would value children more who were "considerate" or "well behaved." Those choosing the more "traditional" qualities are characterized as being more authoritarian.

Moreover, authoritarianism plausibly underlies preferences on policies of emerging import such as gay rights, how to combat terrorism and immigration, all of which are dividing Americans today. Authoritarians and nonauthoritarians differ in their ability to tolerate difference, which would be germane to differences in preferences on gay rights and immigration as well as differences in racial resentment. Authoritarians tend to favor the use of the military over diplomacy, which would be germane to understanding differences on the proper approach to combating terrorism abroad. It is also plausible that authoritarians will differ in their willingness to cast aside certain civil liberties in the name of preserving the safety of the nation, which would be germane to combating terrorism at home. In fact, we demonstrate all these relationships (and several more) empirically in Chapter 5.

It is also worth noting that this pattern of party sorting is not evident on "nonauthoritarian" issues. Figure 2.3 tracks the percentage differences between self-identified Republicans and Democrats on a range of 7-point issue scales measured by the NES, including government-sponsored health care, government-guaranteed jobs and standard of living, and government services and spending. Although we see a sharpening of party differences from the late 1980s to the mid-1990s, there is no such movement more recently. Our analysis very clearly suggests that sorting is occurring, but mostly on the issues in which preferences are structured by authoritarianism.

AUTHORITARIANISM AND POLARIZATION

In assessing polarization, the scholarly literature has generally focused on the distance between groups, usually the average Republican and average Democrat. This is, of course, entirely appropriate; the greater the distance, the

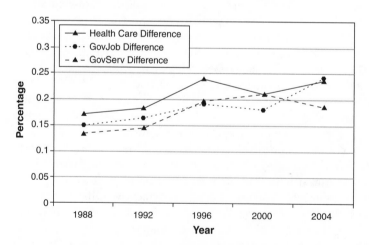

FIGURE 2.3. Differences between Self-Identified Democrats and Republicans on "Nonauthoritarian" Issues, Nonblack Respondents 1988–2004
Notes: Health Care Difference = Differences in support for government-sponsored health care; GovJob Difference = Differences in support for government-guaranteed jobs and standard of living; GovServ Difference = Differences in support for government services and spending.

more differently the two sides see a problem or a political issue. Conversely, if there is no difference, there is, on average, no disagreement. However, it is also probably the case that differences in certain things might be more polarizing than other things. We suggest that this is particularly true when preferences are structured by authoritarianism because those who score low and high in the concept understand the world in such different ways. Moreover, we show throughout the book that authoritarianism structures such a wide array of preferences on increasingly salient issues that those who score high must feel as though they agree with the Democrats on very little and those who score low must feel as though they agree with the Republicans on very little.

As for the nature of the disagreements, Feldman (2003) argues that those who score high in authoritarianism tend to be social conformists and expect others to conform to the established social code. Since gays and lesbians fail to conform to existing social conventions on sexual behavior, authoritarians are inclined to dislike them (Barker and Tinnick 2006). The extension of rights to gays and lesbians could imperil other time-honored traditions, such as traditional marriage, which have served societies well for centuries. In contrast, those who score low in authoritarianism tend to place more emphasis on personal autonomy, making them more open to challenges to existing norms (Feldman 2003). The norm-challenging sexual behavior of gays and lesbians would be less an affront to the less authoritarian because personal autonomy, not social conformity, is a more important virtue. In this view, people should be able to pursue their personal lifestyle choices provided they not harm others. As for gay marriage, specifically, those scoring low in authoritarianism might even believe that norms surrounding marriage have, in fact, changed significantly over the years without causing moral collapse.

Herein lies the rub. Those who are more authoritarian are likely to perceive that previous changes to traditional marriage have, in fact, eroded the institution over time and led society in the direction of moral collapse. While a nonauthoritarian would be concerned about impeding a gay person's personal choice without a demonstrated good cause, an authoritarian would surely see good cause – a fundamental disagreement about a hot-button issue.

Similarly, authoritarianism ought to help structure conceptions of how best to protect national security while at the same time preserving democratic ideals. Among those who are more authoritarian, it is simple common sense that providing security is the most important consideration because, without security, lofty ideals are meaningless. When presented with trade-offs that might limit certain civil liberties to buttress safety, those who are more authoritarian will tend to choose safety for straightforward and commonsensical reasons. In fact, those unwilling to take such steps might be viewed as somewhat dangerous because the more authoritarian see the path to keeping the nation safe as so clear. A nonauthoritarian's view will usually differ significantly. In most cases, those scoring low in authoritarianism will not view the nation's security situation as being as tenuous as a more authoritarian person might. As a result, the stakes for protecting security are likely significantly lower. This makes it easier for people scoring low in authoritarianism to express support for abstract ideals over measures to enhance safety. At least in the abstract, failing to protect the ideals that make the United States distinctive might, to nonauthoritarians, render its future security less meaningful. As with gay marriage, there is a fundamental disagreement about an issue sure to arouse great passion.

We demonstrate in the next chapter how and why these preferences emanate from a fundamental difference in outlook. Specifically, those scoring high in authoritarianism tend to favor the concrete and immediate, seeing the world in black and white terms. Those scoring low in authoritarianism are more inclined to favor the abstract, seeing the world in more complex terms. Solutions to problems that might be obvious to one side might seem overly simplistic to the less authoritarian or relativistic to the more authoritarian. Even if issue preferences are not miles apart, political conflict can seem polarized if it has a fundamental difference in outlook at its foundation. It is this more subtle understanding of polarization that we believe characterizes American politics today.

CONCLUSION

We have argued that much of the scholarly disagreement about whether ordinary Americans are polarized can be explained by the fact that different scholars have meant different things by the term *polarization*. Fiorina adopts a more literal definition, requiring both large distances between groups in their issue preferences and a clustering of those preferences toward the ideological poles. This, by and large, has not occurred. Fiorina's critics label as polarization increasing distances between the preferences of ordinary Republicans and Democrats without clustering toward the poles. Americans are better sorted, which has produced partisan differences on some issues, notably gay marriage and gay adoption, which are even greater than those that existed between southerners and nonsoutherners on civil rights in the 1960s. But ordinary Americans are not polarized in the same way members of Congress are. In fact, in the 109th Congress (2005–06), every Republican scored more conservative than even the most conservative Democrat, and the distance between the average Republican and Democratic member reached its highest point in 100 years.

In our use of the term *polarization*, we do not mean to suggest that there has been a large-scale movement of preferences toward the ideological poles in the American electorate. Instead, we stress the nature of disagreements to suggest why ordinary Americans might feel differently about politics even if they are not polarized in Fiorina's understanding of the term. When deeply valued considerations are very salient, different political camps may not need to be particularly far apart in reality to perceive that they are. Issues such as gay rights, terrorism, and war are all now prominent on the issue agenda and all have the ability to provoke strong feelings. And, as we demonstrate in later chapters, all are structured by authoritarianism, which has, itself, come to divide Republicans from Democrats.

3

Authoritarianism and Nonauthoritarianism: Concepts and Measures

Thus far, we have introduced why we think authoritarianism is central to an understanding of the contemporary political divide, particularly in regard to the polarization of U.S. politics in the early twenty-first century. In this chapter, we explain in more depth our understanding of the concept of authoritarianism itself. Recognizing the implications that the term has had in the literature, we define and defend our use of it, and explain how more recent innovations in measuring the concept lend themselves to a better understanding of its utility in explaining crucial features of the contemporary American political divide. Finally, we consider nonauthoritarianism as a distinct worldview with particular attributes of its own. Up to now, nonauthoritarianism has been largely seen as a default category, which we believe is mistaken. In fact, much of the explanatory power of authoritarianism in understanding contemporary political conflict derives from changes in attitudes among nonauthoritarians.

We should note at the outset that when we define authoritarians and nonauthoritarians, we are dealing in ideal-typical categories. Many Americans are near the midpoint of the scale, not obviously evincing more characteristics of one category than the other. And even those at the extremes may, in some ways, maintain beliefs and attitudes more typical of the opposite extreme. In other words, we do not assume that most Americans are two-dimensional caricatures one way or the other. Instead, in this chapter, we sketch the ideal types in order to specify the attributes that we think are most relevant.

CHARACTERISTICS OF AUTHORITARIANISM

Authoritarianism has traditionally been conceptualized, quite simply, as a tendency to submit to authority (Altemeyer 1981), but it is much more complicated than that. Indeed, in their landmark study, *The Authoritarian Personality*, Adorno et al. (1950) identified nine separate dimensions. Subsequently, Altemeyer (1996) characterizes authoritarianism as a social attitude, composed of three clusters – submission, conventionalism, and aggression. In their reckonings, Feldman (2003) and Stenner (2005) focus on the first two of these clusters, conceiving of authoritarianism as a tendency toward intolerance predicated upon one's need for social conformity and consequently, aggression toward those perceived as challenging the social status quo.

Left less clear in these important treatments of the concept is what, at base, motivates the worldview. Our treatment places a need for order at the center. Much emerging work in cognitive science depicts a struggle in all humans to achieve clarity in the face of confusion. To use terms more often used by social scientists, people hope to impose order on ambiguous situations. No one particularly likes to feel confused, but some, notably those with greater cognitive capacity, can tolerate it better on average than others. In the search for order, however, different types of people might choose different paths. Some might choose fairness, others equality. The thing that makes authoritarians distinctive is their reliance on established authorities, which might include things like time-honored conventions, texts, or leaders who make decisions with these considerations in mind, to impose order. Taken together, we suspect that those who score high in authoritarianism have (1) a greater need for order and, conversely, less tolerance for confusion or ambiguity, and (2) a propensity to rely on established authorities to provide that order.

At root, these differences probably derive from cognitive differences between the more and less authoritarian, which, in the end, may lead to differences in emotional response as well. Specifically, those scoring high in authoritarianism will probably tend to rely more on emotion and instinct than those scoring low because they (1) have, on average, fewer cognitive tools and (2) feel more threat from the often ambiguous nature of the complicated world around them. When people feel substantial threat or anxiety (or fatigue), cognition breaks down, causing greater reliance on emotion and instinct to pick up the slack. Of course, this suggests (and we later show) that authoritarians and nonauthoritarians alike ought to reach similar preferences when they report feeling substantial threat. The reason people at opposite ends of the authoritarianism distribution differ in their feelings about a range of issues under most circumstances is because those scoring high tend to perceive threats fairly constantly in their battle to achieve clarity and impose order.

Thinking about authoritarianism in terms of order rather than authority itself also helps explain why those scoring high are more inclined to simplify the world into black and white categories while those scoring lower in authoritarianism feel more comfortable with shades of gray. Black and white categories provide order. So, too, does a propensity to submit to authorities, but only to those who promise a black and white understanding of the world. Authoritarians do not view Barack Obama as the same type of authority as, say, George W. Bush. Hence it is not so much the submission that is important but rather a preference for concreteness that is important.

Though we believe that a perceived need for order is more central to understanding authoritarianism than are uniform notions of authority, we still believe that ideas about authority play a distinctive role in understanding the disposition.

As Feldman observes, "If there is some ultimate wisdom in social norms, they may not even be a creation of ordinary people. They are likely to come from some 'higher authority'" (2003, 49; see also Hunter 1991). The potential importance of some "higher authority" to authoritarian conceptions of order echoes Gabennesch's (1972) notion of "reification," which "discourages or obviates any activity which would tamper with a social world that is super-ordinate and infused with transcendental authority. In other words, a reified world is self-justifying. Being morally and ontologically superior to men, it demands that men strive to adjust themselves to it" (Gabennesch 1972, 864).

Given these insights, it is perhaps unsurprising that authoritarianism is highly correlated with belief in biblical inerrancy.[1] It is not that all authoritarians are fundamentalist religious believers; that is not close to true. However, a shared mind-set by which strict adherence to the letter of the law, as opposed to context-specific interpretations of it, reflects authoritarian conceptions of order. This mind-set is a kind of secular or ecumenical analogue to a fundamentalist religious worldview. Whether one is talking about the Bible or the Constitution, for instance, one can identify an outlook that would reject multiple, layered interpretations in favor of an outlook motivated by the belief that too much slack and uncertainty in rule application could yield disorder, chaos, and social breakdown.

Adorno et al. (1950) framed the issue in terms of "harsh application of rules" versus "assimilation of principles." As Gabennesch puts it, "the externality and rigidity of the normative dimension induces a concern for the letter, rather than the spirit, of norms and discourages an appreciation of the subjective and the internal" (1972, 866). We suspect, for example, that a strong correlation would exist between authoritarianism and belief in "strict constructionist" views of the Constitution. Furthermore, when one considers the degree to which strict constructionists have vilified the Warren Court, with its mantra of substantive due process over procedural due process, and the extent to which that Court's activities are seen to have shaped the chaotic (some would say anarchic) 1960s, one can see how an authoritarian outlook might underlie the hot-button, culturally divisive, and contested symbols and issues over which Americans are fighting today. The growing secularism of the past forty years, accompanied by far-reaching challenges to older authorities, the transformation of gender roles, and changing family structures have all had a profound impact on American life, providing the context in which significant differences in attitudes about order and authority would take their place as central nodes of conflict in American politics.

Importantly, scholars have had an easier time characterizing authoritarians than they have characterizing authoritarian*ism*. As Schuman, Bobo, and Krysan (1992) remarked in 1992, and as remains true today, scholars are unsure whether authoritarianism is a personality trait, an attitude, or an ideology. The earliest work by Adorno and his colleagues conceptualized authoritarianism as

[1] The Pearson correlation is .43.

a personality trait resulting from the "repression of hostility toward parental authority and its displacement on societal outgroups" (Stenner 2005, 2). The latest line of work by Stenner (2005) and Feldman (2003) characterizes it as a "disposition." (For the roots of this approach, see Duckitt 1992.)

We do not attempt to solve this puzzle here because we are studying the *effects* of authoritarianism. In studying the effects of a variable, we assume that variable to be causally prior to the variables it affects. To put mass political behavior in the simplest causal terms, people must translate their deeply held values first into preferences about contested political issues and next align these preferences with positions proposed by candidates. For example, let's say a person values equality. She then translates this value into a preference for equal pay for equal work. And finally, she chooses candidates who articulate positions that are closest to her preferences on the issue. Now, why does she value equality? Is it because she is hard-wired, by dint of genetics or upbringing, to do so? Is it because equality is part of a larger view of how the world should work? While it might be interesting to find the root of her value system, the crucial relationship is how this value translates into political action.

We view authoritarianism in the same way. Here we characterize it forming the basis of a worldview. A worldview is quite simply a set of beliefs and ideals that a person uses as a guide to interpret the world. A worldview ought to be firmly and deeply held within an individual. As such, if we are right, it should translate into certain political preferences, regardless of its origin. The key point is that it is situated near the beginning of the causal chain of political reasoning where it will serve as a determinant of public opinion and political behavior.

This debate over authoritarianism and its origins is emblematic of its troubled history in the academy. Although *The Authoritarian Personality* sparked much initial scholarly interest, it was ultimately discredited. Some of the criticism was substantive, including the charge that the Freudian approach of relating childhood experiences to the emergence of authoritarianism was theoretically over-determined and inherently nonfalsifiable (Duckitt 1992, Stenner 2005; Altemeyer 2006). Another critique was methodological, suggesting that the survey items used to create the F-scale, Adorno et al.'s measure of authoritarianism based on a battery of survey questions, were poorly constructed (Hyman and Sheatsley 1954) and tapped into a range of attitudes beyond authoritarianism (e.g., Altemeyer 1981; Duckitt 2003; Stenner 2005). As Alan Wolfe (2005) put it, "When I attended graduate school in the 1960s, *The Authoritarian Personality* was treated as the social-science version of the Edsel, a case study in how to do everything wrong." As a result, the topic nearly disappeared from major scholarly journals for some time.

After decades of dwelling in the scholarly hinterlands, the study of authoritarianism has reemerged. Today, Lavine et al. (2005) note that, with "several theoretical alternatives to the original psychoanalytic framework, as well as more valid instruments to measure it ... [i]t would appear that authoritarianism is a core political predisposition, on a par with party identification and political ideology as a lens through which the political world is perceived and evaluated" (237).

While scholars have addressed substantive and methodological criticisms, they have had a somewhat harder time addressing normative ones. Simply put, how many of us, in polite conversation would tell a colleague "of course you support torture. You're an authoritarian!" Or how many people would explain their opposition to gay marriage as an outgrowth of their being an "authoritarian"? Certainly many of authoritarianism's most prominent scholars view those deemed to be authoritarian with great concern, if not outright derision. Altemeyer (1996), for example, has made no bones about what he regards as the pathological tendencies of authoritarians. He argues that those who score high on measures of authoritarianism (as measured by his right-wing authoritarianism [RWA] scale) are desperate for an authoritarian leader to follow to the ends of the earth (and perhaps off) so long as that leader projects an image of strength to salve their deep-seated fears and anxiety. He believes that the right-wing authoritarians he has identified would have made ideal Nazis and would make ideal Jihadists, and are characterized by impaired reasoning skills, greater than normal levels of hypocrisy, strong antidemocratic tendencies and other clear psychological and moral deficiencies.

One illustrative quote asserts that authoritarian followers

have mainly copied the beliefs of the authorities in their lives. They have not developed or thought through their ideas as much as most people have. Thus almost anything can be found in their heads if their authorities put it there, even stuff that contradicts other stuff. A filing cabinet or a computer can store quite inconsistent notions and never lose a minute of sleep over their contradiction. Similarly a high RWA can have all sorts of illogical, self-contradictory, and widely refuted ideas rattling around in various boxes in his brain, and never notice it. (Altemeyer 2007, 75)

The literature is replete with such indictments, regardless of the measures used to identify authoritarians. Notably, Stenner (2005) also associates authoritarianism with a range of personality defects, including lack of intelligence, greed, unwarranted suspiciousness, a generally sour disposition, and a tendency, under threat, to experience significant "cognitive deterioration."

Our claims for authoritarians are different, although we find much useful in this work. We find persuasive the broad-based findings that show authoritarians to be more likely to feel threatened by, and dislike, outgroups; more likely to desire muscular responses to conflict; less politically well informed; and less likely to change their way of thinking when new information might challenge their deeply held beliefs. But we confine our treatment of authoritarianism to the *political* world. Our measure of authoritarianism suggests individuals' expressed preferences for parenting styles, but it does not necessarily tell us what kind of parents authoritarians actually are (see Stenner 2005), nor what kind of neighbors or co-workers they might be. Some scholars have explored the deeper dimensions of personality in connection with political values and outlooks. However, personality remains, in important respects, a black box. We are, consequently, agnostic about the sources of authoritarianism and nonauthoritarianism in individuals' basic personalities. Instead, the concept provides important insight into the kinds of political issues certain individuals are likely to be motivated by and the accompanying political outlook likely to sustain those more specific issue positions. So, although we acknowledge some of the more troubling normative dimensions inherent in our use of this semantically pointed term, we believe it accurately reflects our empirical findings.

Authoritarianism and Current Issues

The rise of certain issues, especially those involving feelings toward minority groups and maintaining safety and security, makes authoritarianism particularly relevant politically because these issues have been closely associated with authoritarianism through decades of research (Adorno et al. 1950, Rokeach 1960, Martin 1964, Altemeyer 1981, 1996). Moreover, several recent studies have added to the voluminous older literature on this issue (see Duckitt 1989, Stenner 2005, and Altemeyer 2007).

When it comes to attitudes toward gays (one of the major new fault lines we discuss throughout the book), there is various evidence that those who score high in authoritarianism are much less positive than those who score low. Barker and Tinnick (2006) show authoritarians are much less supportive of a range of gay rights initiatives than are nonauthoritarians. In addition, authoritarians judge lawbreaking much less harshly when it involves gay bashing or police brutality, suggesting sympathy for dealing harshly, even illegally, with perceived deviants (Altemeyer 1996, 2007). Similarly, authoritarians are more inclined to favor quarantines for AIDS patients, a likely proxy for attitudes toward gays generally (Peterson, Doty, and Winter 1993).

Such aversion to difference extends to a variety of racial and ethnic groups. Sniderman and Piazza (1993) find that authoritarian attitudes are strongly predictive of negative racial stereotypes in general. For example, they find that "the person who believes that most Jews engage in shady practices and that Jews are indifferent to the well-being of those who are not Jewish tends also to believe that most blacks have a chip on their shoulder and take advantage of welfare" (1993, 37). They further note that "what underlies perceptions of blacks as lacking a willingness to work hard is not the ethic of hard work associated with individualism but the ethic of discipline and conformity associated with authoritarianism."

Circumstances may change the explicit targets of that intolerance. In the 1940s and 1950s, Jews were the outgroup du jour. In the 2000s, that is no longer true (Raden 1999). While those of Arab descent were not on Americans' radar until recently, they are now an object of authoritarian scorn, at least since September 11 (Huddy et al. 2005). Furthermore, it does not follow from these findings that all authoritarians are would-be members of the Ku Klux Klan. As our analyses indicate, however, those who score higher are, as an empirical fact, negatively disposed toward a broad range of ethnic and racial groups relative to those who score lower.

Apart from a clear inclination toward moral, ethnic, and political intolerance, those who score high in authoritarianism tend to favor more aggressive responses to external threats (Huddy et al. 2005; Perrin 2005). This is, of course, an especially important cleavage in a post-9/11 world, with the parties occupying such distinct positions, in the public mind, on the global war on terror, the war in Iraq, and the larger question of how to make America secure. Since the general view among authoritarians is that group cohesion is very fragile and must be protected at all costs, it follows that the use of any force necessary to preserve the group might be justified.

Authoritarianism versus Conservatism

Although political conservatives are closely identified with anti–gay rights positions and more hawkish responses to foreign policy, it is important to note that authoritarianism and conservatism are not the same thing. As Stenner (2005) argues, authoritarianism is "not preference for laissez-faire economics" and conversely, that conservative "distaste for change" does not automatically imply "distaste for other races"; nor is it true that "commitment to economic freedom somehow suggests an interest in moral regulation and political repression" (2005, 327). Those who score high in authoritarianism do not approve of the status quo merely for the sake of preserving the status quo. On the contrary, they are, first and foremost, concerned with maintaining the social order and opposing that which they believe undermines that order (what Stenner refers to as "normative threat").

Because existing norms are time tested in their ability to maintain the social fabric, authoritarians tend to favor orthodox, venerable understandings of right and wrong. But under the right circumstances, they will support radical changes in the existing social fabric if they can be persuaded that those changes are necessary to maintain order and quell threats to the social fabric (Stenner 2005). In this way, authoritarianism is conceptually distinct from conservatism (Feldman 2003; Stenner 2005), though the two are becoming more and more closely intertwined in contemporary American politics as conservatives increasingly choose to make use of issues like gay rights, supporting broad surveillance of the country's citizens to maintain security, and immigration, in which mass preferences are structured by authoritarianism. If conservatives made more use of issues like limiting the size of government while emphasizing libertarian social attitudes, for example, conservatism and authoritarianism would be much less intertwined.

We can draw at least indirect evidence of this from the 1960s. In the years leading up to the race-based issue evolution, Americans were significantly more willing to call themselves "liberal." From the late 1930s, through 1965, Ellis and Stimson (2007) find a relatively constant stream of liberal responses to public opinion items. This changed fundamentally and durably in 1965, the year after the adoption of the Civil Rights Act and the increased focus on race in the political system. This suggests that when politics was about the traditional New Deal cleavage, people were more comfortable identifying themselves as liberals. Conservatism and authoritarianism were relatively distinct. When politics evolved such that race – and later, moral permissiveness – were central to perceptions of liberalism, people were much less comfortable identifying themselves as liberals. Conservatism and authoritarianism were becoming increasingly indistinct. In short, the relationship between authoritarianism and conservatism is historically contingent, not immutable.

As Stenner (2005, 85–86) helpfully notes, the scholarly literature suggests three different sorts of conservatism. Two of those strains, a desire to preserve the status quo rather than encourage change and a preference for free markets and small government, are not authoritarian in nature. Only the third, which has an intolerance of difference at its core, can be considered authoritarian. Importantly, all our models explaining public opinion in succeeding chapters include statistical controls for each of these strains of conservatism when appropriate. We take great pains to carve off the authoritarian strain from the other two.

Situationism

Another important aspect of authoritarianism is situationism. Situationism is the idea that the impact of authoritarianism (always latent in certain people) manifests itself in politically relevant ways only under threatening circumstances (Duckitt 1989, 2001; Doty, Peterson, and Winter 1991; Feldman and Stenner 1997; Lavine et al. 1999; Feldman 2003; Stenner 2005). A voluminous body of research connects authoritarianism to prejudice as part of a larger negative affect for, and intolerance of, those who are seen as different and, therefore, as threats to existing social order. Recent work, however, suggests that such tendencies are much more contingent than the original approaches to authoritarianism assumed (Duckitt 1992; Feldman and Stenner 1997; Feldman 2003; Stenner 2005). Perceived threat varies over time depending on the nature of issues and events, so the political relevance of authoritarianism is subject to changing circumstances rather than being a static reality.

Speaking to the interaction of threat with authoritarianism as it relates to intolerance and prejudice, Feldman (2003) concludes that both are a function of "the degree of perceived threat to social cohesion" (51). In fact, Feldman goes so far as to argue that authoritarians "should not be highly intolerant or prejudiced, absent a perceived threat to social cohesion. Those who strongly value social conformity should be highly sensitive to those threats and should react by denigrating groups that are seen as a threat and by supporting action to eliminate the threat by limiting the liberties and rights of those seen to be responsible" (2003, 66). In short, Feldman finds that authoritarianism does not directly affect prejudice but rather does so only in interaction with threat.

We are sympathetic to Feldman's arguments about situationism and agree that there is a logic to asserting that prejudice and intolerance are not sui generis but rather are an outgrowth of some more fundamental cognitive/psychological need – in this case, for order and sameness. Furthermore, we regard it as sensible and consistent with our own understanding that particular circumstances would intensify underlying dispositional traits. However, it is important to note that most of the conclusions about authoritarianism and situationism derive from controlled experiments, usually of student subjects. In a controlled experiment, authoritarians are apt to react most strongly to manipulated levels of threat, especially when the threats devised are ones that are likely to be more threatening to those scoring high in authoritarianism rather than to those who score low.

In cross-sectional survey analysis, however, we cannot control who receives threatening stimuli and what the threatening stimuli are. In fact, one could argue that given the dynamism and uncertainty of an ever-more rapidly changing world (and all the more so in post-9/11 America), it is plausible to assume that there is always some measure of threat to social cohesion and that an increasingly acrimonious political climate would only exacerbate such perceptions. Moreover, it is plausible to assume that authoritarians' innate wariness about social order and threats to it would be activated as soon as they are prompted to think about politics, as they would be when asked to answer questions for any political survey.

Therefore, without rejecting the premise of situationism, we suggest that in the real world, perceptions of threat among authoritarians are likely to be high with low variance relative to nonauthoritarians so that scholars utilizing cross-sectional surveys are unlikely to find a positive interaction between threat and authoritarianism. In fact, as we discuss and demonstrate in Chapter 6, we consistently find the reverse. For the purposes of fleshing out our understanding of authoritarianism, it is important to note that although Feldman may be right conceptually, in practical terms the relationship between authoritarianism on the one hand and prejudice and ethnic intolerance on the other is, our analyses show, a direct one.

In sum, authoritarianism is fundamentally motivated by a desire for order and a support for authorities seen as best able to secure that order against a variety of threats to social cohesion. For authoritarians, proper authorities are necessary to stave off the chaos that often appears to be just around the corner. Furthermore, authoritarians often imbue authorities with transcendent qualities, not subject to questioning and doubt. Emanating from such a conception is a suspicion of ideas that appear to pose a threat to such authorities and of groups that may, by their very nature, unravel the social fabric. A tendency to rigid thinking and an unwillingness or inability to process new information that might challenge such thinking also appears to be characteristic of authoritarians' mode of political understanding. In fact, Kruglanski et al.(2006) argue that there is an important connection between desire for group cohesion and sameness on the one hand, and a need for cognitive closure and aversion to ambiguity on the other, insofar as group cohesion is predicated, importantly, on a shared outlook or worldview.

CHARACTERISTICS OF NONAUTHORITARIANISM

Critics have long maintained that one of the problems with the literature on authoritarianism is its ideological bias – its tendency to associate psychological pathology with a set of attitudes commonly associated with political conservatism. In this vein, scholars like Shils (1954) and Ray (1976, 1983) have argued that there was also an authoritarianism of the left.

There are a couple of important points here. First, when concerns about authoritarianism of the left emerged, Stalinism and Maoism were major forces in world politics, with nontrivial followings in Western liberal democracies. Those movements, animated by rigidity, varying degrees of ethnocentrism, political intolerance, and intolerance of ambiguity, could fairly be said to share many of the characteristics associated with authoritarianism of the right. However, Stalinism and Maoism, outside of North Korea, are long dead. We do not believe that it is plausible to argue that the dominant left-of-center party in the United States today shares any meaningful characteristics with Maoism and Stalinism, and movements further to the left have been thoroughly marginalized.

This does not mean that farther left groups cannot be criticized for shrillness or intransigence; they can. Indeed they can even behave in ways that we typically associate with those who score high in authoritarianism. For example, the literature on authoritarianism often highlights a willingness for authoritarians to follow leaders in lockstep (Adorno et al. 1950). Notably, Rush Limbaugh has his "ditto heads." But it is also true that those who score low in authoritarianism follow their opinion leaders very closely, too. Markos Moulitsas, who created the liberal blog The Daily Kos, also has his "Kossacks." But what might make the nonauthoritarian left shrill or intransigent emanates from something or somewhere different from a need for order, making it conceptually different from authoritarianism. It is critical not to confuse behavioral manifestations of attitudes with the attitudes themselves.

Second, none of this is to say that nonauthoritarians lack specific, identifiable characteristics or that nonauthoritarians possess characteristics that are uniformly beyond criticism or reproach. Instead, we simply wish to clarify that the fundamental divide in America is not between two groups with the same psychological disposition who merely disagree on the objects of their scorn. They do disagree on those objects. But, more fundamentally, they appear to be animated by fundamentally different dispositions which, in turn, inform their dramatically different worldviews.

We accept the notion of Jost et al. (2003) that authoritarianism represents a form of "motivated social cognition," in which, as Lavine et al. (2005) explain, "ideological beliefs are seen as grounded in epistemic and existential psychological needs" (220, fn. 2). The term *motivated social cognition* is a clunky one, but it connotes the idea that people believe what they believe because to do so serves certain key psychological purposes. In the case of authoritarians, for example, much of the literature suggests that their need for certainty and aversion to ambiguity serves a functional purpose – to help ward off concerns and anxieties about disorder. Significantly, our work suggests that not only authoritarians are so motivated, but that nonauthoritarians may be as well, though for different reasons.

Because of the lack of attention to understanding what motivates nonauthoritarians, we are somewhat hamstrung in our efforts to sketch a profile of nonauthoritarians comparable in detail to the composite picture we can trace for authoritarians. However, as we have asserted and show throughout, much of the explanatory power of authoritarianism in American politics over the past fifteen years or so derives from changes among those with moderate or low levels of authoritarianism, and not among authoritarians. Therefore, it would be useful to say something about the phenomenon as its own kind of motivated cognition.

Several features are common to nonauthoritarians that may derive from a specifically motivated worldview, and we discuss each briefly, in turn. These are a strongly held notion of fairness that manifests itself as outgroup preference; a tendency toward accuracy motivation; an aversion to prejudicial thinking; valuing personal autonomy over social conformity; an aversion to judgments that make them relativistic; and a tendency to be broadly opinionated.

Fairness as Outgroup Preference

Those who score low in authoritarianism apparently have a different notion of fairness from those who do not, at least as it relates to preferences that are structured by authoritarianism. Those scoring high in authoritarianism have a strong need for order, resulting in a tendency toward black and white thinking. Conversely, those who score low in authoritarianism have more tolerance for ambiguity, which allows for more nuanced understandings of political phenomena. For those scoring high, treating people differently, under any circumstances, would be classified as unfair. For those scoring lower in authoritarianism, such a calculation might be more complicated in ways that favor those who are often the objects of concern for authoritarians. Race provides the best opportunity to test our thinking.

One empirical measure of support for the supposition that nonauthoritarians have a particular notion of fairness that favors outgroups can be drawn from the Race and Politics Survey carried out in 1991. Through a survey experiment, randomly selected groups of respondents were asked whether certain groups (specifically poor people and blacks) would rather take government assistance than work. While those scoring high and moderate in authoritarianism tended to think both groups were equally likely to take government handouts, those at the low end said blacks were *less* likely than poor people to take handouts. Another survey question asked whether blacks (in one condition) or new immigrants from Europe (in the other condition) should work their way up, as in the past. Nonauthoritarians were significantly less likely to say blacks needed to work their way up than they were to say new immigrants needed to. Only nonauthoritarians treated the two groups differently.

There are, of course, different ways to characterize these findings. Those scoring high in authoritarianism would probably argue that nonauthoritarians maintain an unfair double standard by treating groups differently. Alternatively, those scoring low in authoritarianism might believe they are being fair, given the social realities that, in their view, hinder African Americans. In this sense, outgroup preference can be seen as a commitment to fairness, not a rejection of it.

The second interpretation suggests more nuanced thinking than the first, although we hasten to add that it might not be more correct. Rather than treating everyone the same way, which to the more authoritarian might be perceived always to be the fair position, those who are nonauthoritarian apparently are more inclined to make exceptions. Consistent with this, it is noteworthy that those scoring lower in authoritarianism are more supportive of affirmative action programs than those who score high (Barker and Tinnick 2006). Part of the reason is likely that authoritarians dislike the intended recipients of the program. But differing calculations of fairness might also be important. In a concrete sense, nothing could seem less fair than giving preference in hiring decisions or college admissions to one group over another, especially if you are part of the group that is being discriminated against. If this is the only metric on which fairness is judged, then it would be hard to justify support. But if one tackles the more ambiguous historical context that gave rise to the need for affirmative action programs, then deciding what is fair becomes more complicated. One's relative willingness to wrestle with the ambiguity inherent in solving discrimination against one group by, in effect, discriminating against another helps determine what "fair" means.

In this context, it is worth noting that one powerful source of resentment directed against liberal social programs in the late 1960s was that white, working-class communities were forced to bear the brunt of reformers' desire to engineer social change. In fact, it was a conservative Democrat, Mario Procaccino, who first used the epithet "limousine liberal" to describe his liberal Republican opponent, John Lindsay, during the latter's reelection bid in the 1969 New York City mayoral race. Procaccino suggested that Lindsay himself would never be forced to live in the kinds of neighborhoods whose integration he was pushing. The more general point here is that what critics might contend is a misguided belief that every human foible can be solved by a government program or, for example, that what are concrete, criminal misdeeds by individuals are really to be blamed on society more generally, could stem from a nonauthoritarian impulse both toward abstract notions of fairness and a tendency toward viewing issues in broad contextual terms.

Accuracy Motivation

Numerous scholars have written about accuracy motivation (see, e.g., Thompson et al. 1994; Kruglanski et al. 2006). Kruglanski et al. (2006), in particular, argue that there is a strong relationship between the need for social cohesion and group identity on the one hand, and a willingness to sacrifice unbiased access to information on the other. Lavine et al. (2005) link that phenomenon to authoritarianism by using an experimental manipulation. They find that both high authoritarians and low authoritarians, in the absence of a "threat" treatment, responded similarly to norms of evenhandedness in selecting information. However, once they introduced a threat condition, authoritarians subsequently became much less interested than nonauthoritarians in seeking information that was balanced in its approach, and much more interested in pursuing one-sided information that reinforced existing beliefs.

Although the literature is rife with examples of those scoring high and low in authoritarianism differing in their command of objective facts, we draw on a recent example that fits well with our approach to understanding contemporary American politics. In an original survey we conducted in 2006, we asked respondents whether weapons of mass destruction had been found in Iraq and whether Saddam Hussein had been involved directly in the September 11 terrorist attacks. Of course, neither was objectively true. Those scoring low in authoritarianism, by and large, answered these factual questions correctly. Among those scoring below the midpoint of the scale, only 15 percent answered the weapons of mass destruction question incorrectly while 19 percent erred on the Saddam and September 11 question. Among those scoring above the midpoint, however, those percentages were 37 and 55 percent, respectively.

Those scoring high in authoritarianism would have been disposed toward a military solution to September 11 and thus would have been likely to avoid information that would have complicated this position, especially that Hussein was not involved in the terrorist attacks on the United States. Such a tendency would have been particularly strong among Republicans, since Republican elites had at least implied that claims about finding weapons of mass destruction in Iraq and Hussein's involvement were true. Among Republicans, however, those scoring below the authoritarianism midpoint were only about half as likely to answer these questions wrong (33 and 36 percent, respectively) as those scoring above the midpoint (62 and 68 percent, respectively).

Perhaps the motivations of those scoring low in authoritarianism are also important. Nonauthoritarians' commitment to balanced information might itself be a cognitively motivated – that is, functionally useful – psychological strategy. Perhaps nonauthoritarians believe that a lack of complete information or comprehensive evaluation of available evidence will produce its own significant threats to well-being. We are not arguing that all individuals are equally anxious, and it may be that authoritarians evince a certain kind of anxiety that is more readily identifiable and classifiable. But we would suggest that the motivation to seek out balance and fully informed sources of information may be as strongly held as the motivation to tamp down one's anxiety and uncertainty by seeking out information that affirms what one already knows.

Importantly, this attribute, which seems admirable in the abstract, may not be so admirable under certain circumstances. One could readily imagine a situation requiring decisive leadership and the need to process information quickly, in which excessive hand-wringing might be an active detriment to social well-being. In any event, the underlying finding is consistent with our hunch about nonauthoritarians and accuracy motivation. As we discuss in more detail below, nonauthoritarians have a greater need for cognition, and they are more accurate in their political knowledge and assessments than are authoritarians. This may be as much a result of psychological motivation as it is of any underlying intelligence, which is beyond our means to assess.

Aversion to Ethnocentrism

The literature on authoritarianism has long held as a bedrock finding that authoritarians tend toward ethnocentric and generally prejudicial thinking. However, it is noteworthy, and consistent with our own perspective on the driving force behind political change that when we examine the correlations between measures of affect toward different groups, it is the nonauthoritarians who show dramatically more constraint than the authoritarians. Among those who scored lowest in authoritarianism in the 2004 National Election Study (NES), the correlations between their (generally favorable) sentiment toward blacks, Jews, and gays, as measured by the NES's feeling thermometer questions in 2004, are in the neighborhood of .5. By contrast, among those scoring highest in authoritarianism, the correlations among their (generally less favorable) sentiments toward those groups are barely above .1.

While the literature on authoritarianism views ethnocentrism as a motivated outcome, the degree of constraint among nonauthoritarians may itself be the result of a strong, discrete motivation. Perhaps nonauthoritarians are less likely to evaluate ethnic groups, for example, in stereotypical ways because they find it so dangerous to do so. Or perhaps they feel constrained by an abstract belief in evenhandedness even if they have prejudicial emotions and feelings that they are uncomfortable acknowledging. In any event, these results suggest at least the possibility that nonauthoritarian tolerance is more robust than authoritarian intolerance.

Personal Autonomy

That nonauthoritarians appear to value personal autonomy over social conformity does not necessarily mean, contra Feldman, that nonauthoritarians have no conception of social well-being. They almost certainly do. It may be that their conception of social well-being is in strong contrast to that of authoritarians and is predicated on a belief in flexible rule application, independence of thought, and reluctance to ostracize out-groups. In fact, the absence of such attributes may cause nonauthoritarians considerable worry and anxiety about the well-being of the social fabric as they understand it.

Perhaps, then, the key distinction between authoritarians and nonauthoritarians is not between those who worry about the social fabric and those who do not, but rather between the objects of worry about threats to social well-being, with authoritarians being more focused on individuals and their behaviors, and nonauthoritarians on large institutions and other powerful forces in society. We cannot substantiate our hunch, but we suspect, for example, that nonauthoritarians would be more concerned with phenomena like global warming or the bird flu.

It would follow from this understanding that personal autonomy would, from a nonauthoritarian perspective, be not only a matter of lifestyle preference but likely a greater bulwark against threats to social well-being – as nonauthoritarians understand them – than conformist behavior would allow for. Perhaps this is because nonauthoritarians are less anxious about how individual behaviors, like gay lifestyles, for example, would affect social well-being. Or, alternatively, nonauthoritarians may be especially loath to make judgments about other people, perhaps even when such judgments are warranted and necessary to protect the community, as might be the case of views about criminality and how best to safeguard communities from it. In any event, it appears that nonauthoritarians maintain a strong preference for personal autonomy in matters of private behavior and that this is a distinctive feature of their worldview.

MEASURING AUTHORITARIANISM

Devising a measure of authoritarianism has proven problematic. Adorno's original "F-scale," used to tap the concept, fell into disrepute within a decade of its introduction for any number of reasons, response acquiescence and poor reliability chief among them (Altemeyer 1981). Subsequent to the abandonment of the F-scale, scholars have measured authoritarianism in many ways. The most widely used measure is the RWA (Right-Wing Authoritarianism) scale. Originally composed of thirty Likert-type items, and later pared to twenty-four, this scale asks respondents to agree or disagree with statements such as the following: "our country desperately needs a mighty leader who will do what has to be done to destroy the radical new ways and sinfulness that is ruining us," "it is always better to trust the judgment of the proper authorities in government and religion than to listen to the noisy rabble-rousers in our society who are trying to create doubt in people's minds," "what our country really needs is a strong, determined leader who will crush evil, and take us back to our true path," and "the real keys to the 'good life' are obedience, discipline, and sticking to the straight and narrow."

Unlike its predecessor, the RWA boasts an impressive reliability. Yet, such high reliability is the source of criticism, with scholars suggesting, with good reason, that the reason the measure is so predictive of prejudice and intolerance is that it is, itself, largely a measure of prejudice and intolerance (Feldman 2003; Stenner 2005). For example, Feldman (2003) suggests that some RWA items, such as "gays and lesbians are just as healthy and moral as anybody else," likely taps tolerance toward deviant groups. If it is itself a measure of intolerance about specific groups, then it has little value as an explanatory variable attempting to explain intolerance toward specific groups. Moreover, Feldman (2003) argues that the measure fails to distinguish between social conservatism (or a moral traditionalism) and authoritarianism. As evidence, he cites items such as "homosexuals and feminists should be praised for being brave enough to defy 'traditional family values,'" "a woman's place should be wherever she wants it to be," and "there is absolutely nothing wrong with nudist camps."

The measure of authoritarianism that we use was designed to address these concerns. In 1992, the NES introduced its four-item authoritarianism index. Specifically, it asked respondents to judge attractive attributes in children, introducing the topic in this way:

Although there are a number of qualities that people feel that children should have, every person thinks that some are more important than others. I am going to read you pairs of desirable qualities. Please tell me which one you think is more important for a child to have.

The pairs of attributes are independence versus respect for elders, obedience versus self-reliance, curiosity versus good manners, and being considerate versus being well behaved. Those who value "respect for elders," "obedience," "good manners," and "being well behaved" score at the maximum of the scale. Those who value "independence," "self-reliance," "curiosity," and "being considerate" score at the minimum.

In creating an authoritarianism scale using the NES data, we array all four items such that the authoritarian response has a score of 1 and the nonauthoritarian response has a score of 0. Since both values in each pair are desirable, a fair number of people volunteer that they value both. We score these responses as .5. We then combine the items additively and take the mean.

Some could argue that these pairings require a false choice. After all, most people would presumably want their children to be curious *and* well-mannered. What is useful about this approach, we believe, is that it appropriately mirrors choices individuals are forced to make in politics. Most people would probably like to pick and choose between Republican policies and conservative attitudes they like and Democratic policies and liberal attitudes they share. But voting forces choices, and we believe that the pairings described above represent people's priorities. In this case, the forced choice prompts respondents to prioritize their normative preferences for the proper relationship of children to parents, of youngsters to elders, of subordinates to superordinates. It also prompts people to choose between a preference for self-directed decision making and strict adherence to rules which, as we noted above, is critical to distinguishing authoritarians from nonauthoritarians (see also Lakoff 1996).

As evidence that the child preferences battery is valid, we draw on findings derived from Feldman's (2003) Social Conformity-Autonomy Scale. He constructed seventeen fixed-choice items, asking respondents which of two statements they most strongly agreed with. Of these seventeen, he categorized twelve as tapping "Social Conformity-Autonomy Beliefs" (SCA Beliefs) and five as tapping "Social Conformity-Autonomy Values" (SCA Values). Among other items, the SCA Beliefs included choices between "it's best for everyone if people try to fit in instead of acting in unusual ways" versus "people should be encouraged to express themselves in unique and possibly unusual ways," while the SCA Values focused on socialization and child-rearing values, such as "it may well be that children who talk back to their parents respect them more in the long run" versus "obedience and respect for authority are the most important virtues children should learn." Feldman reports correlations among the SCA Beliefs, SCA Values, and RWA scales as well as correlations among the RWA scale and a combined SCA Beliefs-SCA Values scale. The correlations are quite high; indeed, the combined Beliefs-Values measure correlates with the RWA at .77.

For our purposes, the most interesting finding is the .68 correlation between the SCA Values (composed in part of child-rearing items) and the RWA. This correlation is suggestive of the potential to tap into authoritarianism by relying on measures clearly untainted by any ideological leanings, or any subsequent attitudes or behaviors. This may seem somewhat unusual, but the idea that child-rearing values are a potential indicator of authoritarianism is not new. The original F-scale and the RWA scale include a question asking whether "obedience and respect for authority are the most important virtues children should learn."

In fact, the fundamentally political nature of child-rearing practices has long been noted in political thought – for example, in Rousseau's *Emile* and from leading twentieth-century thinkers such as John Dewey and Jean Piaget. For our purposes, it is noteworthy, as Richard Hofstadter wrote in *Anti-Intellectualism in American Life*, that "Dewey's anxiety about adult authority stemmed from his desire to avoid something with which we are still trying with much difficulty to avoid – the inculcation of conformist habits in the child. If there was anything he did *not* want, it was to breed conformist character" (Hofstadter 1955, 382). For Dewey, according to Hofstadter, what was at stake was no less than the possibility of raising a truly democratic society, an impossibility in the face of conformist education driven by, in Hofstadter's words, a "harshly authoritarian" approach to pedagogy.

Along these lines, Martin (1964), relying on a three-question child-rearing battery similar to the one we employ,[2] argues that

there is probably no other question on which tolerants differ from intolerants more sharply than on child-rearing practices. Attitudes on this subject directly and efficiently

---

[2] Martin relied on data from a large-scale 1956 Indianapolis study that asked respondents to agree or disagree with the following three items: (1) spare the rod, spoil the child; (2) A child should never keep any secrets from his parents; (3) Obedience is the most important thing a child should be.

reflect general ethnocentrism. How to "bring up" or socialize children is a matter of profound consequence, involving basic human values and objectives. The kinds of techniques which a person endorses reveals his values, especially the goals of socialization, i.e., what he considers to be the ideal person as an adult. (1964, 86)

Martin contends that these relationships make sense because "a person's child-rearing attitudes reflect an idealized self-image" (p. 87). He explains:

The subject of child-rearing techniques pinpoints a fundamental proposition in human relations: how should people (superordinate parents in this case) treat other people (subordinate children, in this case)? Should parent-offspring relations be based on mutual trust, genuine affection, and cooperation – democratic, in a word – or is the ideal relationship an "authoritarian" one, based upon power, fear, obedience to a power figure, and mutual distrust, or some compromise between these "polar" positions? (1964, 87)

Thus, child-rearing values suggest a fundamental way in which people view the world (Stenner 2005). Do they favor general authority and submission to it, expressed in a child's obedience or respect for elders? Or do they favor individual autonomy, expressed in a child's creativity and imagination? They likely appreciate the need for both, but, when pressed, which of the two do they value more? Kohn and Schooler (1983) find this dimension in parenting values to exist in all the industrialized countries they studied and one preindustrialized country (Taiwan), suggesting the fundamental human nature of this disposition.

One apparent criticism of this measure of authoritarianism is that it potentially taps into child-rearing practices rather than child-rearing values. Evidence reassures us that this is unlikely. The earliest work demonstrating the centrality of child-rearing values to authoritarianism was published in the mid-1960s (e.g., Martin 1964), and survey items about the importance of obedience in children date to the 1950s. Child-rearing practices in the United States are much less homogenous and less authoritarian today than they were forty years ago, yet child-rearing values are largely the same (Stenner 2005). In addition, the correlation between people's stated child-rearing values and the way they actually parent is far from perfect (Stenner 2005). That is, someone who claims to value "independence" in a child may actually parent in a way that would produce "discipline" and "conformity" instead. Indeed, the stated desire for independence in the survey is, attitudinally, more important than the actual parenting approach. In that sense, these items seem to tap a worldview that is broader than typical political attitudes.

DATA SOURCES

During the course of the book, we make use of several surveys, all of which include child-rearing batteries, in addition to the three NES surveys (those taken in 1992, 2000, and 2004) that included these batteries of questions. The first is an original survey that was conducted for us by the Internet-based polling firm Polimetrix as part of a large 2006 data collection for a range of nearly forty different universities called the Cooperative Congressional Election Study (CCES). We provide more details about this survey in Chapter 5. The second is another original survey, also conducted by Polimetrix, titled AmericasBarometer by LAPOP (Latin American Public Opinion Project). Commissioned by Mitch Seligson for the Latin American Public Opinion Project, the survey was designed to provide a benchmark of American attitudes toward democracy to compare with attitudes of those from Latin America. It also included many items useful to our purposes.

Since both these surveys conducted by Polimetrix were carried out using an online computer interface in which response options were provided for respondents to click, they did not allow respondents to volunteer to a human interviewer that they valued both attributes equally as was the case in the NES. Hence none of the individual items include responses that we place at the midpoint of the scale. Despite this difference, the data from the NES and from the CCES produce relatively similar results for both the central tendency and the spread of the distribution of authoritarianism in the electorate. In the 2004 NES, the mean is 0.58 with a standard deviation of 0.29. In the 2006 CCES, the mean is 0.53, which is somewhat lower than the NES, with a standard deviation of 0.33, which is somewhat larger. In the 2008 AmericasBarometer by LAPOP survey, the mean is .59, with a standard deviation of .31.

In Table 3.1, we present the frequency distributions for three of the surveys we use most throughout the book: the 2004 NES, the 2006 CCES, and the 2008 AmericasBarometer. Since a fair number of people volunteer "both" to one or more of the items in the battery in the NES, there are significantly more categories than for the two data sets administered by Polimetrix, in which such responses were not allowed.

By this measure, authoritarianism is not a fringe disposition. Nearly 50 percent of each of the samples scores either .75 or 1 on the scale. Those scoring at .25 or below are a rarer breed, making up about 25 percent of cases in the 2004 NES and 2008 AmericasBarometer surveys. We had more people scoring low in authoritarianism in the 2006 CCES. Unlike most survey items or batteries, the midpoint is not the modal category in any of the surveys. Instead it is the .75 category. Although there are differences in the distributions here, we should add that they do not seem to matter much substantively. Our results replicate across data sets, something we show repeatedly through Chapters 5 and 6.

Finally, we also make some use of the 1991 Race and Politics Study, which was carried out by Paul Sniderman and a bevy of co-investigators. This survey included three of the four child-rearing items. Like the Polimetrix surveys, the Race and Politics Study did not allow people to provide a response of both. We mostly use this survey to test the construct validity of the child-rearing battery against a set of items with which any measure of authoritarianism ought to be correlated.

TABLE 3.1. *Frequency Distribution of the Four-Item Authoritarianism Battery in Three Separate Surveys*

	2004 NES	2006 CCES	2008 AmericasBarometer
0	8.2	14.8	9.7
.125	0.2		
.25	14.9	19.4	14.1
.33	0.3		
.375	1.8		
.50	23.5	23.1	26.8
.625	6.5		
.667	0.2		
.75	24.9	25.4	28.4
.875	3.8		
1	15.8	17.3	21.0
TOTAL	100	100	100

Sources: 2004 NES, 2006 CCES, 2008 AmericasBarometer by LAPOP

CONSTRUCT VALIDITY

In this section we explore the relationship between this measure of authoritarianism and a range of different variables that a good measure of authoritarianism should be correlated with. In demonstrating that the child-rearing battery works well as a measure, we are also able to sketch a profile of those who score high and low in authoritarianism.

Cognitive Differences

Scholarship about authoritarianism suggests that those scoring high tend to exhibit lower levels of cognitive power (see Stenner 2005 for a review). This specific difference may be at the root of the tendency for those scoring high in authoritarianism to favor black and white interpretations of events and those scoring low to favor more nuanced interpretations One, albeit indirect, indication of such a pattern is the marked differences in educational attainment between those scoring high and those scoring low in authoritarianism. An indication that the child-rearing battery is measuring what it is supposed to is that it has a strong negative correlation ($r = -.35$, in the 2004 NES) with education.

In establishing construct validity, it is best to test a range of different indicators that all suggest that the measure is tapping the concept. It would also be helpful if we could find some measures that more directly address cognition since education is a very imperfect proxy. Fortunately, the NES began to employ a set of items in 2000, asking respondents to assess what is called a need for cognition. If our measure of authoritarianism is valid, we should find that those scoring high in authoritarianism score low in need for cognition.

One component of the need for cognition measure asks people whether they like simple or complex problems more. In the population as a whole, Americans are almost evenly split, with 52 percent choosing simple problems and 48 percent choosing complex ones. Authoritarianism is strongly related to these preferences. Among those scoring at the authoritarianism minimum, nearly three-quarters favor complex problems over simple ones. In contrast, less than 40 percent of those scoring .75 or above on the authoritarianism scale would prefer to grapple with complex problems.

We find a similarly robust relationship between authoritarianism and another of the NES's need for cognition items, namely how much a person likes "responsibility for thinking." For this measure, respondents were asked to place themselves on a 5-point scale ranging from "like it a lot" to "dislike it a lot." Of course, not many Americans admit that they do not like responsibility for thinking, with only 11 percent falling into the latter category. But of those who expressed such a sentiment, more than 60 percent scored at .75 or above on the authoritarianism scale. Those scoring low in authoritarianism were much more likely to express pleasure about having responsibility for thinking. Among those who scored at authoritarianism's minimum, 70 percent of them said they "liked it a lot," while only 26 percent of those scoring at the maximum said they did.

The last of the NES's need for cognition items asks respondents to assess how opinionated they are, providing them four response options: having opinions about "almost everything," "many things," "most things," or "very few things." Of those scoring lowest in authoritarianism, fully 82 percent placed themselves in the two most opinionated categories. Those scoring at the maximum of the scale indicated that they were much less opinionated, with less than 50 percent falling into these categories. When we combined these three items into a need for cognition scale, its correlation with authoritarianism is a very robust −.26, which is quite strong for variables this difficult to measure with precision.

The relationship between our authoritarianism scale and other measures of cognitive capacity provide us more confidence in the measure. Although the NES does not ask respondents to answer an IQ test, it does ask its interviewers to assess the intelligence of respondents based on their experience during the interview. Although some might be skeptical of the ability of interviewers to provide such an assessment, they are trained by the NES to make them. Moreover, interviewers spend several hours with the respondents conducting the interviews, giving them ample time to observe their abilities and deficits. Perhaps not surprisingly, scholars have found the interviewers' assessment of respondents' intelligence to be an excellent proxy for cognitive ability (see Luskin 1987).

Although the NES instructs its interviewers to make these evaluations on a 5-point scale from very high intelligence to very low intelligence, less than

1 percent of evaluations fall into the latter category. In fact, only about 5 percent of cases fall into either of the not very intelligent categories. Apparently, grade inflation extends to NES evaluators as well. Hence we collapse the two high intelligence categories into one category and the two low intelligence categories into another category, leaving the midpoint of the scale as average intelligence. Again, the authoritarianism score of the respondent clearly structures interviewer assessments. Among those scoring lowest in authoritarianism, 84 percent were placed by interviewers in the high intelligence categories, while only 3 percent fell into the low intelligence categories. Even those scoring at .25 on authoritarianism were judged to be very intelligent by NES interviewers with 72 percent in the high intelligence categories and 3 percent in the low. The story is different for the other end of the authoritarianism scale. Among those scoring at the maximum of the scale, only 42 percent were placed in the high intelligence categories and 12 percent were placed in the low. Among those who scored at .75 in authoritarianism, only 55 percent made it into the high intelligence categories.

In addition to an interviewer assessment of intelligence, the NES asks something akin to a political IQ test. Specifically, the NES regularly asks people a number of factual questions of varying difficulty about politics. In 2004, they asked four such questions. These included asking people to name the job or office held by four political figures: Dennis Hastert (Speaker of the House of Representatives), Dick Cheney (vice president in the George W. Bush administration), Tony Blair (British prime minister), and William Rehnquist (chief justice of the United States). It would be confirmatory if we were to find that authoritarianism has some bearing on people's knowledge of politics as well.

In fact, it does. The Hastert question was by far the most difficult, with only 11 percent of Americans correctly identifying him as Speaker of the House, despite the fact that he had held the position for six years up to that point. Importantly, those scoring at the authoritarianism minimum were three times as likely to answer correctly as those scoring at the maximum. The easiest question was the one about Dick Cheney, which 86 percent of Americans got right. Of the eighty-seven respondents who scored at the authoritarianism scale's minimum, eighty-six answered correctly, a 99 percent success rate. Among those scoring at the scale's maximum, however, only 70 percent answered correctly.

The other two questions about political figures turn up the same pattern. Tony Blair, who was the only world leader that the NES asked about, was identified correctly by 91 percent of those scoring at authoritarianism's minimum. Of those scoring at the maximum, only 45 percent got it right. Authoritarianism plays a similar role for identifying what job or office William Rehnquist held in 2004. Whereas about 30 percent of the entire sample answered correctly, 55 percent of those scoring lowest in authoritarianism did, while only 16 percent of those scoring at the maximum did. If we sum all the answers together into a scale ranging from 0 correct answers to 4, its correlation with authoritarianism is a very robust −.30. Again, we take this as good evidence that our measure of authoritarianism is measuring the concept that it is designed to measure.

Need for Order and Aversion to Ambiguity

Our theory about authoritarianism and cognition suggests that the presence of high levels of authoritarianism should lead to a strong need for order and, conversely, an aversion to ambiguity. Psychologists have developed batteries of questions designed to tap a person's need for order, and, in an original survey that we conducted in 2006, we asked two such questions. Specifically, we asked a random cross-section of Americans to place themselves on a 5-point scale ranging from "strongly agree" to "strongly disagree" with "neither agree nor disagree" as the midpoint: (1) "Personally, I tend to think that there is a right way and a wrong way to do almost everything" and (2) "Nothing gets accomplished in this world unless you stick to some basic rules." We expect that those scoring high in authoritarianism will be more inclined to agree with these statements while those who score lower ought to be less inclined to agree.

That is exactly the pattern of responses that we find. Only about 16 percent of respondents disagree either strongly or somewhat with the "right way" question, but fully 62 percent of these people provided either zero or one authoritarian responses to the child-rearing battery. Only 16 percent of these responses came from those providing either three or four authoritarian responses. In contrast, nearly one-third of respondents agree strongly that there is a right and wrong way to do almost anything. Of those scoring at the maximum of the authoritarianism scale, 54 percent fall into this category. Only 16 percent of those scoring at the minimum of authoritarianism do. Put another way, among people who disagree strongly with that proposition, the mean authoritarianism score is a mere .263. Among people who agree strongly, the mean authoritarianism score is .642. This is just an enormous difference and may well lie at the heart of the differences between authoritarians and nonauthoritarians.

The differences between authoritarians and nonauthoritarians are equally sharp for the "need for rules" item. Of course, it can be argued that people would want rules in an effort to maintain order; as with the "right way" item, most people see a need for rules. But among the 7 percent who do not agree with the proposition, nearly two-thirds provided either zero or one authoritarian response. Less than a sixth of those disagreeing with the proposition came from respondents who provided either three or four authoritarian responses. Conversely, those scoring high in authoritarianism were much more likely to agree with the proposition than were those who scored low. If we sum these two items into a need for order scale, its correlation with authoritarianism is a robust .35.

Tolerance, Difference, and Tradition

One reason that scholars focused significant attention on authoritarianism in the 1950s and 1960s was the importance of political tolerance in the scholarly dialogue at that time. Stouffer's (1955) landmark study raised important concerns about levels of tolerance in postwar American politics, and several later studies demonstrated that those who scored high on the F-scale, the traditional measure of authoritarianism of the time, were significantly less likely to be tolerant of the political rights of unpopular groups (Greenstein 1965). One of Stouffer's (1955) important innovations was the measurement of tolerance. In the context of the early 1950s, he tapped tolerance by asking people whether they were willing to allow the expression of ideas by communists, the United States' Cold War enemy at the time. Specifically, Stouffer asked respondents whether communists should be allowed to make speeches in the community or work as radio singers, and whether a book by a known communist should be removed from public libraries.

With the decline of communism in the 1990s, measures of tolerance that employed communists as the target group became obsolete, a concern that had been raised by scholars even a decade before (see, e.g., Sullivan et al. 1981; Sullivan, Piereson, and Marcus 1979; Gibson and Bingham 1982; Mueller 1988; Gibson 1989, 1992). In the early twenty-first century, the September 11 terrorist attacks made terrorists, particularly Muslim terrorists, the "communists" of the day. Although the NES did not ask an entire battery of tolerance items, in the 2006 NES Pilot Study they did ask the following question:

This next question is about a man who admits he is in favor of terrorism against the United States by Muslims. Suppose he wrote a book criticizing the United States that is in your public library. Somebody in your community suggests the book should be removed from the library. Would you favor removing the book or oppose removing the book?

If our measure of authoritarianism is valid, it should discriminate between those who are more and less tolerant of the expression of even generally unpopular ideas.

The results suggest that the measure we use here is valid on this score as well. Among those who scored at the authoritarianism minimum, only 12 percent thought the book should be banned. Among those scoring at the maximum, 79 percent did, producing an enormous 67 percentage point gulf in opinion across the range of the scale. Although the differences between these two categories are the most dramatic, the differences are still large at less extreme points on the scale. For example, 54 percent of those who scored at .75 on the authoritarianism scale said the book ought to be removed, more than twice the percentage with that opinion among those who scored at .25 (23 percent thought so).

Consistent with the breadth of Stouffer's (1955) interest in tolerance, the AmericasBarometer by LAPOP survey asked a more general battery of questions to tap tolerance as well. Specifically, it asked whether "critics of the United States" should be able to (1) conduct demonstrations, (2) run for public office, and (3) give speeches on television. The survey also asked a fourth question about whether homosexuals, specifically, should be allowed to run for public office. In all four cases, respondents were directed to place themselves on a 10-point scale anchored by strongly disagree at one end and strongly agree at the other.

In the main, Americans were very supportive of critics conducting demonstrations with a mean of 8.0, and were reasonably supportive of homosexuals running for office as well, with a mean of 7.1. Americans were somewhat less supportive of critics running for office or giving speeches on television, with means of 6.3 and 6.4, respectively. Most important for our purposes, the correlation between authoritarianism and these items individually averaged −.33. Taking the four items as an index, the correlation between authoritarianism and tolerance is −.40. To provide a sense of what such a correlation means, consider the following. Among these who provided zero authoritarian responses to the battery, their mean tolerance score was 8.99. Among those who provided four authoritarian responses, however, their mean tolerance score was only 5.61, more than three full points lower than the score of the least authoritarian respondents.

Our measure of authoritarianism also carries the expected correlations with measures of feelings about groups that could be seen by some, or most, as out-groups. Moving back to the 2004 NES data, we find that the correlations between authoritarianism and measures of nonblacks' attitudes toward blacks are strong. For example, the correlation between authoritarianism and the racial resentment battery that we introduced last chapter is a robust .35. We also find that those who score high in authoritarianism are more likely to hold anti-black stereotypes. Specifically, the NES asks respondents to place people from different races on an industriousness scale, anchored at one end by "lazy" and the other by "hardworking." To the extent that people evaluate whites as more hardworking than blacks, it suggests a propensity toward anti-black stereotyping. The correlation between the difference in whites' evaluations of whites' industriousness relative to blacks and authoritarianism is .27. This result further suggests that we are tapping authoritarianism with the child-rearing battery.

We would also expect those who score high in authoritarianism to embrace venerable gender roles. In 2004, the NES asked people whether they agreed or disagreed that it is better for women to care for the home and family while men achieve in the workplace. About 30 percent of Americans agreed with the proposition, nearly 60 percent disagreed, and a little over 10 percent said they neither agreed nor disagreed. Our measure of authoritarianism clearly structures these preferences, which again provides us confidence that our measure is tapping the concept. Among those who scored either 0 or .25 in authoritarianism, about 10 percent agreed that women ought to care for the home and men should achieve. Of those scoring .75 or above in authoritarianism, about 40 percent agreed. We find a similar 30 percentage point gap in disagreement with this proposition as well.

Finally, the 1991 Race and Politics Study asked a range of items that should correlate with a valid measure of authoritarianism. Specifically, the survey presented respondents with a set of ideas and asked them to rate, on a scale from 0 to 10, how important the ideas were to them. These items included things like "preserving the traditional ideas of right and wrong," "respect for authority," "following God's will," "improving politeness," "strengthening law and order," and "maintaining respect for America's power in the world." The three-item child-rearing battery used in this survey was correlated with all these items at a minimum of .2 and most often at greater than .3. These correlations are remarkably strong, given that these items measure how people see themselves rather than how they actually behave.

Taking this wide range of results together, we believe strongly that the child-rearing battery measures what it is intended to measure. Although Stenner (2005) notes that these questions are less effective in measuring authoritarianism among college students and, perhaps more generally, those without children, to the extent that there is slippage between the concept of authoritarianism and its measure, it is sure to attenuate our results rather than help them. In any event, the battery of questions we use meets Feldman's (2003) requirement of a clear, conceptual focus, zeroing in on the importance of authority in maintaining order within clearly defined boundaries, minimizing discretion and following from the insight of Adorno et al. that what distinguishes authoritarians and nonauthoritarians is different views about the importance of a strict application of rules rather than an "assimilation of principles."

RELEVANT CHANGES IN THE PARTIES' ELECTORAL BASES

We next briefly highlight how a few different groups that have been particularly important in the changing nature of the party coalitions score in authoritarianism. Since this was measured in a period when Democrats had been losing supporters, not gaining them, all were groups that had been moving toward the Republicans over time. And all, on average, score relatively high in authoritarianism. Since we have scored authoritarianism on a continuum ranging from 0 to 1, the differences can be interpreted as percentage differences between groups. Table 3.2 displays the results.

Especially during the 1980s, Republican presidential candidates made significant inroads among less well educated, working-class voters. These so-called Reagan Democrats often came from union households who were disaffected by the Democrats' "tax and spend" ways, not to mention the heavy emphasis placed in the party on race and inclusion (Edsall and Edsall 1991). This demographic was more likely to be repelled than attracted by Jesse Jackson's vision of a "Rainbow Coalition." In addition to union members, specifically, becoming a smaller part of the Democratic coalition, the less well educated in general became a larger part of the Republican coalition (Stanley and Niemi 2006). Although education was once highly predictive of party identification, we show in Chapter 7 that by 2004 this was no longer true among nonblacks, other things being equal. With education strongly related to authoritarianism, it ought to be no surprise that those who have graduate degrees, a Democratic constituency (Judis and Teixeira 2002), are nearly 40 percentage points less authoritarian than those who failed to complete high school and nearly 30 percentage points less so than those who attained only a high school diploma, the object of significant Republican gains.

TABLE 3.2. *Average Authoritarianism by Relevant Party Coalition Groups*

Variable	Mean Authoritarianism
Religious Tradition	
Evangelical Protestant	0.709
Catholic	0.571
Mainline Protestant	0.530
Secular	0.481
Jewish	0.383
Church Attendance	
Weekly or More	0.689
Less than Weekly	0.549
Region	
South	0.657
Non-South	0.547
Population Density	
Rural	0.603
Small Town	0.584
Suburb	0.524
Large City	0.502
Inner City	0.549
Education	
Less than High School	0.754
High School Degree	0.657
Some College	0.590
College Degree	0.505
Graduate Degree	0.373

Source: American National Election Study, 2004

There have also been important changes in the religious profile of the parties. The first relates to denomination. From the turn of the twentieth century until the 1970s, the Republican Party was traditionally dominated by mainline protestants. Catholics, particularly around the candidacy of John F. Kennedy in 1960, provided staunch support to the Democratic Party. While mainliners are still more likely to be Republicans than are many other religious groups, evangelical Protestants have evolved over the past twenty-five years into an even more ardently Republican group (Wilcox 2000). Indeed, this group's influence in the party increased nearly threefold between the 1970s and 2004 (Stanley and Niemi 2006). At the same time, Catholics have been drifting steadily away from the Democratic fold over the same period.

Table 3.2 reveals that white evangelicals, with a mean score of .709, are significantly more authoritarian than all other religious groups. Such a result makes good theoretical sense, given that our theory of authoritarianism places aversion to ambiguity at its core. Adopting a literal interpretation of the Bible suggests little tolerance for ambiguity. The NES asks people to choose among three options to judge their belief in biblical inerrency: "the Bible is the Word of God to be taken literally word for word," "the Bible is the Word of God, but is not to be taken literally," and "the Bible is a book written by men and is not the Word of God." In 2004, fully 63 percent of evangelicals adopted the most literal position. This position was adopted by only 33 percent of mainline Protestants, the religious group second most likely to adopt a literal interpretation of the Bible. Although Catholics do not score as high in authoritarianism as do evangelicals, they do score relatively high compared with mainline Protestants, Jews, and secular individuals.

In addition to denomination, a religiosity gap developed in the 1980s and grew much wider through the 1990s (Hetherington and Keefe 2007). Those who go to church more often, irrespective of religious denomination, tend to identify more with Republicans today. While no differences existed in the 1970s and only muted differences existed in the 1980s, religiosity-based differences are now quite large. Among those who go to church once a week or more, the average authoritarianism score is .689. For those who go to church less frequently, the mean is .549, or about 14 percentage points lower. Not surprisingly, regular churchgoing Catholics, who have been significantly more likely to move toward the Republicans over the past generation, score somewhat higher in authoritarianism than do Catholics who do not attend church on at least a weekly basis.

Other important changes to the party coalition are geographic in nature. The South was not particularly hospitable to Republicans until the 1970s. By 2000, however, the Republican tide was so strong that the Republican presidential candidate, George W. Bush, won every southern state. This change was almost entirely the result of increasing Republican identification from southern whites, a group that had been heavily Democratic until the 1980s (Stanley and Niemi 2006; see also Green, Palmquist, and Schickler 2002). The South is a more authoritarian region than the rest of the country. The mean authoritarianism score among southerners is .657, while it is only .547 among nonsoutherners.

Finally, population density is importantly tied to party choice (Judis and Teixeira 2002). One need only glance at a county-level map of presidential outcomes to get a sense of how profound a difference it makes. Majority Democratic support tends to be focused in small geographic areas in and around center cities. Most of the map is Republican red, with large but sparsely populated counties favoring them. We find that those from rural areas and small towns are significantly more authoritarian than people from the suburbs and cities. All these emerging coalitional differences suggest that authoritarianism might be a fault line of some consequence in understanding contemporary American politics.

CONCLUSION

Although we have covered significant ground in this chapter, it is worth briefly reiterating two findings we have already reported. First, nonauthoritarians evince a dramatically higher need for cognition than authoritarians. This is evident in their greater desire to wrestle with complex problems and the greater likelihood that they would have clear opinions about lots of things. The latter in particular could be understood to be a grating quality for many people. A valued part of the American ethos is the idea that people should "do one thing and do it right" and there has long been a particular antipathy toward intellectual know-it-alls (McClosky and Zaller 1984). Of course, a nonauthoritarian might interpret such an attribute as evidence of broad-mindedness instead of narrow-mindedness. But again, the salient point here is to identify distinctive attributes of nonauthoritarians and to think about how their cognitive style and outlook might appear to someone who thinks very differently from the way they do.

The second point in this regard is the extraordinary difference between authoritarians and nonauthoritarians on the question of whether there is a right way and a wrong way to do things. Again, nonauthoritarians' resistance to making snap judgments is evident here. One could certainly imagine circumstances in which this attribute could be viewed as admirable and others in which it could be deemed an irresponsible failure to hold individuals accountable when circumstances warrant such accountability. How people form such judgments is beyond the scope of our study, of course. And positive and negative judgments about these qualities will depend fundamentally on individuals' underlying disposition. But we at least want to suggest a distinctive outlook and worldview among a group of individuals who have received scant attention in decades of research on authoritarianism and also to suggest how they might be comparably provocative and polarizing subjects in the larger story of American political divisiveness as are more authoritarian-minded individuals.

In the next chapter we provide a historical sketch of the emergence of those issues which, we believe, have fundamentally shaped the current authoritarianism-driven divide. In that sketch, we give primary weight to the emergence of issues that were of particular salience to authoritarian-minded individuals. We argue that the current divide began its life largely as a consequence of strategic issue adoption by the Republican Party, which had the intended effect of allowing it to be more competitive electorally and simultaneously to draw into its ranks authoritarian-minded individuals.

But that is not the end of the story. Although Democrats may have been on the defensive over the past generation, it now appears that nonauthoritarians, apparently animated by a coherent disposition of their own, have become angry about the threat that authoritarians might cause to America's well-being. It does not follow from this fact that nonauthoritarians would advocate measures to deal with their opponents similar to those of authoritarians. The evidence on that score is clear enough. Furthermore, the parties may not have identical incentives to appeal to those at the comparable poles of the authoritarianism scale. This is so because there are, quite simply, fewer Americans at the nonauthoritarian pole than at the authoritarian pole and the center of gravity of the distribution remains on the authoritarian side of the scale. But it is important to stress that the current divide owes as much to a group about which we understand much less well – the nonauthoritarians – as it does to a group that has received extraordinary attention – the authoritarians.

4

A Historical Account of the Roots
of Worldview Evolution

In the previous chapter, we discussed in some detail the attributes of both the more and less authoritarian. An important insight of our work is that authoritarianism is important in explaining political change in America, not only, or even primarily, because of authoritarians themselves. Rather, we believe that the increasingly politicized worldview of less authoritarian and nonauthoritarian voters, which has occurred in response to the use of issues like race, gay rights, and the war on terror by conservatives to attract more authoritarian voters, explains much of the recent rise of authoritarianism in defining political conflict.

In an effort to change an electoral playing field that Democrats had dominated since the 1930s, Republican elites and the allied movements of what became known as the New Right and their subsequent offshoots played a pivotal role in bringing these hot-button issues to the fore. In the process, they shaped a political environment in which emotionally laden, symbolic concerns – what Richard Nixon and his advisors originally termed *positive polarization* (Carter 1996) – assumed particular importance to political conflict and, as it happens, made authoritarianism central to understanding that conflict.

In thinking about the historical roots of the current political divide we have drawn upon Carmines and Stimson's (1989) notion of issue evolution. They saw important changes in the nature of American political party competition as rooted in a single issue – race – and the power of that issue to restructure American politics beginning in the 1960s. Our argument traces the deepening and widening of that divide, from "issue evolution" to "worldview evolution." We argue that this set of issues connected by authoritarianism has reshaped American political competition and changed the nature of political debate itself. In this chapter, we trace the emergence of some of those issues.

FROM ISSUE EVOLUTION TO WORLDVIEW EVOLUTION

Worldview evolution is a more elusive concept than issue evolution. As conceived by Carmines and Stimson (1989), issue evolution is the notion that under certain circumstances, a kind of adaptation takes place whereby out of the countless possibilities, one issue emerges that has the power to reshape the political environment profoundly. Our conception of a worldview is based on the idea that a cluster of issues tethered to an underlying disposition animates a distinct way of understanding political reality and of shaping political behavior and identity. The emergence of race as an issue was a foundational event in the longer term worldview evolution that we note. But alongside its emergence, other issues that arose have also become woven into the larger tapestry of a worldview divide.

This cluster of issues has arisen in fits and starts, for varied and sometimes initially unrelated reasons, and it is beyond our scope to treat them all in depth. We do not believe that any of them alone restructured party competition the way race has, with the possible exception of the war on terror, which we treat separately and in greater depth in the next chapter. Rather, they accumulated over a period of time in a way that had an increasingly weighty impact on political life. We trace a handful of key links in the evolutionary chain of issues that cumulatively contributed to a new equilibrium based on the sorting of nonauthoritarians and authoritarians into distinct political homes.

Although the process of party sorting is ultimately crucial in allowing issues to recast political competition, Carmines and Stimson (1986) outline important intervening steps in this process. The first occurs when mass publics alter their perceptions of the parties regarding the new issue dimension based on the decisions that political elites are making. Starting in the 1960s, conservative and Republican Party elites apparently made the strategic decisions that set in motion the current dynamic. They did so not because they had a master plan to attract authoritarian followers. Instead, like all political elites, they had as their primary goal winning elections. As Lee Atwater said shortly after the highly charged 1988 elections: "We had only one goal in the campaign and that was to elect George Bush.... Our campaign was not trying to govern the country."[1]

Ultimately, we cannot know the mix of motives, calculations, and deeply held beliefs at the elite level that brought to life the current divide. We do know that Republican strategists and grassroots activists were trying to forge new coalitions of disaffected voters to offset the historical advantages of the Democratic Party from the New Deal forward. That is what political losers do, and the Republican Party had been mostly losing since the early 1930s, disastrously so in 1964. In the course of casting about for new issues and approaches to forge a new majority in America, political operatives stumbled upon a set of appeals that proved highly attractive to authoritarian-minded voters who were likely disproportionately Democrats at the time, setting in motion the process we explicate throughout the book.

Political commentator and former Nixon speechwriter Patrick J. Buchanan recently told the *New Yorker* about his first meeting with Nixon in 1966: "From

[1] Quoted in Greider (1992, 271).

Day One, Nixon and I talked about creating a new majority.... What we talked about, basically, was shearing off huge segments of F.D.R.'s New Deal coalition, which L.B.J. had held together: Northern Catholic ethnics and Southern Protestant conservatives – what we called the Daley-Rizzo Democrats in the North and, frankly, the Wallace Democrats in the South" (Packer 2008). Elite-level strategic visions fortified by and responding to newly insurgent forces on the right, such as the Moral Majority, neoconservatism in its various guises, and Phyllis Schlafly's Stop ERA, took the lead in defining the new issue environment, which increasingly pivoted on what we earlier referred to as "easy" as opposed to "hard" issues and Stimson calls symbolic as opposed to programmatic issues.

This is not to say that Democratic elites played no role in this process. Certainly the very public displays of radicalism from certain corners of the student, antiwar, civil rights, and feminist movements are relevant to our story. And beginning in the late 1960s and early 1970s, the Democratic Party embraced self-consciously the concerns of civil rights organizations, feminist organizations, and later, and more cautiously, gay rights groups. Among other things, these increasingly visible appeals would have had the effect of attracting more nonauthoritarian voters and further repelling authoritarian ones. But Democratic elites found themselves constantly on the defensive because of their ties to these organizations, which Ronald Reagan recast as "special interests."

Several limitations need to be aired at the outset of this historical narrative. First, we lack measures of authoritarianism on public opinion surveys back to the 1960s. Thus, we cannot match up the historical sketch below with definitive claims about what issues and frames motivated specific voters along the dimension that is our primary concern. Second, we cannot take into account content from talk radio, which we suspect has significantly influenced political thinking in America in the past twenty years. The vast audiences of Rush Limbaugh, Sean Hannity, and Michael Savage, espousing deeply emotion- and symbol-laden views of American politics speak to the place in American life of the political style that we believe is best explained by an authoritarian divide. To a lesser extent, cable television, especially Fox News, has served this function as well.

Third, we cannot systematically account for the significance of "narrowcasting" for targeting political messages at carefully chosen political groups. This approach is especially effective on radio (for a good analysis and overview of the phenomenon in relation to political ads on radio, see Overby and Barth 2006). But although we surmise the importance of these widely consumed sources of information for an increasingly calcified worldview-based chasm, we lack the data to connect them directly to our quantitative analysis.[2]

---

[2] We would note here that one would expect the style of much right-wing political talk radio to be congenial to an authoritarian disposition, given the medium's tendency to hammer on symbolically charged themes in a simple, easy to digest way. Nuance, complexity, hand-wringing, and lack of clarity are not the staples of the medium, and leaving aside the substance of the issues

Finally, we do not mean to discount the importance of other issues. Traditional New Deal issues and another hot-button issue – namely, abortion – have undeniably been critical to defining the parties and voter identification over the past forty years, and they continue to do so (Layman and Carsey 2002). Since preferences on these issues are not structured by authoritarianism, we wish to acknowledge that the authoritarian divide is not all-encompassing. It is a significant part of the story of American political conflict, but it is not the only part.

THE KEY ISSUES

We treat four issue clusters: (1) racial and ethnic differences; (2) crime, law and order, and civil liberties; (3) ERA/feminism/family structure; and (4) American militarism, diplomacy, and the aftermath of Vietnam. These clusters clearly relate to some of the crucial animating concerns of authoritarianism that we outlined in the previous chapter. All these clusters became salient over the past forty years, with the major parties becoming clearly identified with distinct and opposing positions on them.

The particular issues have changed over time. For example, concerns about American weakness and capitulation influenced discussions about the Panama Canal treaties in the 1970s,[3] but that issue has itself long since passed from the scene, replaced successively by debates about the proper response to the Soviet invasion of Afghanistan, what to do about Saddam Hussein's incursion into Kuwait, and how best to fight the war against terrorism. However, the underlying concern – the question of American strength and the proper balance between force and diplomacy – has remained significant throughout the past four decades in defining perceptions of the parties.

More broadly, each of these clusters provokes views that tend to be deeply held and of symbolic significance; this means that negotiating about them and finding common ground related to them is generally more difficult than with the programmatic economic issues one associates with the New Deal. However, it may be better to understand each issue as having symbolic and programmatic dimensions rather than labeling some issues, such as race, as symbolic, and other issues, such as taxes, as programmatic. We believe that the

---

discussed, they would be expected to appeal far differently to nonauthoritarians and authoritarians, given the two groups' very different needs for cognition. These worldview differences may help explain the oft-noted fact that no left-wing radio comparable in popularity to their right-wing counterparts has emerged.

[3] Many observers believe that Helms was critical to the ultimate success of Ronald Reagan. On the verge of dropping out of the 1976 GOP primaries, Reagan won a surprise landslide victory in North Carolina, largely thanks to the active support of Helms's political operation. Reagan's opposition to the proposed Panama Canal treaties and Helms's aggressive attacks on President Ford for supporting those treaties probably helped Reagan in North Carolina. In turn, while Reagan did not win his party's nomination in 1976, he did save his political career and position himself as front-runner for 1980 by his very strong showing after the North Carolina win (Nelson 2005).

issues that have become dominant in American political discourse over the past generation are issues that are laden symbolically: race, gender, safety, and security. But, as we elaborate below, presumptively symbolic issues have programmatic dimensions, just as programmatic issues can have symbolic dimensions. Therefore, what is noteworthy about the contemporary political discourse is not only the emergence of symbol-laden concerns, but also the degree to which the symbolic dimensions of a range of issues have become so prominent.

Racial and Ethnic Difference

Carmines and Stimson (1989) argue that the new racial fissures first opened up during the 1958 midterm elections, when a number of racially progressive northern Republicans were defeated by liberal Democrats. This event began the process of sorting the political parties on the question of racial tolerance. The emerging bloc of northern Democratic liberals began to deprive the southern wing of the Democratic Party of its traditional congressional dominance. The erosion of southern Democratic hegemony eventually allowed Lyndon Johnson to pursue his agenda to promote racial equality. Until then, the party of Lincoln was often a better bet for the interests of blacks. According to Carmines and Stimson's examination of political party platforms in the late 1940s and throughout the 1950s, the Republican Party devoted more space to advocating racial tolerance than did the deeply divided Democratic Party.

In 1960, Republican nominee Richard Nixon acceded to Nelson Rockefeller's demands for a stronger civil rights plank as a condition of Rockefeller's support, in a deal that became known as the Compact of Fifth Avenue. As a consequence, Nixon won about one-third of the African American vote, which is a lot by today's standards.[4] In fact, while Kennedy famously called Coretta Scott King to inquire about her husband Martin's condition as he sat in jail in the fall of 1960, his campaign also distributed photos to voters in Virginia showing Nixon posing with black leaders and informing them that Nixon had been an NAACP member for ten years (Schaller 2006, 75).

Though Carmines and Stimson believe that the rumblings of a new order were already evident for those who were paying closest attention, it was not until after the Goldwater takeover of the Republican Party in 1964 that the new alignment began to be clarified.[5] Out of the rubble of Goldwater's landslide

---

[4] In 2004, exit polling indicates that President Bush won about 11 percent of the black vote. In 2008, John McCain won an infinitesimal 4 percent of the African American vote.

[5] In the Port Huron statement, written in 1962, Tom Hayden wrote that the "status quo" consensus-based politics of the period were producing "discontented, super-patriotic groups" and that their "ultra-conservatism" had become a "politically influential force in the Republican Party, at a national level through Senator Goldwater, and at a local level through their important social and economic roles." Hayden observed that though these groups justified their appeals as the surest way to defeat communism and defend bedrock American values like individual freedom in the market, their anticommunism really became an "umbrella by which to protest liberalism, internationalism, welfarism, the active civil rights and labor movements" (in Miller 2001, 337).

defeat, Republicans established a beachhead in the formerly solidly Democratic South and strategists found traction in race, an issue they realized had the power to weaken, then shatter, the New Deal coalition. The southern strategy emerged – variously pushed by Goldwater advisor Clifford White, and Nixon advisors Harry Dent (a Strom Thurmond protégé), Pat Buchanan, and Kevin Phillips. Phillips's 1969 book, *The Emerging Republican Majority*, systematized this approach, demonstrating that the Republican Party could run against the interests of African Americans and, in the process, mobilize vast new white constituencies to vote Republican and eventually become Republicans.[6]

By 1968, Richard Nixon had completed his evolution from racial progressive to duck hunter in chief of the new racialized politics,[7] disavowing busing and federal intervention in southern racial matters and, the next year as president, undermining desegregation orders and other civil rights legislation. In 1968, Nixon's support among black voters had dropped to 13 percent, which Phillips saw as a good thing. Republicans should, Phillips argued, welcome the expanded black suffrage that resulted from the Voting Rights Act because "Negro-Democratic mutual identification was a major source of Democratic loss" and, in fact, was "essential if southern conservatives are to be pressured into switching to the Republican party."[8]

In 1972, Nixon asked for a moratorium on court-ordered busing efforts, and the Republican platform that year stated its categorical opposition to busing as part of an even more aggressive pursuit of white southern votes. That contrasts sharply and unmistakably with the 1972 Democratic platform, which was "the most consistently liberal statement ever made by an American political party" and featured thoroughgoing calls for full equality including "equal and uniform enforcement in all states and territories of civil rights statutes and acts" (Carmines and Stimson 1989, 51).

Although Jimmy Carter defeated Gerald Ford with the help of white southerners in 1976, this was only a temporary hiatus in the longer term trends in racialized voting. Ronald Reagan's emergence as the Republican standard-bearer in 1980 marked the resurgence of the southern strategy. He won his landslide 1984 victory with what was "the lowest percentage of black votes...of any Republican candidate in American history" (Carmines and Stimson 1989, 53). The 1980s also witnessed two major attempts to capture the Democratic nomination by the Reverend Jesse Jackson, in 1984 and 1988. Jackson won

[6] Phillips predicted that the trends he described would lead to GOP ascendance for the next thirty-two to thirty-six years. From the late 1960s, from Nixon's appeals to law and order and the "silent majority," to Reagan's call for states' rights at the Neshoba fairgrounds in 1980, just a few miles from the site of the murder of three civil rights workers in 1964, to the elder Bush's conscious racial strategy in 1988 starring Willie Horton, the GOP had "shrewdly used racial appeals to help split a minority of white middle- and working-class voters – mostly males – away from the Democrats" (Ferguson 1994, 289–90).

[7] In 1961, Barry Goldwater told a group of political activists in Georgia that the GOP should stop pursuing the votes of African-Americans and instead "go hunting where the ducks are," attempting to win southern white voters.

[8] Quoted in Schaller (2006, 91–92).

over three million votes in 1984, and roughly seven million in 1988. The high-profile civil rights activist became closely associated with, and for many, symbolic of, the Democratic Party. In fact, much political commentary during that era described the Democrats as having a "Jesse Jackson problem," predicated on the idea that Jackson was too closely connected in the public mind to the kind of indulgence of minority and special interests that foreclosed the party's ability to appeal to the broad (white) majority of Americans.

After the racially charged 1988 campaign, race faded from view in terms of *national* political contestation (at least before Barack Obama's 2008 candidacy), partly because Democrats realized how acute their problem with race was.[9] In 1992, Bill Clinton took pains to signal that he would stand up to certain black interests, notably criticizing the rap artist Sister Souljah at an NAACP event during the 1992 campaign and making clear that Jesse Jackson would have no formal role in the party's convention that summer. In so doing, and in his pledge to "end welfare as we know it" as well as in his support for the death penalty, Clinton partly muted the issue.

This is not to say that race no longer matters. Black identification with the Democratic Party is now nearly unanimous. And, as we demonstrated in Chapter 2, mass party differences in racial resentment among nonblacks have never been wider. Such findings are consistent with a bevy of other studies (e.g., Sniderman and Piazza 1993; Hurwitz and Peffley 1997), which show an unmistakable Republican advantage in this issue area. As political commentators have become more cognizant of the use of even implicit racial appeals, however, making use of the race issue in election campaigns has become more difficult. Still racial differences remain an important dividing line in the party system even if discussion of race has not been prominent in recent elections. Although the fact that Barack Obama is an African American made race more salient in 2008, it is still true that racially tinged policy debates that once occupied significant space in our national dialogue – like crime, welfare, and affirmative action – continue to play almost no role in contemporary national politics.

Crime and Civil Liberties

A burgeoning scholarship on the rise of modern conservatism in the 1960s has emerged recently. Older academic formulations of conservatism, especially during the liberal consensus era of the 1950s and 1960s, often cast right-wing supporters as down-and-out dead-enders, John Birch society fanatics, and the like, unable to adapt to or cope with modernity. By contrast, much of the new scholarship (see, e.g., Perlstein 2001, 2008; McGirr 2002; Lassiter 2007) argues that many people who became part of the mass base of the New Right were at least solidly

[9] Perhaps the last prominent campaign run using race as a central appeal was North Carolina Senator Jesse Helms's successful reelection effort in 1990 against African American Harvey Gantt. Helms famously aired an eleventh-hour commercial decrying racial "quotas" by featuring a white hand crumbling up a presumed job rejection letter. The spot is now typically referred to as the "white hands" ad (Mendelberg 2001).

middle class with a real stake in the American dream. They were respected members of their communities and firmly entrenched in the mainstream of American life. Perlstein summarizes the outlook of many in this growing conservative base as rooted in a paradox of New Deal liberalism's success in the decades after the Great Depression: "with the boom they had helped build, ordinary laborers were becoming ever less reliably downtrodden" (Perlstein 2008, 41). It was the pollster, Samuel Lubell, who in the 1950s first observed that "the inner dynamics of the Roosevelt coalition have shifted from those of getting to those of keeping" (Perlstein 2008, 42). That orientation toward a politics of preserving hard-won economic prosperity became linked in the 1960s to a growing concern over crime, against both property and individuals. The crime issue and its connection to race, along with perceived social breakdown and declining faith in the ability of the federal government to solve basic problems, made debates about law and order a potent part of the changing electoral fortunes of the Republicans beginning with the 1966 midterm elections. And, as it happens, the emergence of the crime issue mapped quite naturally on to the worldview divide we explicate, raising as it did fundamental questions about the trade-offs between security and order on the one hand and civil liberties, as well as a more contextualized concern for minorities and social problems, on the other.

The debate about crime and civil liberties that emerged in the 1960s may reflect what Sniderman et al. (1996) understand to be the inherent conflict within democracy itself. Many students of democracy have concluded that a failure to stand by individual rights represents a failure, usually on the part of the ill-informed masses, to understand the proper foundations of a democratic polity. In contrast, Sniderman et al. (1996) argue that differing views on individual rights derive from an "inescapable collision of values" and warn that even if we "eliminate misunderstandings, [and] guarantee the learning of societal values" it will still be true that "clashes over claims to rights will nonetheless remain at the center of democratic politics" (1996, 11).

The 1960s, of course, witnessed major changes in American jurisprudence about criminal defendants. In a series of landmark rulings, the liberal Warren Court established the right of indigent defendants to an attorney, the exclusionary rule barring illegally seized evidence from use in criminal cases, and the requirement that law enforcement officers read defendants their rights or risk having criminal cases against those defendants thrown out. At the same time, crime rates were beginning a dramatic increase through the 1960s, capped off by a series of riots and other civil disturbances that shook the nation to its core.

The rights revolution combined with the surge in crime and civil disorder provided Republicans a political opportunity to peel off disaffected Democrats. The parties in this period were not well sorted ideologically. The first time the NES asked people to place themselves on its 7-point ideology scale in 1972, its correlation with partisanship was less than .3, with about 20 percent of self-identified Democrats placing themselves on the conservative end of NES's ideological self-placement scale. In contrast, in 2004, the correlation was more than double that, with less than 10 percent of Democrats identifying themselves as conservatives. If campaigns are largely about identifying and exploiting issues in which a large percentage of party identifiers are out of step with their party (Hillygus and Shields, 2008), then the related issues of crime and civil liberties provided fertile ground to those on the right.

Using data gathered in the 1970s, McClosky and Brill (1983) found that self-identified conservatives were much less supportive of civil liberties than self-identified liberals. For example, among ordinary citizens, 75 percent of strong conservatives said that communities had a right to censor a teacher. Only 35 percent of strong liberals did so. Sniderman et al. (1991) exploit these data further, showing that differences between elites and mass, which was the thrust of McClosky and Brill's research, were actually more modest than differences between those of different ideological bents regardless of whether they were elites or ordinary people. Specifically, they showed that elite-level conservatives were less supportive of a number of questions about civil liberties than were mass-level liberals. These findings suggest that not only might Republicans attract self-identified conservative Democrats by questioning the rights revolution of the Warren Court and challenging liberal tendencies to prioritize civil liberties over social order, but that such an approach might come quite naturally to the elites carrying out these efforts.[10]

Scarcely discussed in 1960, crime became an important part of the Goldwater campaign in 1964. In fact, while Richard Nixon would make it a household phrase in 1968, both Goldwater and George Wallace used the term *law and order* during their speeches four years earlier (Walker 1978, 4). Riots wracked American cities in the summer of 1964, increasing concerns about personal crimes against individuals and their property. In this environment, Goldwater attacked the Kennedy/Johnson administration for "laxity in law enforcement" and for encouraging "rioting and a general rise in crime in the big cities" (Finckenauer 1978, 17).

Goldwater also launched a concerted attack on Supreme Court decisions that expanded rights of defendants. He decried decisions, like the exclusionary rule, which could allow "an obviously guilty defendant" to be freed (Finckenauer 1978, 18). Soon, permissive, soft-on-crime liberal judges who were usurping the popular will and making up rights not grounded in a strict constructionist reading of the Constitution would become a persistent theme of New Right and later Republican appeals. Though Goldwater lost in a landslide, his emphasis on crime appears to have struck a chord with President Johnson, who made the issue a major point of emphasis beginning in 1965. That year, the Gallup poll showed that Americans identified crime as the most important problem facing the country, prompting Johnson to declare a war on crime.

In addition to introducing new legislation, Johnson empowered a presidential commission on the subject, whose report, "The Challenge of Crime in a Free

---

[10] It is worth noting that even among liberals, criminal rights were not particularly popular, with nearly 60 percent favoring stopping crime over criminal rights. Viewed in this context, both Wallace's and Nixon's law and order campaigns struck a resonant chord.

Society," appeared in 1967. It reflected many of the basic beliefs of the emerging strand of liberalism of the 1960s, including an understanding of crime as rooted in socioeconomic realities. The report viewed the causes of crime through a characteristically liberal lens, underlining their complexity. It also committed to liberal solutions based on a faith in social engineering and the core assumptions of the Great Society and the War on Poverty (Walker 1978, 4–8).

To many, Johnson's commission reflected a case of Nero fiddling while Rome burned. Nixon, then positioning himself for the 1968 Republican nomination, was increasingly putting his stamp on the law and order issue. His byline appeared over an article drafted by Pat Buchanan, which appeared in *Reader's Digest* in 1967.[11] Nixon observed that a country that had been, three years before, "completing its greatest decade of racial progress" was now among "the most lawless and violent in the history of the world." According to Nixon, the major sources of this lawlessness were racial animosity, "decline in respect for public authority and the rule of law in America," and the public's attitude toward police. Consequently, Nixon said, "far from becoming a great society, ours is becoming a lawless society."

Nixon also rehearsed what would become a growing theme among Republicans in subsequent elections: an attack on cultural elites, increasingly identified as liberal and deemed responsible for exacerbating societal ills. He argued that "our opinion-makers have gone too far in promoting the doctrine that when a law is broken, society, not the criminal, is to blame," and further declaimed, "our teachers, preachers, and politicians have gone too far in advocating the idea that each individual should determine what laws are good and what laws are bad, and he should then obey the law he likes and disobey the laws he dislikes." In conclusion, Nixon urged that "this country cannot temporize or equivocate in this showdown with anarchy.... Immediate and decisive force must be the first response."

Nixon's *Reader's Digest* article outlines some of the important features that, we believe, would have been attractive to authoritarian-minded voters, especially an emphasis on a breakdown in order and attendant collapse in respect for proper authority as well as a rejection of perceived hand-wringing and a need for decisive action in the face of such a breakdown. In fact, the crime issue contributed to an increasing sense of political defensiveness on the part of Democrats that persisted into the 1990s. During this period, the term *liberal* became a bad word. It had been, for much of the previous thirty years, mainly identified with the New Deal. But in the 1960s, it became increasingly associated with matters of race, a particular response to dealing with social problems and, for many of its critics, increasingly a set of "abstract, even exotic, commitments felt most strongly by the well educated members of the upper middle class" (Dionne 1991, 79). This was the source of the "limousine liberal" charge, first leveled against a Republican, John Lindsay, in New York City. Crime, and the growing threats to life, limb, and property, linked the charge powerfully to race

---

[11] All quotes from the article in this and the next paragraph are from Perlstein (2008), 202.

and social transformation more generally, in a way that would be increasingly advantageous to Republicans (Hurwitz and Peffley 1997; Peffley, Hurwitz, and Sniderman 1997).[12] This was the basis of the phrase coined by Phillips's boss, John Mitchell – "positive polarization" – that the potent mixture of culture and race would divide the electorate into warring camps and that, when the dust cleared, Republicans would end up with more than 50 percent of the electorate (Carter 1996, 43–44). The issue of crime, striking in the most fundamental way at people's basic sense of security and well-being, was surely a key ingredient in that mixture.

By the time of the 1968 presidential election, all the major candidates recognized crime as a serious problem. Gallup confirmed that crime was the number one domestic concern in America at that time, and a Harris poll in the summer of 1968 found that 81 percent of Americans believed that "law and order had broken down." While Nixon and Humphrey evinced similar concerns about crime, their approaches to dealing with the problem contrasted sharply. Humphrey in particular took issue with those who would "sneer at the constitutional guarantees, and propose shortcuts to justice across the quicksand of contempt for due process of law" (Finckenauer 1978, 20). A campaign commercial that Humphrey ran in 1968 articulated well the liberal sensibility against which Nixon was now so successfully mobilizing:

When a man says he thinks that the most important thing is to double the rate of convictions, but he doesn't believe in, and then he condemns...the Vice President, myself, for wanting to double the war on poverty, I think he has...lost his sense of values. You're not going to make this a better America just because you build more jails. What this country needs are more decent neighborhoods, more educated people, better homes... . [I]f we need more jails we can build them, but that ought not be the highest objective of the presidency of the United States. I do not believe that repression alone can bring a better society. (Perlstein 2008, 342–43)

Thus, by the end of the 1960s, the parties, on the national level, had staked out distinct positions on crime's sources and solutions, as well as on the more general question of the proper balance between protecting society and respecting individual rights.

At the core of the differing perceptions were the competing ideas of distributive and retributive justice. Distributive justice – associated with liberals

---

[12] There were larger trends at work during the 1960s. Trying to explain the sudden "de-alignment" of American politics that took place in 1965, when there was a significant drop in support for both parties, Converse argued that demographic factors could not account for the change. Instead, he argued, historical developments, including "the density of events surrounding both Vietnam and race relations... might be shown more objectively to have stood out on the record even against the backdrop of a generally troubled time" (1976, 106, quoted in Bishop 2008, 90). The journalist Bill Bishop identifies other "seismic" social changes anchored around the year 1965, including the beginning of a long-term decline in affiliation with mainline protestant churches in favor of independent and evangelical ones and a more general decline in a slew of indicators measuring social capital (Putnam 2000) and the beginning of a long-term decline in political trust (Hetherington 2005).

and, by 1968, with the Democratic Party – saw bad behavior as a consequence of socioeconomic circumstances. When people are ill-clothed, ill-fed, unemployed, and poorly educated, they become more likely to transgress. In this view, healthy societies are responsible for minimizing the circumstances in which people are more likely to commit crime. By contrast, retributive justice, associated with the Republican Party and conservatism after 1968, locates crime more readily in individual moral failings, and espouses the belief that "because man is responsible for his actions, he ought to get his just deserts" when he commits a crime (Finckenauer 1978, 21).[13]

Although crime was, relatively speaking, less of a national issue after 1968, the differing perceptions of the parties' approaches to law and order persisted long after 1968 in a highly charged, symbolic embodiment of the larger crime issue – the death penalty. Given its relatively rare application in most of the United States as well as ongoing debates about whether it serves as an effective deterrent to crime, it is not clear that, on programmatic grounds, capital punishment is a vital tool in efforts to deal with lawbreaking and violence in society. However, as a symbolic issue, it is powerful, representing barbarism for some and for others a decisive application of the venerable scriptural principle "an eye for an eye."

Beginning in 1967, America entered a ten-year period in which no executions were carried out, and this may have had something to do with why it would soon become an issue of party contestation. Changes in public opinion about the death penalty over time reveal the effects of rising crime rates, the Republicans' championing of the issue, and the changing strategies of liberals in confronting it as it became more prominent. Gallup has been asking Americans since 1936 whether they support the death penalty for a person convicted of murder. For most of that period, a clear majority of Americans has answered in the affirmative. However, one notable exception was the 1960s, when the issue became seriously contested. In fact, in 1966, Gallup reported its lowest ever affirmative response rate (42 percent) to that question. This division likely helped put the issue in play. The first time the phrase "death penalty" or "capital punishment" appears in a party platform was 1972, when the Democratic Party called for its abolition. It was also in 1972 that the Supreme Court, in a 5–4 ruling, struck down the death penalty as unconstitutional, instructing states that wished to persist in using capital punishment to redress the problems that plagued its application.[14]

---

[13] We've mentioned George Wallace before, but it's worth noting again his significance during this transformative period in American history. Wallace, of course, was never a Republican, but his extreme conservatism during this period paved the way, according to many observers, for the GOP's success in the South and among many white, working middle-class voters in subsequent years. In Phillips's path-breaking book, *The Emerging Republican Majority*, he argued that "people will ease their way into the Republican Party by way of the American Independents.... We'll get two-thirds to three-fourths of the Wallace vote in 1972" (1969, 265, 267; quoted in Carter 1996, 44).

[14] The four Nixon appointees on the Court all dissented from the majority opinion in the case. "Supreme Court, 5–4, Bars Death Penalty as It Is Imposed under Present Statutes," Fred Graham,

The brief period of public ambivalence about the death penalty in the 1960s ended in the early 1970s. In 1972, Gallup reported a 25-point gap in favor of the death penalty, and by 1976, the spread had grown to 40 percentage points. In fact, Gallup has never recorded less than a 30-point gap in favor since that time. In response, the Democratic Party did not mention capital punishment again until 1996 when it proudly trumpeted the establishment of the death penalty for certain major federal crimes. Little wonder. In 1994, 80 percent of the public backed capital punishment, the highest figure ever recorded in a Gallup poll on the issue, and a 64-point spread over those opposed. Consequently, the death penalty, like the larger crime and civil liberties issue, surely contributed to Republicans' increasing success after 1968. Though the 1972 Republican platform maintained silence on the issue, every subsequent Republican Party platform endorsed capital punishment.

In 1988, after having been relatively dormant in presidential campaigns for several cycles, crime reemerged as a significant issue, pushed by the Bush campaign and its chief strategist Lee Atwater. In fact, if one considers the most memorable images from the 1988 campaign, two involve crime: (1) the Willie Horton ad, which attacked Dukakis's permissive attitude toward violent felons by highlighting his furlough of a violent rapist who struck again, and (2) Dukakis responding "no" in a seemingly unemotional, technocratic way to a debate question about whether he would favor capital punishment for someone who murdered his own wife. Whatever else it did, the Bush campaign succeeded in painting its opponent as an out of touch liberal and a "card-carrying member of the ACLU." These charges were best summarized in a speech George H. W. Bush gave in North Carolina that summer, shortly after he had secured the nomination. With an approving Jesse Helms looking on, Bush said, "I don't understand the type of thinking that lets first-degree murderers who haven't even served enough time to be...out on parole so they can rape and plunder again, and then isn't willing to let the teachers lead the kids in the Pledge of Allegiance" (Dionne 1991, 301). That one line managed to tie together Dukakis's weakness on patriotism and his softness on crime. In the process, it derided his preference for abstract rights over people's concrete well-being and personal safety.

When Bill Clinton emerged as the Democratic nominee in 1992, he was determined to neutralize race in the general election campaign, convinced that the issue had badly damaged the Democratic Party over the previous quarter of a century. Relatedly, Clinton sought to neutralize crime as an issue. As governor, he had long supported the death penalty, and shortly before the New Hampshire primary in 1992, he returned to Arkansas to sign the death warrant for an inmate who had been partially lobotomized in a shoot-out with state police.[15] Once he was president, Clinton took aggressive, and popular, steps to

---

New York Times, June 30, 1972, p. 1. The Supreme Court reaffirmed the constitutionality of the death penalty in 1976.

[15] The condemned, Ricky Ray Rector, also happened to be African American.

deal with crime, including support for a ban on assault weapons and backing for three-strikes-you're-out legislation, as well as a commitment to putting more police officers on the streets. Clinton was successful in these efforts. According to several 1994 polls, crime had overtaken the economy as the most important problem facing America, and in a reversal of long-standing opinion, voters said that Democrats were as capable as Republicans in dealing with it. These developments, in fact, led Newt Gingrich spokesman Tony Blankley to complain in 1995 that the crime issue "has been a Republican issue for over 100 years. It's counterintuitive to think that the head of the Democratic party is tougher."[16]

Clinton's success in neutralizing crime was important in its disappearance as a contested national issue.[17] As another reason for its disappearance, about the time Clinton was able to reverse public perceptions of the Democratic Party in this domain, the United States entered a long and unexpected period in which crime rates declined dramatically in many parts of the country. Nowhere was this more striking than in New York City, long viewed as the epicenter of menacing street life in America. In 1990, there were over 2,000 murders in the Big Apple. By 2007, there were scarcely more than 500, making New York City, in per capita terms, one of the safest big cities in America. Other major areas witnessed dramatic decreases as well.

The muting of the domestic crime issue[18] and the death penalty,[19] though, does not mean that Americans no longer evince profound differences about the proper balance between ensuring public order and Americans' security on the one hand and respect for civil liberties on the other. Instead, the new battleground for that divide has now shifted, especially since 9/11, to debates about the proper response to terrorism, detainee rights at Guantanamo Bay, the use of torture, and disagreements over the government's surveillance rights. We detail in Chapter 5 that authoritarianism provides a powerful explanation for party and mass differences on those inter-connected concerns.

ERA, Feminism, and Family Structure

The 1960s and 1970s witnessed profound changes in American debates about the family and the role of the family in society. But, as Christopher Lasch

---

[16] The polling information and quote are in Katherine Seelye, "Anti-Crime Bill as Political Dispute: President and G.O.P. Define the Issue," *New York Times*, February 21, 1995, p. A16.

[17] It is a truism among political operatives that crime is always an important issue in state and, especially, local politics.

[18] The one context in which domestic crime still appears to capture national attention, aside from the general problem of crimes against minors, is in the highly charged area of perceived lawlessness by illegal immigrants. We discuss this issue in Chapter 8.

[19] In June 2008, in a high-profile case, the Supreme Court struck down as a cruel and unusual a Louisiana death penalty statute that applied to those convicted of raping minors. The conservative Anthony Kennedy, increasingly uneasy with the death penalty in a wide variety of circumstances, wrote the decision for the 5–4 majority. Notably, Democratic nominee Barack Obama disagreed with the Court's decision and said he supported the Louisiana statute.

(1977) documented extensively in *Haven in a Heartless World*, this was not the first time there was a serious challenge to preexisting notions of family. For example, the 1950s, subsequently viewed as a pillar of "tradition" in terms of family norms, may have been an outlier in the twentieth century (Dionne 1991). In that decade, marriage rates reached an all-time high, with 70 percent of women married in those years, compared to 50 percent in the 1980s and, notably, *an even lower figure of 42 percent in 1940* (1991, 102; emphasis added). Rates of increase in divorce were lower in the 1950s than in any other decade in the twentieth century.

In short, what was new about the evolving nature of families and women's roles in the 1960s and 1970s was not the evolution itself but the degree to which those changes affixed themselves to identifiably partisan political positions. One cause of this new politicization was the emergence in the late 1960s and early 1970s of a newly assertive wave of feminism. In 1970, in a move that received significant press coverage, feminists launched the "strike for equality," a nationwide day of public actions designed to draw attention in support of women's rights. Soon after, the 92nd Congress, spanning 1971–72, passed an unprecedented package of legislation expanding women's rights. Bella Abzug, an outspoken Democratic congresswoman from New York City during that period, noted the bipartisan nature of the debate at that time: "we put sex discrimination provisions into everything. There was no opposition – who'd be against equal rights for women? So, we just kept passing women's rights legislation."[20]

In 1972, the Equal Rights Amendment (ERA) overwhelmingly passed both houses of Congress, with both Americans for Democratic Action, a venerable liberal advocacy group, and the Republican National Committee working to secure passage. During this period, two contradictory dynamics were at work. On the one hand, both party platforms supported ERA, equal pay, child care tax deductions and federal assistance, elimination of sexual discrimination, and appointment of women to government positions, with Republican feminists even more successful than those on the Democratic side (Wolbrecht 2000).

On the other hand, a backlash was brewing against feminism. Indeed, some argue that it was opposition to women's rights, especially the ERA and abortion, that had the largest impact on organizing the New Right. No better exemplar of this dynamic exists than Phyllis Schlafly. Schlafly was a grassroots force behind the Goldwater nomination in 1964, and a staunch anticommunist. In 1964, she penned *A Choice, Not an Echo*, a short book in support of Goldwater and against the liberal Eastern Republican establishment; it sold over three million copies. However, it was her opposition to feminism, abortion, and the ERA that made Schlafly a household name, as she turned her attention away from the Cold War and toward domestic policy concerns in the early 1970s. She founded STOP (Stop Taking Our Privileges) ERA in 1972, and her cause gained greater momentum with the *Roe v. Wade* decision in

[20] Quoted in Wolbrecht (2000, 35).

1973, which she used to tie the abortion issue to ERA and recruit evangelical Christians to her side.[21]

Schlafly was notable not only because of the issues that have ultimately defined her legacy but because of the means by which she pressed her case. For her, politics was not simply about issues but about something much greater: a fundamental battle between right and wrong, good and evil.

> Starting with Melvin Price (whom [Schlafly] ran against for Congress), back in 1952, her opponents have invariably been not just wrong or misguided but downright evil.... From the Communists and "perverts" who infiltrated the state department to the Republican Kingmakers, who used "hidden persuaders and psychological warfare techniques," and the "women's libbers," who placed "their agents and sympathizers in the media and the educational system," Schlafly's foes have always aimed at nothing less than the destruction of "civilization as we know it." (Kolbert 2005)

Schlafly's efforts are an important historical pivot, ushering in a new, concerted opposition to much of the feminist agenda on the part of the Republican Party, anchoring growing social anxieties about changing sexual mores and gender roles to a specific partisan political agenda. As such, the early 1970s represented a time when "for many conservative Americans, the personal became political for the first time when questions of family, children, sexual behavior and women's roles became subjects of political debate" (Mansbridge 1986, 5).

Though the ground for such issues was shifting under foot by the early 1970s, the Republican Party maintained its formal commitment to ERA through the 1976 platform. In 1976, President Ford's wife, Betty, sat for a wide-ranging interview with *60 Minutes*. In response to a question about what she would do if her eighteen-year-old daughter were having an affair, Mrs. Ford said: "Well, I wouldn't be surprised.... I think she's a perfectly normal human being, like all young girls" (Dionne 1991, 203). However, Mrs. Ford's moderate views, and those of her husband, were increasingly out of place in the Republican camp. In fact, many observers believe that Ford lost the 1976 election in part because he failed to hold on to social issue conservatives who had overwhelmingly chosen Nixon over McGovern in 1972. And Dionne concluded that Ford's defeat marked the end of moderate "modern Republicanism," observing that "the Republican future clearly lay in polarization around the conservative social issues" (1991, 206).

The parties made noteworthy changes on women's rights after 1976. Wolbrecht's (2000) systematic analysis of party platforms from 1952 to 1992 reveals that through 1968, while neither party devoted significant attention to women's rights, "Republicans were generally more favorable to the few women's rights issues discussed, such as the ERA" (2000, 71). In 1972, both parties devoted extensive space in their platforms to affirming women's rights.

---

[21] This is another noteworthy example of a prominent figure tying together two seemingly disparate issues, in this case, communism and feminism, for which preferences are both structured by authoritarianism.

Throughout the remainder of the decade, "women's rights were hotly debated at both parties' conventions by activists." But by 1980, "the parties had shifted from a generally favorable consensus regarding women's rights to a situation of increasing polarization" (71). Democrats came largely to support feminist positions, while the Republicans increasingly opposed women's rights, on issues such as ERA, abortion, child care funding, and more.

In sum, issues concerning women's role in society, the proper place of family in American life, and the types of family structures that the United States ought to encourage have become central loci of debate over the past forty years. Preferences on these issues are structured by authoritarianism. As these issues have become salient and the public has come to view the parties as occupying distinctive positions, the potential exists for worldview evolution to deepen.

Foreign Policy, Force, and Diplomacy

Over the past generation, probably no set of issues has given Republicans as clear an advantage as questions of foreign policy, national security, and whether to use force or diplomacy to resolve conflict. Beginning with Nixon, Republicans have repeatedly succeeded in portraying themselves as strong, resolute, and willing to stand up and fight America's enemies whenever necessary. Conversely, Democrats have had great difficulty in dispelling their image as soft, weak, irresolute, and incapable of keeping America safe and secure. In some variants of this meme, the implication is not merely that Democrats lack resolve and strength of character; it is also that key elements in the party are actively hostile to America's interests and wish it harm.

For most of the past forty years, party differences in this area have probably been more symbolic than programmatic. It would be hard to argue that liberal politicians are actively invested in the failure of U.S. security or its position abroad. But political campaigns tend to focus on symbolic dimensions of issues rather than their programmatic dimensions, which makes party differences easier to comprehend. Symbolic messages are more effective in persuading and mobilizing voters than is walking them through complex, drawn-out, and arcane legislative and executive maneuverings, a point we return to below.

In the pivotal historical period of the late 1960s and early 1970s, it is not hard to understand how perceptions of the parties on this cluster of issues would have begun to shift. Since the major wars of the twentieth century began on the Democrats' watch, perceived softness was not a grave concern. In 1968, however, the Democratic primaries were dominated by staunchly antiwar candidates, Bobby Kennedy and Eugene McCarthy. And, although Vice President Hubert Humphrey, the Democratic nominee, was hamstrung by his loyal support for Johnson's Vietnam policies, he ultimately called for a halt to all bombing in Vietnam during the fall campaign. Programmatically, this position did not differ much from Nixon's, who promised to end the war quickly. Still, the surge of support from student activists for McCarthy's antiwar candidacy during the 1968 primary season and the images of the anarchic Democratic convention in Chicago that year, with antiwar protestors battling Chicago police, surely had an effect on perceptions of the parties.

Following Nixon's inauguration in 1969, deeper party divisions began to emerge. By 1970, as it became increasingly clear that Nixon had no immediate plan for ending the conflict, major efforts were afoot in Congress to end the war. Senator George McGovern (D-S.D.), a leading critic of the war, co-sponsored an amendment to the military procurement authorization bill with Republican Mark Hatfield of Oregon, calling for a halt to all U.S. military operations in Vietnam by the end of the year. At that time, several dozen members of Congress formed the Congressional Committee to End the War and the future Democratic nominee for president, McGovern, became its chair. In a speech he gave on the floor of the Senate during debate on the amendment, McGovern stunned his colleagues when he said that "every Senator in this chamber is partly responsible for sending fifty thousand young Americans to an early grave. This chamber reeks of blood." Above the din of the presiding officer's gavel indicating that his time had expired, McGovern invoked the great conservative theorist Edmund Burke to intone that "a conscientious man would be cautious how he dealt in blood" (Perlstein 2008, 522–23).

McGovern's efforts pulled other important members of his party into the antiwar camp. For example, Senator Edmund Muskie, Humphrey's running mate in 1968 and the widely acknowledged front-runner for the 1972 nomination, had earlier supported timid measures to express Senate concern about the war. But after McGovern-Hatfield was proposed, he signed on as a co-sponsor. Therefore, by the time of the 1970 midterm elections, political battle lines were being drawn. Vice President Spiro Agnew campaigned around the country, attacking "ultraliberalism" for its "whimpering foreign policy" and "pusillanimous pussyfooting on the critical issue of law and order."[22]

In 1972, McGovern's long-shot candidacy for president turned into a successful march to the nomination, which was sure to move public perceptions of the Democratic Party on defense far to the left. Although McGovern had moved other Democratic elites somewhat to the left, most remained to his right. Indeed, the charge that McGovern was for "amnesty, abortion, and acid," appeared as an unattributed quote in a column by Robert Novak after McGovern's victory in the Massachusetts primary; it actually came from Thomas Eagleton, who was McGovern's original choice for vice president. In addition, Hubert Humphrey, who emerged as the head of the Anybody-but-McGovern movement, accused McGovern of planning to disarm America, as he was calling for significant reductions in Pentagon spending in his efforts to redirect government to domestic concerns, such as poverty and care for the

---

[22] Perlstein 2008, 524. Agnew's attacks on radical liberals were not only directed at antiwar Democrats, as there were a number of antiwar Republicans in addition to Hatfield. But the growing association between the Nixon/Agnew characterization of liberals with the Democratic Party was also unmistakable.

elderly. That position was reflected in the 1972 Democratic platform, which called for deep cuts in military spending over the following three years.

Humphrey's position reflected deep fissures within the Democratic Party about militarism, not only in relation to Vietnam but also in connection with the global fight against communism more generally. In fact, today's neoconservatism has important roots in the Democratic Party of this era, with many Cold War liberals supporting Humphrey and also the hawkish Washington Democrat, Henry "Scoop" Jackson, for president in 1972 and again in 1976. By 1980, after a four-year period under Jimmy Carter's watch that witnessed the signing of the Panama Canal Treaties, the Sandinista takeover of Nicaragua in 1979, the Soviet invasion of Afghanistan, the overthrow of the pro-American Shah of Iran, and the subsequent seizure of American hostages there, neoconservatives were out of the party, having thrown their support firmly behind the resolutely anticommunist Ronald Reagan. This mass exodus also left McGovern and Carter as exemplars of the party's position on foreign matters, which surely contributed to the widely held perception that Democrats were soft on defense.

What linked all of these concerns, especially from a neoconservative perspective, was the specter of history. Specifically, this view emphasized that evil is real in the world and in order for it to thrive the good merely have to stand idle. This was the lesson of the 1930s and of appeasement, and that lesson animates neoconservative concerns to this day. From this perspective, everything from Vietnam in the 1970s to the question of negotiating with Iran today invokes the catastrophe of "Munich." From this perspective, the Democratic Party by the 1970s increasingly reflected such tendencies toward appeasement, first in the dangers of McGovernite pacifism and isolationism ("come home America"), and then in the cowardly irresoluteness of Jimmy Carter. Neoconservatism is not the only strand of contemporary Republican foreign policy, of course. Other elements, embodying a more nationalist strain encouraged by people like Jesse Helms and embodied in the campaign against the Panama Canal Treaties, were also significant. The point here is to highlight some of the roots of the disaffection of certain elements within the old Democratic coalition with a foreign policy tendency identified, from 1972 on, with McGovernism.[23]

Although programmatic concerns about McGovern's position on Vietnam and Carter's string of failures in the foreign policy realm were a critical part of this evolution, the symbolic story is perhaps even more important. In the parties' actual records on war, peace, and defense, they are not nearly as distinct as their images in the public mind suggest. Nixon, of course, went to China and pursued détente with the Soviet Union. Moreover, Nixon not only ended U.S. involvement in Vietnam but he did so within two months of his reelection, demonstrating a position on the war not far from McGovern's in 1972. Similarly, the military buildup with which Ronald Reagan has been associated

---

[23] Bacevich (2005, 71–80) discusses in some depth the roots of neoconservatism in relation to Democratic foreign policy during this period.

began under Carter. The second cold war[24] also began under Carter's watch. And, at least as significantly, Reagan nearly agreed to abolish all nuclear weapons in talks with the then-new Soviet leader Mikhail Gorbachev in Reykjavik in 1986, before there were any obvious signs that Gorbachev was going to embark on a program of radical domestic reform. Moreover, Reagan did sign a landmark elimination of an entire class of nuclear weapons in 1987, the first such agreement in the history of U.S.-Soviet relations. In the meantime, the characteristic image of Democrats became Michael Dukakis riding in a tank wearing a helmet that is about five sizes too big during his failed bid for the presidency in 1988.

Notable as well is Bill Clinton's record as president. Clinton regularly resorted to force (see, e.g., Bacevich 2005): in Somalia, Bosnia, Haiti, and Afghanistan; in daily bombings of Iraq; and in a full-scale air war over Kosovo, a war that the Republican leadership in Congress vocally criticized. However, none of this appeared to do much to alter perceptions of Clinton as someone who worked hard to avoid military service in Vietnam and who, as a result, was soft in the area of national security.

Many have observed over the past two decades that Democrats insist on fighting "on the issues" (Tomasky 2004). But it is perhaps better to conceive this approach as emphasizing the programmatic dimension of issues, while Republicans have done battle on their symbolic aspects. Building on President Clinton's record of military deployment in the 1990s, Vice President Al Gore proposed significantly larger defense budgets than did George W. Bush in their contest for the presidency in 2000. Bush notably articulated a foreign policy doctrine of restraint, including his oft-noted insistence that he was opposed to "nation-building." But the public did not see this as evidence that the Democrats are "tough" on defense because the public was not forming judgments based on careful inspection of policy differences. Instead, it drew on symbolic understandings of the parties that had been developing over decades.

Similarly, in 2004, among Kerry's criticisms of President Bush was that our force in Iraq was inadequate. He promised to increase the size of the U.S. presence in Iraq by up to 40,000 troops. At the same time, he advocated diplomacy and a rejection of the unilateralism of the Bush administration that he believed was detrimental to America's international standing. It appears that public perceptions of Kerry were influenced little by his call for more troops and more by his advocacy of diplomacy.[25]

---

[24] The second cold war, as it is sometimes called, refers to the especially chilly period in U.S.-Soviet relations beginning in the late 1970s following the breakdown of détente, the Soviet invasion of Afghanistan in 1979, the Olympic boycotts of 1980 and 1984, and Reagan's characterization of the USSR as an "evil empire" in 1983. This period wound down after Gorbachev came to power in 1985.

[25] During the 2008 campaign, Senator Obama proposed significant increases in the overall size of the U.S. military as well as increases in Pentagon spending, contrary to the wishes of his party's increasingly nonauthoritarian base. However, in the public mind, his initial opposition to the war in Iraq was far more salient.

Perceptions of Kerry were likely shared by both those scoring high and low in authoritarianism, although the resulting feelings about him would have differed markedly. Those scoring high likely found the emphasis on diplomacy weak, a continuation of the McGovern/Carter days. But Kerry's insistence on diplomacy, talk, negotiation, listening, contemplating, and deliberating would have had significant appeal to those scoring low. This would not operate merely or primarily on a programmatic level but would resonate most on a symbolic level, conveying the kind of worldview with which Kerry could be identified. From that standpoint, even if Kerry's and Bush's programmatic plans for what to do about Iraq did not differ fundamentally, the contrast between the two could not have been more stark. This is the level at which the sorting and polarization operates.

Defense has powerful symbolic meaning, and Republicans have succeeded in framing it in terms of masculinity, personal toughness, and belief in simple clarity in the face of difficult decisions, which would be attractive to those scoring high in authoritarianism. Over the last forty years, those scoring low have likely come to view hawkishness as indicative of impulsiveness, macho posturing, and a lack of understanding of the realities of a complex world. As a result, the choice between them has become increasing clear along the authoritarian dimension. In either case, the policy facts outlined above appear to be secondary to symbolic considerations to public evaluations of the parties. Thus, as with race in the South, one party has established its bona fides to such a degree that it no longer needs to reprove itself on the issue.[26]

Unlike the other issues we have identified in this historical narrative, issues regarding the use of force have not grown fainter and are likely central to worldview evolution. Next chapter, we take up issues broadly associated with the war on terrorism, which map clearly onto the public's perceptions of the parties that have developed over especially the last several decades of the twentieth century.

CONCLUSION

In this chapter, we have developed a historical sketch suggesting that issues for which authoritarianism might be an important consideration have been present, if not entirely dominant, since the 1960s. These issues rose to the surface partly because of events, but partly because they helped win elections. Race, feminism, criminal rights, and defense all seem to be complementary elements that set the stage for a divide that has become even sharper in the beginning years of the twenty-first century.

---

[26] In the case of George W. Bush, one could argue that 9/11 and its aftermath proved that symbolic-level judgments about his tough, manly qualities were borne out. Faced with America's most catastrophic attack in sixty years, Bush came out swinging, abandoning, in the face of extreme and imminent threat, whatever prudence he had counseled while running for president. When it comes to foreign policy in the post 9/11 period, there is an arguably tighter fit between the programmatic and symbolic dimensions of the issue and the actual partisan divide on both those dimensions than there has been in more than a generation.

Despite important programmatic ambiguities between the parties on many of the issues in which authoritarianism structures preferences, the symbolic divide between them has become stark. The historical circumstances in which Republicans have successfully portrayed themselves as strong and Democrats as weak may be the product of a larger context and framework for understanding the worldviews undergirding perceptions of the two parties.

Writing in 1978, Senator Thomas McIntyre[27] argued that the New Right was beginning to wage successful political combat by digging under the topsoil of interest politics to the bedrock of status politics: "New Rightists sensed that many Americans were beginning to see the lack of spending restraint at all levels of government as evidence of a mass collapse of discipline, order, and purpose and as a threat to what they long believed was the right and respectable way to perform as citizens and parents." McIntyre identified a "rich roster of evils" including "government waste," "denigration of patriotism," "lack of courage and purpose in foreign policy," acceptance of gay rights and pornography and "welfare cheating," rejection of traditional marriage, and insistence on "abortion on demand" that were increasingly causing people alarm. These, in turn, were attributable in people's minds to "permissiveness as the malady weakening the entire moral structure of the nation" and "as threats to long-held standards and values" (1979, 5–7). This was the very fertile soil in which the "new rightists" were beginning to sow the seeds of the new status-based politics.

Authoritarianism does not predict individuals' preferences on all these issues. But on a critical cluster of issues – relating to racial tolerance, family structure, the trade-offs between rights and safety, foreign policy, and strength and security – it is a powerful predictor of individual preferences. We will demonstrate that as these issues have become increasingly salient, authoritarianism has come to shape fundamentally important attributes of the American political system. Moreover, the clear resonance of a symbolically based political discourse with authoritarian cognitive dispositions and nonauthoritarian responses to that cognitive style is powerfully reinforcing and deepening what we have called a worldview-based divide. McIntyre's sketch of the forces that fed the emerging New Right may be over-determined, but as a context for understanding the connective tissue linking disparate issue strains into a coherent entity, it is a useful and early naming of the roots of the current divide.

---

[27] One early critic of the New Right was the above mentioned moderate Republican Mark Hatfield. In the foreword to the book McIntyre wrote in 1979, *The Fear Brokers*, Hatfield identified three crucial elements of the New Right: (1) hypernationalism which, Hatfield argued, caused all foreign policy issues to be transformed from policy debates into tests of loyalty to the nation; (2) manipulation of religion; Hatfield, himself a devout Christian, found especially disturbing the New Right's characterization of opposition to their agenda as both un-American and un-Godly; (3) "persistent threads of racism" which, according to Hatfield "lie right below the surface of the New Right's ideology" (1979, xiii–xvi).

5

Authoritarianism's Structuring of Contemporary Issues

For authoritarianism to become relevant to helping us understand political conflict, people's preferences on a wide range of salient issues must be, in some significant part, structured by it. This was not the case for the last seventy years of the twentieth century. New Deal–style conflicts mostly dominated American politics, although, as we detailed in the last chapter, the groundwork for the development of an authoritarian cleavage was being laid during this time. But the fundamental disagreements between Republicans and Democrats concerned the size of government, the amount of taxes, and government's role in assuring a minimum standard of living. As overtly racist appeals fell out of favor, even racial issues were discussed using a New Deal frame (see, e.g., Hurwitz and Peffley 1997; Peffley, Hurwitz, and Sniderman 1997; Gilens 1999; Peffley and Hurwitz 2002). Since these issues have comprised the dominant party cleavage since the 1930s, we would not have expected authoritarianism to be central in understanding New Deal–style political conflict.

Especially since the dawning of the twenty-first century, the issue agenda has changed a great deal, with authoritarianism stitching together some existing patches with new ones to create the political tapestry we have described. We focus here on several issues, which on the surface do not seem to be interrelated. They include gay rights, the role of Christian fundamentalism in American politics, the use of force, and trade-offs between security and liberties. In this chapter, we first demonstrate that these issues are now more prevalent than earlier in the information environment. Next, we present evidence that authoritarianism does, indeed, structure the public's preferences on a range of these increasingly salient issues. And finally, we demonstrate that when we prime people to think about these issues, they perceive more ideological distance between the parties than when we prime them about traditional New Deal concerns. This suggests that the rise of issues in which authoritarianism structures preferences is a plausible explanation for why people now perceive the political world as so polarized.

GAY RIGHTS

The rise of gay rights from a nonissue to a central issue threatens one set of traditional values and taps into the authoritarians' concerns about difference (Altemeyer 1988, 2007). Gay rights represents a relatively new issue cluster, which has emerged over the last three decades. As recently as the early 1970s, the American Psychiatric Association classified homosexuality as deviant behavior (see Zaller 1992, Chapter 12, for a time line). Not surprisingly, attitudes toward gays and lesbians throughout the 1970s and much of the 1980s were overwhelmingly negative (Yang 1997; Bowman and Foster 2006). As measured by the General Social Survey – a well-respected academic survey conducted by the National Opinion Research Center (NORC) – even at the beginning of the 1990s, fully 71 percent of respondents characterized same-sex sexual relations as "always wrong" (Loftus 2001; Brewer 2003).

As a result, it was too risky for either party to provide much support for gay rights initiatives. Politicians of both parties were even reluctant to respond to the AIDS crisis, which was initially labeled a gay issue. As celebrities, such as Rock Hudson, contracted the disease, public support for AIDS research increased to some degree (Shilts 1987). But it was the Ryan White case, in which a child contracted HIV from a blood transfusion and was subsequently barred from attending a public school, that ultimately transformed AIDS into a more general public health concern. Only when AIDS became something more than a gay rights issue did public support for AIDS research increase dramatically (Stipp and Kerr 1989; Price and Hsu 1992).

In 1992, gays in the military received some attention, as Democratic presidential candidate Bill Clinton championed a policy to allow gays and lesbians to serve in the armed forces. The Democratic standard-bearer could make a decision like this because public opinion toward gays and lesbians had grown somewhat more positive, and the group's financial backing of his candidacy provided further encouragement (Broder 1999). Still, gays in the military did not occupy center stage during the campaign. The economy did. Moreover, the salience of the gay rights agenda did not increase appreciably over the course of the 1990s despite the controversy generated by the "Don't Ask, Don't Tell" policy that emerged from the gays in the military debate and despite the fact that gays and lesbians became an increasingly well accepted group in American life (see Brewer 2003, 2008).

When gay rights was discussed, it was often because of efforts to stymie the agenda. For instance, President Clinton signed into law the Defense of Marriage Act of 1996 after it was passed by both houses of Congress with strong majorities on both sides of the aisle. This act held that neither any state nor the federal government was obliged to recognize a same-sex marriage even if the marriage was recognized as legal in another state. This policy, of course, runs counter to how marriages between a man and a woman are treated. Instead, any advances that were made by gays and lesbians during this period occurred via small-scale interest group conflict rather than large-scale and fundamental changes (Haider-Markel and Meier 1996; Dorris 1999).

Things changed substantially in the year preceding the 2004 election. In a decision returned in November 2003, the U.S. Supreme Court struck down a Texas anti-sodomy law, which had previously banned private sexual relations between consenting adults of the same sex. In early February 2004, the Massachusetts Supreme Court required that the state legislature redraft existing statutes to allow for gay marriage. Only one week later, San Francisco Mayor Gavin Newsom authorized his city to grant marriage licenses to gay couples in defiance of California law. This move, in particular, received intense attention from the national news media (Campbell and Monson 2007). Most television news programs led their newscasts with images of gay and lesbian couples before, during, and after their nuptials. These events firmly catapulted gay marriage, in particular, onto the public issue agenda.

The events created an opportunity for Republican political operatives to win votes. The institutions (the courts) and the places (Massachusetts and San Francisco) that were championing gay rights were all intimately identified with liberals and Democrats. Moreover, gay marriage as a policy was wildly unpopular with the public (Bowman and Foster 2006). In a poll taken the week after the Massachusetts Supreme Court decision, Princeton Research Associates found that less than a quarter of Americans supported gay marriage, with about twice as many opposing any legal recognition of gay couples. Indeed, despite the marked gains in public support since the 1990s, surveys generally show that about 40 percent of Americans continued to believe that even consensual sexual relations between people of the same sex ought to be against the law (see Fiorina 2006, Chapter 6). On February 24, 2004, George W. Bush announced his support for a constitutional amendment that would ban gay marriage, which ensured that the issue would be a topic of intense interest during the upcoming presidential race.

Gay rights issues became identified with groups beyond just gays and lesbians. A number of different religious faiths have championed efforts to restrict gay rights. These include the Catholic Church, which continues to treat homosexuality as an illness, and a range of Protestant churches, especially those that are more fundamentalist in their approach to religious faith (see, for example, Wald 1987; Wilcox and Jelen 1990; Layman 1999). But whereas the public's feelings toward Catholics has generally improved over time (Wuthnow 1988), feelings toward Christian fundamentalists have not (Bolce and De Maio 1999), probably because they have come to be synonymous with religious conservatism today (Hunter 1991).

It is not as though fundamentalists were a new political force in the late twentieth and early twenty-first centuries. Christian fundamentalists have been the scourge of liberal secularists since at least the time of the Scopes trial in 1926 because of their more conservative positions on a range of religious and cultural issues (see Hunter 1991). Although they identified with Democrat Jimmy Carter in 1976, the first presidential candidate to describe himself as a "born again" Christian, Christian fundamentalists became an important and more permanent part of the Republican electoral coalition starting in 1980, attracted centrally by the GOP's stand on abortion, its stand against the Equal

Rights Amendment, and its call for a return to traditional family values (Wilcox 2000).

What has changed is an increasing antipathy toward this group on the part of liberals, many of whom do not attend church themselves. This is true because Christian fundamentalists are more intimately tied to their views on controversial political issues than are other religious groups, such as Catholics and Jews (Bolce and De Maio 1999). Kellstedt et al. (1994) argue that this identification is an indication that fundamentalist Christians are widely considered ideological partisans battling against the creep of moral relativism, as represented by such issues as gay rights, feminism, and the like. In contrast, Catholics are public in their advocacy of at least some concerns that are usually identified with liberals and Democrats, such as social justice, opposition to the war in Iraq, and an end to capital punishment.

The studies we have cited all draw on data gathered before George W. Bush's presidency. We suspect that the public's view of the group's partisan and ideological nature will have increased dramatically since 2000. Although Bush has never explicitly said that he had a "born again" experience, which characterizes an evangelical approach to religious faith, well-known stories about the role of his faith in overcoming alcoholism in the 1980s have caused people from fundamentalist religious traditions to embrace him. Moreover, Bush appears to share many of their preferences, whether it is his position on gay rights and stem cell research or his desire to make religious institutions more central to governing by using faith-based initiatives in his administration. If secular liberals had negative feelings about religious fundamentalists before, we suspect that those feelings have grown sharper recently, especially given the success that Bush and his allies in Congress had on these issues during his administration. As a result, we expect that feelings about groups associated with those issues, including Christian fundamentalists, might also be structured by authoritarianism.

While this chronology suggests gay rights' increasing salience, we need evidence that ordinary citizens, often inattentive to politics, were exposed to such information in the mainstream media. To provide systematic evidence of the changed salience of gay rights, we used Lexis-Nexis to conduct a content analysis of newspaper reporting from the presidential years 1988 through 2004. We focused our attention on the *New York Times*, although we are certain other media would provide similar results. Specifically, we searched for articles that used the names of both major party presidential candidates and either the word "gay" or "homosexual" during the election year, which we delineate as running from January 1 to election day.

As expected, gay rights was simply not a topic of media attention in the 1980s. In 1988, for example, only thirty articles met the search criteria across more than ten months of reporting. In 1992, this number jumped to 177 articles largely on the strength of Clinton's identification with gays in the military. This number fluctuated a bit in the next two election cycles, falling to 156 in 1996 and rising to 203 in 2000. Not surprisingly, given the intense interest in gay marriage in 2004, the number of articles meeting the search criteria surged to 428 for the Bush-Kerry contest, more than double the previous high. In a search using the term *gay marriage*, the most divisive of issues on the gay rights agenda, 2004 skunked the other years by a score of 222–0.

We performed a parallel content analysis to see if, indeed, Christian fundamentalists have become increasingly tied to politics. This search was a bit more complicated because many labels are used to describe this group. So we searched for articles that included the names of both presidential candidates in a given year and any of the following labels "Christian fundamentalist," "Christian conservative," "evangelical," "Religious Right," "religious conservative," "Christian Coalition," and "fundamentalist Christian." The results again show a marked upturn over time. In 1988, only thirty-one articles met the search criteria. This number nearly doubled to sixty-one articles in 1992, a change that likely results from the fact that Pat Buchanan gave his culture wars speech at the Republican National Convention in that year. Such mentions reached a maximum in 2000, the first year that Bush was on the ballot, with 154 articles. In 2004, the number dropped to 144, but this is a very small drop indeed. The key point is that the profile of Christian fundamentalists is much higher now than it was in the early to mid-1990s.

Taken together, these results suggest that gay rights and religious groups galvanized by this issue cluster received a significant increase in coverage in relation to presidential politics after the dawn of the new century. This will have important implications for public opinion. Zaller (1992) suggests that opinions are, in part, a function of the things that are most accessible to people when they are asked to think about politics. More coverage of gay rights makes it more likely that it will be on the tops of people's heads when they are considering the political world. Likewise, more coverage of Christian fundamentalists makes it more likely that such religious groups will be in the forefront of people's minds.

THE WAR ON TERROR

The rise of gay rights issues and the increased importance of Christian fundamentalists are not the only areas for which authoritarianism might structure the public's issue preferences. Since terrorists operate outside mainstream strictures and institutions and thrive on disorder and chaos, matters that relate to combating them might as well. One specific area might be whether people think the better weapon against terrorism is force or diplomacy. In the case of Iraq, some elites suggest that the invasion of that country has failed and that American troops ought to return home soon while others argue that victory is at hand if people will be patient. The conflicts have been protracted and costly, particularly in Iraq, where a bloody insurgency has claimed thousands of American lives. Indeed, the prolonged nature of the struggles has plausibly served to keep authoritarianism an important consideration in people's political calculus for an extended time.

The use of force or diplomacy is not the only area in which authoritarianism may be relevant to preferences in fighting the global war on terror. When it comes to trade-offs between enhanced security and protecting abstract democratic principles, authoritarianism ought to be important just as it likely was for the trade-off between protecting criminal rights and protecting people from criminals, which we explored last chapter.[1] Several initiatives that presented such trade-offs became public during Bush's second term in office. In mid-2005, a surveillance program in which the government admitted to wiretapping electronic communications without a court order, was brought to light by the *New York Times*. Critics suggested that such a program violated the Foreign Intelligence Surveillance Act (FISA) of 1978. Subsequently, it became widely known that the U.S. government was examining international bank records of American citizens and noncitizens through the Society for Worldwide Interbank Financial Telecommunication (SWIFT) program. This data mining operation, which was justified through the president's emergency powers during wartime, was an effort to find patterns in monetary transactions by potential terrorists. Like the earlier FISA revelation, it raised questions about balancing the need for security with protecting civil liberties and rights to privacy. We expect that whether people believe these programs are justified will be, in part, structured by authoritarianism because trade-offs between security and liberty lie in the balance.

The war on terrorism has made other civil liberties, such as the proper wartime role of the press, more salient than usual. The *Times*, in particular, absorbed attacks from conservative talk radio, after it published stories about wiretapping and the surveillance of bank records. Critics charged that the media's investigative work undermined the war effort by alerting terrorists to the type of surveillance they might expect to face. In addition, questions about free speech came into sharp relief. Some condemned war critics for their criticism of the president's efforts to combat world terrorism, arguing that it undermined his efforts to defeat the enemy. Never was this clearer than in March 2003, when Natalie Maines, the lead singer for the Texas-based country music act the Dixie Chicks, said during a concert in London that she was "ashamed that the president of the United States is from Texas." In response, many fans and radio stations boycotted the Dixie Chicks' music. Outside one radio station in Kansas City, Missouri, personnel set trash cans on fire and encouraged listeners to bring their Dixie Chicks albums to burn. In Bossier City, Louisiana, more than 200 country music fans gathered to watch a sixteen-ton tractor run over the group's CDs and tapes.[2]

Similar to the environment surrounding gay rights, we find that the information environment was very different on these issues in 2004 compared with previous election years. To provide some sense of how different, we again

---

[1] Data from the 2000 NES reveal that authoritarianism has a strong effect on people's disposition toward capital punishment.

[2] Kimberly Strassel, "Messing with Texas: A Dixie chick regrets anti-Bush remark," *Wall Street Journal*, March 20, 2003.

used Lexis-Nexis to search for articles that used the names of both presidential candidates and several key terms. The first was the word "terrorism." We found a sawtooth pattern. In 1988, we found sixty-four such articles between the first of the year and Eelection Day. But in 1992, only thirty-nine such articles appeared. In the Clinton versus Dole contest in 1996, the number of stories jumped to 114, but it declined again to 81 in 2000. Not surprisingly, a whopping 906 stories, roughly eight times the previous high, met the search criteria in 2004.

We performed a similar search, substituting the "war in Iraq," "Iraq war," and "Persian Gulf War" for the word "terrorism." This is a very conservative approach, of course, because a war was also going on in Afghanistan in 2004. Even so, the results conform to expectations. Since we had not yet been at war in the region in 1988, we start the analysis in the next presidential election year. In 1992, the year after the first war in the Persian Gulf, we found 140 mentions in the *New York Times*. But war becomes a much less important part of the election year dialogue in 1996 and 2000, racking up just thirty-seven and fifty-eight mentions, respectively. Of course, with U.S. troops in the field in 2004, the number of articles meeting the search criteria increased dramatically to 684, nearly five times the level in 1992. A similar search involving words such as "civil liberties" paired with the major party presidential candidates turned up the same pattern of results. In 1992, only fifteen stories included "civil liberties" along with the names Bush and Clinton. In 2004, that number quadrupled. Since the revelations of wiretapping and mining data from international bank records did not occur until 2005, it is certain that these issues would have received even more attention in Bush's second term.

In focusing on these issues, we do not mean to suggest that these are the only ones for which the public's preferences ought to be structured in part by authoritarianism. We focus on these specific areas because we suspect the worldview evolution we hypothesize has crystallized recently and these issue domains have received significantly more attention lately.

PRELIMINARY EVIDENCE OF AUTHORITARIANISM'S EFFECT ON PREFERENCES FOR GAY RIGHTS

As a first cut at the data, we present a series of bivariate tests of the relationship between authoritarianism and preferences on issues that involve gay rights. Specifically, we show that preferences differ markedly depending upon whether a person scores at authoritarianism's minimum, midpoint, or maximum. This strongly suggests that authoritarianism structures preferences on these issues.

We turn to data from the 2004 National Election Study (NES). The NES asked people's preferences on a number of gay rights issues, including gays in the military, employment protections for gays and lesbians, adoption of children by gays, and gay marriage. The top panel of Table 5.1 focuses on these issues. Among those who score at authoritarianism's minimum, support for gay rights is consistently strong. For example, nearly 90 percent of this group favors gay adoption, about

TABLE 5.1A. *Support for Gay Rights Agenda Items, by Authoritarianism, 2004*

Item	Support
Adoption by Gays	
Minimum Authoritarian	89
Midpoint Authoritarian	51
Maximum Authoritarian	28
All	50
Gay Marriage	
Minimum Authoritarian	71
Midpoint Authoritarian	36
Maximum Authoritarian	19
All	35
Protect Gays from Job Discrimination	
Minimum Authoritarian	94
Midpoint Authoritarian	77
Maximum Authoritarian	67
All	75
Allow Gays in the Military	
Minimum Authoritarian	95
Midpoint Authoritarian	79
Maximum Authoritarian	67
All	81

Source: American National Election Study, 2004

TABLE 5.1B. *Mean Feeling Thermometer Score for Christian Fundamentalists, by Authoritarianism, 1992 and 2004*

	1992	2004
Minimum Authoritarian	39.87	30.76
Midpoint Authoritarian	52.66	59.52
Maximum Authoritarian	63.74	65.66

Source: American National Election Study, 1992 and 2004

95 percent favors protections for gays and lesbians from job discrimination and allowing them to serve in the military, and over 70 percent supports gay marriage. Those who score at the midpoint of the scale are significantly less supportive of gay rights. Only about 50 percent favor gay adoption and 35 percent favor gay

marriage. As expected, those who are most authoritarian are even less supportive. On the two most contentious issues, gay adoption and gay marriage, these respondents provide only 28 and 19 percent support, respectively.

Most of these results should come as no surprise. The scholarly conventional wisdom about authoritarianism suggests it ought to structure preferences involving groups that challenge established norms, as gays and lesbians do. Even so, the data do provide a couple of interesting twists. It is noteworthy how strong support is for gays in the military and protecting gays and lesbians from job discrimination, even among those who score at the maximum of the authoritarianism scale. For both, fully two-thirds of the most authoritarian respondents report supporting these issues. In the case of gays in the military, this was a very contentious issue only twelve years earlier. Then, only 43 percent of people who scored at the maximum on the authoritarianism scale supported it. It appears, however, that once an issue becomes a relatively established practice, even those with the greatest concerns about difference will come to accept that change. Such a pattern of findings is similar to the evolution of feelings about groups that were once objects of intense discrimination, such as Jews. While Adorno et al. found a strong relationship between authoritarianism and anti-Semitism in 1950, recent scholarship has found a much weaker relationship (Raden 1999).

The lower panel of Table 5.1 examines the relationship between authoritarianism and feelings about a group intimately identified with the other side of the gay rights agenda, namely Christian fundamentalists. We show the differences in affect among people scoring at different points on the authoritarianism scale, and we also track this relationship over time using the three years the NES has asked the authoritarianism battery. First, it is important to note that the differences in mean feeling thermometer score for "Christian fundamentalists" is very large depending on where someone scores on the authoritarianism scale. Those who are least authoritarian return a mean of only about 31 degrees in 2004. In contrast, those who score at the maximum of the scale produce a mean of about 66 degrees, creating a yawning 35 point difference.

Second, the depth of negative affect nonauthoritarians expressed for Christian fundamentalists in 2004 is noteworthy. To put the mean of 30 degrees into perspective, those who score *highest* in authoritarianism in 2004 provided "Gay Men and Lesbians" a mean thermometer score of about 37 degrees, fully seven degrees warmer than nonauthoritarians gave Christian fundamentalists. Moreover, this depth of negative feelings among nonauthoritarians for Christian Fundamentalists is a relatively new development. In 1992, the mean feeling thermometer for Christian fundamentalists among nonauthoritarians was about 40 degrees, not warm to be sure, but 10 degrees warmer than in 2004. As gay rights became salient and Christian fundamentalists became identified as opponents, however, nonauthoritarians developed extraordinarily negative feelings about Christian fundamentalists.

These results are indicative of a more general pattern that we will demonstrate throughout the book. The development and deepening of the authoritarian cleavage in contemporary American politics is caused more by a change in the opinions and behaviors of nonauthoritarians than those of authoritarians. As is the case here, authoritarians' assessments tend to remain relatively constant over time. It is those at the other end of the scale who show variation.

A MORE RIGOROUS TEST USING GAY RIGHTS ISSUES

We have shown a bivariate relationship between authoritarianism and support for policies on the gay rights agenda. Next we estimate a series of multivariate models with the gay rights items as dependent variables to demonstrate that authoritarianism structures opinions on these issues even after accounting for a range of other potential explanations.

To do this, we use a powerful statistical technique called regression analysis. Regression is a tool that allows us to estimate the independent effect of a range of explanatory variables at the same time, while holding constant all the others. For example, whether someone votes for a Democrat or Republican will depend on both a person's party identification and ideology. Even though these two explanations are correlated (that is, Republicans will tend to be conservatives and Democrats liberals), regression allows us to sort out what independent influence each has on vote choice, controlling for the other.

Obviously, things other than authoritarianism explain support for or opposition to gay rights initiatives. For the sake of simplicity, we estimate parallel models for each of the dependent variables. Specifically, we account for a range of social characteristics (race, age, education, income, and gender). African Americans, older people, the less well educated, those with lower incomes, and men are all likely to be less supportive of gay rights than their counterparts. Since authoritarianism is strongly related to one's relationship with church, we also control for a person's church denomination (mainline Protestant, evangelical Protestant, and Catholic) and whether or not a respondent attends church at least weekly. We expect that evangelicals and Catholics will be less supportive of gay rights than the comparison group, which is people who do not identify with a Christian religion. In addition, party identification and ideology ought to affect issue preferences profoundly, so we include the 7-point scales for each as explanatory variables. Given the cues provided by partisans and ideologues at the elite level, Republicans and conservatives ought to express less support for gay rights than Democrats and liberals. We also include moral traditionalism on the right-hand side of the models to account for this strain of conservatism.[3] People can certainly oppose gay rights for reasons that do not

---

[3] Two of the items that usually make up the moral traditionalism scale are essentially about gay rights. Hence, we follow Layman in only including in our measure the two items that tap Hunter's notion of orthodoxy most directly, "The world is always changing and we should adjust our view of moral behavior to those changes," and "We should be more tolerant of people who choose to live according to their own moral standards, even if they are very different from our own."

have at their root an intolerance of difference caused by a need for order, and this variable is designed to tap such opinions. Finally, we include a measure of threat that people report feeling from gays and lesbians. The NES asks a question that taps this well: "The newer lifestyles are contributing to the breakdown of our society."

Each of the gay rights items is a binary choice, so we employ logistic regression to estimate these models.[4] So that we can more easily compare and interpret the effects of the explanatory variables, we map all the independent variables onto (0,1) intervals.

RESULTS

Table 5.2 displays the logistic regression estimates for the gay rights items. A negative sign on a variable indicates that increases in it lead to decreases in the dependent variables. A positive sign on a variable indicates that increases in it lead to increases in the dependent variables. In each model the effect of authoritarianism is negatively signed and both statistically and substantively significant. To demonstrate its substantive effect, we simulate a typical respondent – a non-African American woman who goes to church regularly at a mainline Protestant church and is "average" in her other characteristics. We calculate first differences by varying variables of interest from their minimum to maximum and recording the resultant change in predicted probabilities.

Take, for instance, the effect of authoritarianism on support for gay adoption. The probability of an average authoritarian (authoritarianism at maximum) supporting gay adoption is .266; in contrast, the predicted probability that a nonauthoritarian (authoritarianism at minimum) supports gay adoption is .581 – a difference of .315 points. Substantively, the range of change is important as well because the predicted probability moves from well above .5 for nonauthoritarians to below .5 for those with the most authoritarian worldview. This means that with authoritarianism at its minimum, we would predict this "typical" individual to support gay adoption. With authoritarianism at its maximum, however, we would predict this "typical" individual to oppose it.

Authoritarianism's effect is also large relative to other variables. By fixing authoritarianism at its mean and keeping the other variables as before, we can compare the effect of partisanship with that of authoritarianism. Moving from strong Democrat to strong Republican decreases the probability of supporting gay adoption by .175 points, about half that of authoritarianism. Not surprisingly, moral traditionalism has the largest effect, causing a decrease of .377

---

[4] For the gay marriage question, a fairly sizable percentage of respondents volunteered that they supported civil unions. We coded them as not supporting gay marriage. We should add, however, that the results are perfectly consistent if we coded them as supporting the idea that gays and lesbians ought to have at least certain rights of married people versus people who did not support this idea.

TABLE 5.2. *Support for Gay Rights Agenda Items as a Function of Authoritarianism, Symbolic Attitudes, and Social Characteristics, 2004, Logistic Regression Estimates*

Variable	Gay Adoption Param. Est. (Std. Err.)	Gays in the Military Param. Est. (Std. Err.)	Employment Protections Param. Est. (Std. Err.)	Gay Marriage Param. Est. (Std. Err.)
Intercept	2.454*** (0.374)	2.897*** (0.444)	3.403*** (0.419)	3.354*** (0.427)
Authoritarianism	-1.343*** (0.313)	-0.665* (0.369)	-1.184*** (0.343)	-1.077*** (0.343)
Race (African American)	-0.544* (0.257)	0.164 (0.286)	0.323 (0.268)	-0.344* (0.294)
Moral Traditionalism	-1.709*** (0.363)	-1.020** (0.386)	-0.529 (0.354)	-1.797*** (0.417)
Perceived Threat from "Newer Lifestyles"	-1.524*** (0.292)	-1.328*** (0.361)	-0.636* (0.317)	-1.904*** (0.314)
Party Identification	-0.747** (0.288)	-0.670* (0.324)	-0.818** (0.296)	-0.745* (0.326)
Ideological Self-Placement	-0.335 (0.486)	-0.524 (0.539)	-1.062* (0.499)	-1.801*** (0.549)
Female	0.626*** (0.165)	0.909*** (0.186)	0.263 (0.169)	0.224 (0.185)
Income	0.271 (0.274)	1.231*** (0.327)	0.501* (0.292)	-0.238 (0.306)
Education	1.173*** (0.325)	0.657* (0.372)	0.462 (0.341)	1.329*** (0.370)
Age	0.862** (0.355)	-0.309 (0.393)	-0.821* (0.366)	-1.543*** (0.405)
Attend Church at Least Weekly	-0.599** (0.205)	-0.360* (0.206)	-0.340* (0.192)	-0.374 (0.254)
Evangelical Protestant	-0.172 (0.219)	-0.591** (0.230)	-0.727*** (0.215)	-0.896*** (0.263)
Mainline Protestant	-0.074 (0.259)	0.124 (0.341)	-0.075 (0.273)	-0.412 (0.292)
Catholic	0.458* (0.213)	0.034 (0.250)	0.254 (0.833)	-0.044 (0.229)
Cox and Snell R²	0.28	0.15	0.16	0.34
Number of Cases	926	926	926	904

*p<.05, **p<.01, ***p<.001, one-tailed tests
Param. Est. = parameter estimate; Std. Err. = standard error

Source: American National Election Study, 2004

points across its range, and the effect of feeling threat from "newer lifestyles" is similarly large at .359 across its range.

Authoritarianism has a large effect on support for the other gay rights initiatives as well. For protecting gays from job discrimination, the predicted probability of support decreases by .213 points in moving from authoritarianism's minimum to maximum. This is greater than the effects of partisanship and ideological self-placement, which are .156 and .197, respectively. In this case, moral traditionalism's effect is statistically insignificant and feeling threat from "newer lifestyles" has an effect even smaller than partisanship, suggesting that moral conservatives are willing to afford some legal protections to gays and lesbians. For gays in the military, moving from minimum to maximum authoritarianism decreases the probability of support by .103 points, and for gay marriage the effect is .201 points. In both these cases, the effect of authoritarianism is again larger than that for partisanship (.107 for gays in the military and .133 for gay marriage). Feeling threat from "newer lifestyles" has the largest effect in both the gays in the military and the gay marriage models (.190 for gays in the military and .376 for gay marriage).

It is also worth noting that variables like ideological self-placement and being an evangelical Christian tend to have smaller effects in these models than does authoritarianism. As we described in Chapter 3, conservatism is a multidimensional construct. Once several of its components, such as authoritarianism and moral traditionalism, are included in the same model with it, the effect of ideological self-placement seems to disappear in the gay rights domain. Although the estimated effect of being evangelical is statistically significant, it is important to bear in mind that the reference category here is the secular and Jewish. The effect of being evangelical is often not that much different from being either a mainline Protestant or being Catholic. Moreover, its effect is modest compared with the attitudinal variables in the model, suggesting that what makes the preferences of evangelicals different is their attitudes rather than the fact that they identify with an evangelical church.

In sum, the relationship between authoritarianism and support for gay rights holds up even when we control for a wide range of other potential explanatory factors. Moreover, the effect of authoritarianism is very large in a relative sense. It is consistently larger than that of partisanship and ideological self-identification, as well as all the demographic variables. And in some cases, its effect is even on par with things like feeling threat from "newer lifestyles" and moral traditionalism, although usually these two variables pack a bigger punch than authoritarianism.

PRELIMINARY EVIDENCE OF AUTHORITARIANISM'S EFFECT ON WAR ON TERROR PREFERENCES

Since the National Election Study asked few questions about terrorism, a general disposition toward force, and the consequences of the fight against terrorism at home, we turn to an original survey that we conducted in 2006 to test our hypotheses in these domains. Specifically, Vanderbilt University participated in the 2006 Cooperative Congressional Election Study (CCES), which was a survey of more than 38,000 Americans conducted during October and November of 2006. Fully thirty-nine universities participated in the survey, in which we administered our questionnaire to 1,000 unique respondents who completed the survey online.

We queried our sample about a range of issues that we believe ought to be structured by authoritarianism as well. The first set of questions asked people to make trade-offs between civil liberties and security. These questions were the following.

1. As you may know, federal government agencies have recently been given more power to use electronic surveillance to monitor phone calls and emails within the United States without first getting a court warrant to do so. Do you consider this an acceptable or unacceptable way for the federal government to investigate terrorism?
2. Some people think installing video cameras in public places is a good idea because they may help to reduce the threat of terrorism. Other people think this is a bad idea because surveillance cameras may infringe on people's privacy rights. What do you think? Would you say this it is a good idea or a bad idea to install surveillance cameras in public places?
3. These days, if someone disagrees with the president on issues relating to terrorism, do you think it is okay to criticize him publicly, or should people not criticize the president on issues relating to terrorism?
4. Do you think the news media should – or should not – report information it obtains about the secret methods the government is using to fight terrorism?

In Table 5.3, we provide descriptive statistics for each of these items, and we also break the results down by authoritarianism as we did for the gay rights items. In the main, Americans' disposition toward limits on civil liberties is somewhat mixed. There is little concern about the use of video cameras in public places with 71 percent suggesting this was a "good idea" to reduce the threat of terrorism. Similarly, 65 percent of Americans thought the media should not report information about secret methods the government is using to fight terrorism. Americans express more concern about the use of wiretaps without a warrant, which is not surprising given that it is a potentially more serious impingement on privacy. In this case, 47 percent believe this is an acceptable tool in the fight against terrorism. Most Americans, however, believe that people should not censor themselves in talking about the president's performance on the issue of terrorism. Only 23 percent of Americans suggest they should not.

In breaking these data down by authoritarianism, the expected pattern emerges. Those who score lowest in authoritarianism are, by far, the least supportive of limitations to civil liberties while those who score highest are the

TABLE 5.3. *Support for Limitations on Various Civil Liberties*

Item	Support
Use Wiretaps without a Warrant to Fight Terrorism	
Minimum Authoritarian	19
Midpoint Authoritarian	47
Maximum Authoritarian	60
All	47
Use Video Cameras in Public Places to Fight Terrorism	
Minimum Authoritarian	53
Midpoint Authoritarian	69
Maximum Authoritarian	79
All	71
Not Okay to Criticize the President on Terrorism Fight	
Minimum Authoritarian	8
Midpoint Authoritarian	19
Maximum Authoritarian	33
All	23
Media Should Not Report on Secret Methods in Terror Fight	
Minimum Authoritarian	27
Midpoint Authoritarian	69
Maximum Authoritarian	79
All	65

Source: CCES, 2006

most willing to support them. We find the largest differences on media censorship in fighting the war on terrorism. Only 27 percent of those who score at the minimum of the authoritarianism scale think the media should not report on secret methods in fighting the war on terrorism. Nearly 80 percent of those who score at the maximum of the scale do. On this issue, more than 50 percentage points divide the least from the most authoritarian. The differences in support for wiretapping without a warrant are very large as well. Only about 20 percent of nonauthoritarians think it is a good idea whereas 60 percent of authoritarians do. Although the differences in preference between the most and least authoritarian are somewhat smaller for the other two issues, they are still about 25 percentage points apart. In sum, there is little doubt that authoritarianism structures opinions on issues like these.

We find a similar pattern of results for another set of original questions we asked in the 2006 CCES survey about the use of force and the war in Iraq. Specifically, we asked people whether they thought the war in Iraq was a

TABLE 5.4. *Support for Forceful Solution to Political Problems*

Item	Support
Strength over Diplomacy	
Minimum Authoritarian	22
Midpoint Authoritarian	45
Maximum Authoritarian	54
All	43
Iraq War Not a Mistake	
Minimum Authoritarian	21
Midpoint Authoritarian	44
Maximum Authoritarian	53
All	44
Follow National Interest over Follow Allies	
Minimum Authoritarian	14
Midpoint Authoritarian	29
Maximum Authoritarian	49
All	29

Source: CCES, 2006

mistake. We also asked whether "the U.S. should take into account the interests of its allies even if it means making compromises, or whether "the U.S. should follow its own national interests even when its allies strongly disagree." Finally, we asked whether "the best way to ensure peace is through military strength" or whether "good diplomacy is the best way to ensure peace."

Table 5.4 tracks these preferences in the entire sample, and we also break them down by authoritarianism. After more than three years in Iraq, a substantial 56 percent of Americans express that the war was a mistake while 44 percent say it was not. In addition, the American public appears at least somewhat dubious about going it alone as opposed to compromising with our allies. Only 29 percent thought that the United States should follow its own national interests when allies strongly disagree. Finally, Americans split somewhat more evenly on whether military strength or diplomacy was the best way to ensure peace with 43 percent favoring force and 57 percent favoring diplomacy.

To provide some indication that authoritarianism structures these preferences, Table 5.4 reveals that there is a substantively large difference between the most and least authoritarian in their disposition toward force and cooperation. The difference is slightly larger for the item that asks people whether national interest is more important than cooperating with allies, but each of the items produces differences larger than 30 percentage points. As with the gay rights items, there is strong preliminary evidence to suggest that these preferences are structured by authoritarianism.

MORE RIGOROUS TESTS – CCES DATA

Even large differences like these could result if authoritarianism is highly correlated with other variables that are really causing them. In other words, the apparent effect of authoritarianism could be spurious. Hence we must estimate models similar to those above, employing statistical controls for other competing explanations. To be clear, we do not think authoritarianism is the only variable shaping these opinions. We do, however, believe that it is an important determinant of them.

For both the civil liberties and force items, controls for party identification and ideology are necessary. Republican and conservative elites have articulated a much different vision than have Democratic and liberal elites. Partisans and ideologues ought to sort themselves accordingly. The CCES uses the same 7-point party identification scale that the NES uses. The ideology item, however, is somewhat different. Rather than a 7-point scale ranging from extremely liberal to extremely conservative, the CCES uses a 5-point scale ranging from very liberal to very conservative.

In Chapter 3, we demonstrated that authoritarianism was highly correlated with race and education. Hence we include these variables on the right-hand side to tap both sets of variables. In addition, we expect that the level of threat that people feel from terrorism will influence their preferences for action. Therefore, we add an item that asks people "How worried are you that you personally might become a victim of a terrorist attack?" The response options created a 4-point scale ranging from very worried to not worried at all. We expect that those who are experiencing a lot of anxiety from terrorism will be more inclined to prefer limitations on civil liberties in return for greater perceived security and to favor the use of force.

For each of the dependent variables, we code the more "forceful" response as 1 and the less "forceful" response as 0. Hence authoritarianism, party identification, ideology, and perceived threat from terrorism ought to carry positive signs. Since all the dependent variables are dichotomous choices, we again use logistic regression to estimate the effects of the independent variables.

RESULTS

The civil liberties models appear in Table 5.5. Even with the range of statistical controls, the results conform to expectations. On issues such as wiretapping without a warrant, on which conservative and Republican political elites have made their positions clear, both partisanship and ideology have large effects. The one exception among the four models is the use of video cameras in public places. There was little discussion of this topic in the media, and the effect of ideology and party are much smaller – indeed, statistically insignificant. As expected, perceived threat also has a significant effect in all the models. Race and education generally have no effect in the models. The only exception is that more educated respondents are more inclined to agree that the president

TABLE 5.5. *Civil Liberties Agenda Items as a Function of Authoritarianism, Symbolic Attitudes, Perceived Threat, and Social Characteristics, 2004, Logistic Regression Estimates*

Variable	Support Wiretaps without a Warrant Param. Est. (Std. Err.)	Support Video Cameras in Public Places Param. Est. (Std. Err.)	Oppose Criticizing the President on Terrorism Param. Est. (Std. Err.)	Support Media Keeping Secrets on Terror Fight Param. Est. (Std. Err.)
Intercept	−4.566***	−0.759**	−4.483***	−3.035***
	(0.412)	(0.276)	(0.473)	(0.353)
Authoritarianism	1.992***	1.536***	1.956***	2.464***
	(0.459)	(0.372)	(0.528)	(0.435)
Perceived Threat from Terrorism	2.759***	1.683***	2.039**	2.551***
	(0.626)	(0.535)	(0.764)	(0.601)
Authoritarianism* Perceived Threat	−2.110*	−1.514**	−2.258	−1.055
	(0.993)	(0.894)	(1.099)	(1.059)
Race (Black)	−0.082	0.288	−0.265	0.376
	(0.323)	(0.289)	(0.470)	(0.293)
Party Identification	3.064***	0.261	1.741***	2.062***
	(0.331)	(0.297)	(0.351)	(0.340)
Ideological Self-Placement	2.873***	0.855*	2.180***	2.190***
	(0.500)	(0.413)	(0.516)	(0.478)
Education	−0.182	0.201	−1.135**	−0.363
	(0.346)	(0.294)	(0.378)	(0.336)
Cox and Snell R^2	0.394	0.074	0.199	0.324
Number of Cases	915	911	912	905

$p < .05$, **$p < .01$, ***$p < .001$, one-tailed tests
Param. Est. = parameter estimate; Std. Err. = standard error
Source: CCES, 2006.

should be open to criticism in his handling of terrorism. Education's effect is insignificant otherwise.

The effect of authoritarianism, in contrast, is large and consistent. In all cases, its effect is properly signed and statistically significant. As with the gay rights analysis, we use the results from the regression models to simulate a "typical" respondent to get a sense of the magnitude of the effect. We do this by plugging in values of some substantive interest for the independent variables and calculating from the model the predicted probability of expressing support for limits on the various civil liberties. We choose as our "typical" respondent a non-African American, moderate, Republican leaner, who is of average education and who perceives average threat from terrorism.

Based on the "typical" characteristics, we find that the effect of authoritarianism is largest for the media self-censorship variable. The predicted probability of the typical respondent who thinks that the media ought to keep secrets is .55 if that respondent scored zero on the authoritarianism battery. That probability climbs to just over .90 if the respondent provides four authoritarian child-rearing responses. Across its range, authoritarianism increases the probability of supporting wiretaps without a warrant and video cameras in public places by .28 and .20 points, respectively. Although the effect is somewhat smaller for video cameras, it is worth noting that if we carry out parallel simulations allowing other variables to vary across their range and fixing authoritarianism at its mean, the effect of other variables is smaller than that of authoritarianism. For understanding whether people think criticizing the president on the war on terror is acceptable, authoritarianism performs as expected as well. In moving our typical respondent from least to most authoritarian, the predicted probability more than doubles.

Finally, in Table 5.6, we present the multivariate results for the use of force models. In all three cases, the results conform to expectations. Given the importance of elite opinion leadership and the closeness with which the Bush administration is identified with the force side of the dichotomies, it is not surprising that both party and ideology have large effects. In all three models, their estimated effects are at least four times their standard errors. In contrast, neither race nor education has a consistently significant effect. African Americans are somewhat more likely to favor diplomacy over strength in achieving peace, but the effect of race is insignificant in the other two models.

Most important for our purposes, authoritarianism's effect is, again, consistently large. Just to demonstrate that its effect is not contingent on what characteristics we assign as typical in the simulations, this time we make our typical respondent a non-African American who claims to be a conservative and who identifies as a weak Republican. We set education at its mean.

The predicted probability of the typical person suggesting that our national interest is more important than the support of our allies is about .2 if that person scores zero in authoritarianism. That probability more than doubles to nearly .5 if that person provides scores at the authoritarianism maximum. The effect of authoritarianism is similarly strong for understanding opinions about whether strength or diplomacy is more important in ensuring peace. If our typical respondent provides zero authoritarian responses to the child-rearing battery, the probability of favoring force over diplomacy is a little over .5. If that same typical respondent provided four authoritarian responses, the probability increases to about .75. The effect of authoritarianism is somewhat smaller in explaining whether people believe the Iraq war was a mistake. But, at least for our "typical" respondent, the effect is politically relevant. Moving from minimum to maximum on the authoritarianism index increases the probability of thinking the Iraq was was not a mistake from .307 to .512, a sizable 20 percentage point increase. Importantly, for those who score low to moderate in authoritarianism, our model would classify our "typical" respondent as

TABLE 5.6. *Attitudes on the Use of Force versus Diplomacy as a Function of Authoritarianism, Symbolic Attitudes, and Social Characteristics, 2006 Logistic Regression Estimates*

Variable	Iraq War Was Not a Mistake Param. Est. *(Std. Err.)*	Follow National Interest vs. Allies Param. Est. *(Std. Err.)*	Better to Rely on Strength opposed to Diplomacy Param. Est. *(Std. Err.)*
Intercept	−4.209*** *(0.389)*	−3.541*** *(0.337)*	−4.328*** *(0.378)*
Authoritarianism	0.863** *(0.315)*	1.154*** *(0.285)*	0.830** *(0.300)*
Perceived Threat from Terrorism	1.590*** *(0.363)*	.650* *(.312)*	1.855*** *(0.347)*
Race (African American)	−0.025 *(0.386)*	0.134 *(0.339)*	−1.545*** *(0.448)*
Party Identification	4.318*** *(0.382)*	1.569*** *(0.321)*	2.597*** *(0.329)*
Ideological Self-Placement	2.527*** *(0.533)*	1.742*** *(0.461)*	3.279*** *(0.515)*
Education	−1.156*** *(0.373)*	−0.296 *(0.325)*	0.127 *(0.344)*
Cox and Snell R^2	.450	.175	0.390
Number of Cases	915	910	915

*p<.05, **p<.01, ***p<.001, one tailed tests
Param. Est. = parameter estimate; Std. Err. = standard error
Source: CCES, 2006.

thinking the war was a mistake. But, if our "typical" respondent scored at the authoritarianism maximum, we would classify him as thinking the war was not a mistake.

In sum, these results quite clearly demonstrate that authoritarianism structures a range of opinions on the trade-offs between civil liberties and security in addition to the general use of force. Since such issues have become prominent political concerns over the last decade, they will make authoritarianism important when people make political decisions.

ISSUE TYPE AND POLARIZATION

We have now shown that authoritarianism is critical to understanding preferences for a range of issues new to the contemporary political universe. We next turn to linking these issues to the larger question of polarization.

Although the major treatments of polarization reach different conclusions about its existence (e.g., Fiorina 2006; Jacobson 2007; Abramowitz and Saunders 2008), all agree on two points: (1) the public *perceives* the parties are now farther apart and (2) elite polarization is at the core of whatever polarization/sorting has occurred in the mass public. Although not acknowledged explicitly in the literature, the electorate's *perceptions* of the parties may actually provide a partial solution. Contemporary partisans, who have remained relatively moderate, though better sorted, in an ideological sense, might find the opposite party unacceptable now because they perceive it as too far from the center. Even if dissatisfied with their own party, such moderate partisans might engage in polarized voting and evaluations of partisan players while maintaining moderate preferences on issues.

While elite polarization is certainly an important part of understanding the public's perceptions of polarization (for a review, see Hetherington 2009), there is reason to suspect that perceived polarization is caused by significantly more than objective reality. Any serious scholar of American public opinion can marshal a bevy of citations that suggest a significant chunk of the public might not have the capacity to perceive correctly the increase in elite polarization (e.g., Converse 1964; Luskin 1987; Zaller 1992). We propose that perceptions of increased party polarization are also a function of the types of issues that now play a prominent role in the public sphere. Specifically, preferences on these issues are structured by authoritarianism. Since people understand these issues on a gut level, it is likely that they will perceive party differences to be greater when these issues are salient than when traditional New Deal issues are.

One commonly cited piece of evidence that Americans now correctly perceive the parties as further apart is drawn from the NES' 7-point ideology scales. In 1984, the mean perceived distance between the Republican and Democratic parties was 1.52 points. By 2004, it had increased to 2.10 points. This increase, however, has occurred in a nonlinear fashion. In 1992, people saw an average distance of 1.93 points. But in 1996, on the heels of a marked surge in elite polarization as measured by Poole and Rosenthal's DW-NOMINATE scores, perceived ideological distance *dropped* to 1.74.[5] Since the increase in elite polarization has been largely linear over time while the public's perceptions of the parties have not, it suggests that something beyond elite polarization must be contributing to these perceptions.

We hypothesize that another part of the answer is understanding which issues divide the parties. Since issues structured by authoritarianism have a more visceral quality, people's general perceptions of party differences may increase when these issues become more salient. This, in turn, may cause people to view the parties as further apart ideologically, regardless of how far

---

[5] Certainly the change in presidential candidates cannot explain why people saw less ideological distance between the parties in 1996 than 1992. Bill Clinton, of course, was the same, but Bob Dole, the Republican standard-bearer in 1996, was, if anything, more conservative than George H.W. Bush was in 1992.

apart they really are. Indeed, on issues like gay rights, it is easy to argue that Republicans and Democrats at the elite level are actually closer together than they are on New Deal issues. Certainly few Democratic candidates actively promote gay marriage, although it is also true that nearly all those who do are Democrats.

One way to test this hypothesis is to prime people with references to specific issues before asking them to place the parties on an ideological scale. By prime, we mean to make certain issues more salient than others by asking about them, which brings those considerations to people's attention when they are asked to make evaluations later in the survey. We expect that when we cause people to think about the issues we cover in this chapter, people will see the parties as further apart. When traditional left-right issues are at play, people will see the parties as closer together.

To test these hypotheses, we constructed a survey that asked a group of student respondents to place themselves and both major parties on the NES's 7-point ideology scale, which runs from extremely liberal at one end of the continuum to extremely conservative at the other end of the continuum. We also set up several different experimental conditions in which we asked people a battery of questions about specific issues just before giving them the three ideology questions. In the gay rights condition, we asked people to answer whether they supported or opposed gay marriage, adoption of children by gays, and employment protections for gays and lesbians. In the spending condition, we asked people to answer whether they supported increased, decreased, or constant spending levels on a number of New Deal–style programs. In the George W. Bush condition, we asked people whether they approved or disapproved of the president's job performance in general, on economic policy and on foreign policy. Finally, in the control condition, we began the survey by asking people to answer the ideological items first.

Our first cut at the data involve the use of a student sample taken from two classes at Vanderbilt University in introduction to American government. Although this is not a representative sample, the fact that we are using an experimental manipulation, in which each member of the class has an equal chance of being chosen into each of the four conditions, obviates some of the concerns about the lack of representativeness in the sample.

The results, which appear in Table 5.7, conform to expectations. In the gay rights condition, subjects, on average, perceived the Republicans as 4.32 points to the right of the Democrats. As expected, the other conditions produce average differences that are quite a lot smaller both substantively and statistically (3.61 for spending, 3.44 for Bush, and 3.71 for the control). An analysis of variance (ANOVA) suggests that the group means are not all equal (F = 3.547, df = 3, 111) at nearly 99 percent confidence (p = .017).[6]

---

[6] It is worth noting that these results stand up to a range of statistical controls. We also estimated a regression equation in which we regressed the perceived distance between the parties on whether someone was in the gay rights condition, the distance the respondent placed himself or herself

TABLE 5.7. *Perceptions of Party Polarization as a Function of Prime on Issue Analysis of Variance*

Type of Prime	Mean	Standard Deviation	Number of Cases
Gay Rights	4.322	1.012	31
Government Spending	3.612	1.358	31
George W. Bush Approval	3.438	1.134	32
Control	3.714	0.956	21
TOTAL	3.774	1.178	115

ANOVA: $F = 3.547$ df$(3,111)$, $p < .017$

Taken together these results suggest that changes in the issue environment can cause significant changes in perceived polarization between the major political parties. When people think about authoritarian structured issues like gay rights, they think the political system is much more polarized than when they think about issues like government spending or even a polarizing political figure like George W. Bush. Although Bush has chosen to make authoritarian-structured issues salient, these results suggest that it is not Bush, himself, who causes people to perceive a polarized political environment. Moreover, this insight helps explain why people saw the parties as furthest apart in 1992 and 2004. In both these elections, war and gay rights issues, both structured by authoritarianism, played a more prominent role in both election years' dialogue. This was much less the case in 1996 and 2000 when the data suggest perceptions of party differences were more muted.

CONCLUSION

In this chapter we have demonstrated that preferences on issues important to contemporary politics are, at least in part, structured by authoritarianism. First, we showed that these issues are much more prominent parts of the information environment than they were during the 1990s. Second, we demonstrated that knowing how authoritarian a person is provides an important window on where the person stands on seemingly disparate issues like gay rights, the Iraq war, the proper use of force in general, and the trade-offs between security and civil liberties. These two points should combine to make authoritarianism more accessible to people today as they make political decisions. And finally, we showed that when people are asked to think about these specific issues

from the center of the ideology scale, and whether the subject identified himself or herself as either a Republican or Democrat. Being in the gay rights condition is the only statistically significant variable in the model. Its estimated effect suggests that being in this group increased the perceived distance between the parties by about three-quarters of a point, other things being equal.

before they are asked to place the parties ideologically, they perceive the parties as more polarized compared with when they are asked to think about traditional New Deal issues.

We do not mean to suggest that gay rights and issues related to combating terrorism are the only issues that appear in the contemporary dialogue that authoritarianism helps to structure. In fact, understanding the role that authoritarianism plays in preference formation can explain other features of American political life. For example, the twenty-first century has witnessed increasing concerns that secular elements in the mass media and people who value political correctness more generally are waging a war against Christmas. One commonly cited example that Christmas is under attack is the fact that many stores instruct their employees to wish patrons "Happy Holidays" rather than "Merry Christmas" during the Christmas season.

We asked our CCES sample whether they were offended by this change. About 60 percent reported that they were and about 40 percent reported that they were not. Most important for our purposes, only 27 percent of those who scored at the minimum of the authoritarianism scale said they were, compared with 70 percent of those scoring at the maximum – a remarkable 43 percentage point difference. When Fox News and other cable outlets express concerns about whether Christmas, and likely Christian religious observances more generally, receive adequate respect, our results make it clear what worldview they are tapping into.

In the next chapter, we explore the political implications of the increased prominence of such issues. Sometimes their presence actually leads to a convergence of preference. Other times, it leads to polarization. We demonstrate the different circumstances that produce these differing outcomes. In doing so, we provide a compelling explanation for the parties' rising and falling electoral fortunes.

6

Threat and Authoritarianism: Polarization or Convergence

As the literature has evolved from treating authoritarianism as a static personality characteristic à la Adorno et al. (1950) to seeing it as a disposition that manifests itself in situation-specific circumstances (e.g., Feldman 2003; Stenner 2005), threat has come to play a starring role in understanding its effect. Scholars today tend to believe that the *level* of authoritarianism in a population generally stays the same over time (but see, e.g., Altemeyer 1996, who measures authoritarianism differently). Its *effect*, however, changes depending upon measurable circumstances. Specifically, most scholars argue that an authoritarian disposition lies dormant in the absence of threat, meaning that under this condition the preferences of the more and less authoritarian will not differ by much. Threat activates an authoritarian disposition, which, in turn, causes it to have measurable effects on opinions, behaviors, and preferences (see, e.g., Feldman and Stenner 1997; Stenner 2005, for the most complete treatment).

Although we wholeheartedly embrace the notion of situationism – that authoritarianism's effect will wax and wane depending on how threatened people feel – we will demonstrate that scholars have misunderstood the relationship between threat and authoritarianism. Worse, this flawed thinking encourages a fundamental misreading of the recent dynamics of American politics. In correcting this misunderstanding, we can better explain why support for gay rights, limitations on civil liberties, the use of force, and even approval of the president have tended to move in the directions they have over the last decade. Our explanation also provides some purchase on why opinions on these matters have been relatively more and less polarized at different points in time.

To use the language of social science, scholars suggest a positive interaction between authoritarianism and threat. As threat increases, the difference between the preferences of the most and least authoritarian is supposed to increase. The reasoning goes that authoritarians become increasingly concerned about maintaining the group's well-being (and, by extension, their own well-being since they are part of the group) during threatening circumstances. This would make them increasingly supportive of policies that would, for example, value security over civil liberties. Although much literature largely ignores nonauthoritarians, the positive interaction also suggests that threat may cause nonauthoritarians to become even more invested than usual in promoting civil liberties, diplomacy, and tolerance (Perrin 2005; Stenner 2005).

We find a positive interaction unlikely. We depart from the new conventional wisdom in two ways. First, we believe those who score high and low in authoritarianism will have different preferences in the absence of threat. Different cognitive styles and capacities ought to produce different preferences under most conditions. Since a central part of the authoritarian disposition is characterized by feelings of pessimism (Adorno et al. 1950; Altemeyer 1996; Stenner 2005), we believe that those scoring high in authoritarianism will tend to believe the world is more threatening than do nonauthoritarians during times that appear unthreatening to most. Indeed, it might be that this relatively constant perception of threat helps account for the simplifying black versus white, good versus evil cognitive style. Stress and fatigue often lead to a breakdown of cognitive capacity and a greater reliance on instinct. Hence, people who are more and less authoritarian ought to display significantly different preferences under "normal" circumstances.

Second, we think that threat has the potential to actually reduce the difference in preferences between the more and less authoritarian rather than increase it. When circumstances make the world a scary place for more people, which a high-profile terrorist attack that kills thousands of people might, the difference in perceived threat between the more and less authoritarian ought to narrow, maybe even evaporate. Under such circumstances, the less authoritarian will tend more toward the use of instinct over cognition, which the more authoritarian apparently rely on commonly. As a result, we believe the preferences of the more authoritarian and the less authoritarian will differ by less than they do under "normal" circumstances. When both feel threatened, both will seek safety and security. Our reasoning suggests a negatively signed interaction between threat and authoritarianism. Furthermore, we argue that our understanding of the interaction between threat and authoritarianism squares better with the aggregate level findings that informed the early thinking on situationism (see, e.g., Sales 1972, 1973).

In this chapter, we provide a range of illustrations in which the percentage of people adopting prototypically authoritarian preferences during times of threat increases. Since those scoring high in authoritarianism generally have those preferences already, increases in the popularity of those positions must, disproportionately, be the result of the changing behavior of the less authoritarian. We next test our hypotheses about the interaction between authoritarianism and threat, using all the dependent variables we demonstrated in the last chapter to be structured in part by authoritarianism. We find strong evidence for a negative interaction. We also consider changes in George W. Bush's job approval rating through this lens. Finally, in carrying out these tests, we demonstrate that different threat conditions produce either convergence or polarization of public opinion. When threat is perceived widely across categories of authoritarianism, as it was with terrorism after September 11, convergence results. When threat is perceived asymmetrically, polarization occurs.

WHAT A POSITIVE INTERACTION AND A NEGATIVE INTERACTION MEAN

When we use the term *interaction*, we mean that the effect of one variable depends on the value of another variable. That is, one variable conditions the effect of another. A positive interaction between threat and authoritarianism means the effect of authoritarianism increases as threat increases. This relationship is depicted graphically as the solid line in Figure 6.1. The theory suggests that threats cause authoritarians to respond in a less tolerant manner but cause nonauthoritarians to act in a more tolerant manner (see Stenner 2005). The key point is that those who score high and low in authoritarianism will differ in their preferences to a greater degree under conditions of threat than in the absence of threat.

This relationship is supposedly supported by both aggregate-level and individual-level data. At the aggregate level, scholars have shown that periods of both social and economic unease, which are treated in this literature as threats, tend to predate increases in authoritarian-friendly policy outcomes. These outcomes include increased support for police budgets and harsher prison sentences (Sales 1973), more public support for censorship, and a wider expression of racial prejudice (Doty, Peterson, and Winter 1991). In addition, periods of high threat apparently cause more people to embrace powerful figures like the

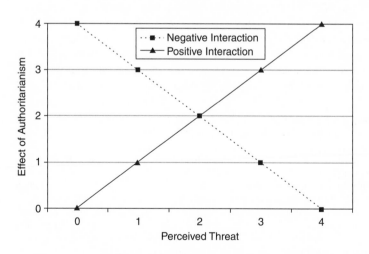

FIGURE 6.1. Graphical Representation of Interactions between Threat and Authoritarianism

president (McCann 1997). Certainly the literature on support for authoritarian leaders in the developing world is consistent with this view.

Such findings, however, do not necessarily suggest a positive interaction between threat and authoritarianism. In fact, we believe they suggest the reverse. The more authoritarian differ from the less authoritarian, often by a lot, on a number of issues even in the absence of an objective threat.[1] For example, those who score high and low in authoritarianism differed in their preferences about gay rights by a lot in 1992 even though gay rights received little attention in the national media. To the extent that differences are *slightly* larger now that gays receive more attention, it is because nonauthoritarians have become more tolerant at a faster rate, not because authoritarians have grown chillier toward them. In fact, on a number of gay rights issues, authoritarians have become increasingly positive over time even as attention to the group has increased, a change that would have presumably made it more threatening. Similarly, those who score high and low in authoritarianism differ in their levels of racial resentment and racial prejudice today just like they did in the early 1990s when race was a much bigger part of the political dialogue.

Rather than needing a readily identifiable threat, we believe that those who score high in authoritarianism are more likely to perceive threat even when situations might not be objectively threatening to most others. The literature on authoritarianism certainly implies that those who score high in authoritarianism find the world a threatening place, suggesting that perceptions of threat are a relative constant for them over time and place (Altemeyer 1996). If true, then the opinions and preferences of authoritarians on issues of contemporary concern are unlikely to change much when more threat is introduced, since their baseline preferences already reflect a high degree of perceived threat. When dealing with fixed choice items as we do in survey research, how much *more* anti–gay rights, pro-security, or anti-affirmative action can one get?[2] Importantly, Altemeyer (1996) – who uses a measure of authoritarianism that mixes authoritarian values, such as order, with authoritarian preferences, such as opposition to gay rights (see Stenner 2005 for a detailed critique) – finds that authoritarianism increases in the aggregate during threatening times. This squares well with our hypothesis. Since those with authoritarian values, by and

---

[1] Indeed, Stenner's (2005) evidence that authoritarians have the same opinions and behaviors as nonauthoritarians absent some threat manipulation is derived from a student sample of fewer than 100 subjects.

[2] We leave open the possibility that those scoring high in authoritarianism might be willing to do increasingly intolerant things when faced with extreme threat relative to those scoring low. For example, in fighting the war on terrorism, we suspect, and show, that when those scoring low in authoritarianism feel a lot of threat from terrorism, they are willing to support things like wiretapping without a warrant. We suspect, and show, that those scoring high in authoritarianism are probably supportive of such measures regardless of whether they feel a lot of threat. But whereas warrantless wiretapping might be the most that a threatened nonauthoritarian would allow, a threatened authoritarian might well support much more serious limitations to civil liberties, such as particularly extreme forms of torture, for example. Matters of degree are hard to adduce with fixed choice survey items.

large, already have authoritarian preferences, his findings suggest that those who score lower in authoritarian values come to adopt more authoritarian preferences in more threatening times.

Similarly the aggregate-level findings often cited in the authoritarianism literature as evidence for situationism suggest that policy outcomes change in an authoritarian direction during tumultuous times. Since policy change tends to reflect changes in the *overall* distribution of opinion (Page, Shapiro, and Dempsey 1987; Erikson, MacKuen, and Stimson 2002), it suggests that *more people* are embracing preferences for such changes when threatened. Those who score high in authoritarianism have these preferences already. Far right political parties, like the National Front in France, tend to attract more votes during tumultuous times than quiet ones (Mudde 2007). But it is not that hardcore authoritarians, the usual base of support for such parties (Dow 1999; Sniderman, Hagendoorn, and Prior 2004), get even more supportive of parties like this; they already support them. Instead people who are *not* hard-core authoritarians start to support them.

Fluctuations in political tolerance over time provide further evidence. Mueller (1988) traces trends in support of civil liberties from the 1940s to the 1980s. Since most of the questions during this period used communists as the unpopular group to test whether people would offer them civil liberties protections, it is most fruitful to compare questions using this group object. Tolerance for communists was reasonably high during the World War II years when the Soviet Union was, from 1941–1945, an ally of the United States. During the early years of the Cold War when communism came to be seen as an increasing threat, tolerance dropped dramatically. Measures of tolerance reached their nadir in the late Korean War years, as Joseph McCarthy pursued supposed examples of communist subversion in the U.S. government, a particularly frightening proposition. As perceived threat from communists ebbed in the 1960s, so, too, did intolerance for communists in the United States. Mueller (1988) concludes that nothing explains fluctuations in the percentage of Americans willing to afford communists civil liberties protections better than measures of perceived threat of communists. We suspect that those scoring high in authoritarianism were likely intolerant of communists throughout the entire period (see Greenstein 1965 for a review). But the number of people with concerns grew as people beyond those scoring high in authoritarianism came to feel more threatened.

All this suggests that increases in the percentage of the public that embraces order during threatening times must be the result of a change in behavior among people who are less authoritarian. This implies a negative interaction between perceived threat and authoritarianism, which we depict graphically as the broken line in Figure 6.1. The negative interaction between threat and authoritarianism suggests that as perceived threat increases, the difference in the opinions and behaviors of authoritarians relative to nonauthoritarians decreases. As people in the middle and lower tiers of authoritarianism come to perceive threat, they adopt policy orientations that are more like an authoritarian's.

Illustrations

To illustrate our thinking, consider an analogy about vehicle preferences. Should someone buy a Toyota Prius or a Hummer? The Prius is a small hybrid car that runs partly on gasoline and partly on electricity and gets well over fifty miles to the gallon of gas; the Hummer is a behemoth sport utility vehicle that weighs in at over 8,000 pounds and gets around ten miles to the gallon. With a few modifications, the Hummer is a military vehicle. Those who value safety over other considerations will feel very secure in one. Since being carbon neutral is unlikely to become a central part of the decision-making calculus of this group, it seems unlikely that their preference will change.[3]

Values are surely different among Prius drivers with principles more abstract than safety guiding the decision-making process. Instead of the effects of an accident on loved ones riding in the car, these people are probably more inclined to consider the effects of driving on the planet. Of course, both drivers are "right," but for different reasons. No one can doubt that Priuses are better for the environment than are Hummers. But it is similarly obvious that people would be better off in a Hummer in a high-speed collision involving the two vehicles. In fact, in the instant before such a collision, an event that would certainly be very threatening to anyone with a pulse, the Prius driver might even wish he had chosen to drive a Hummer. The key point here is that under conditions of high perceived threat, the preferences of the Hummer driver remained constant while the preferences of the Prius driver changed (or should have).

Liberal television talk show host Bill Maher has seemed to suggest this relationship between threat and authoritarianism. Maher's politics as articulated on his HBO series, *Real Time,* suggest a strongly nonauthoritarian bent. He is pro–gay rights, makes frequent reference to drug use, and criticizes the Republican base whenever presented the opportunity. However, months after the September 11 attacks, Maher stated that airport security screeners should profile passengers based on whether they appeared to be Muslims. Certainly racial or, in this case, religious profiling is antithetical to what appears to be his worldview, and he probably did not feel this way before terrorism became a more salient concern. But Maher likely flies a lot and would feel safer doing it if every potential Islamic extremist was patted down before getting on a plane

---

[3] This comparison is probably not at all farfetched to make. The CCES survey that we have employed asked whether the respondent drove a pickup truck. Among those scoring at the minimum of the authoritarianism index, only about 24 percent reported driving a pickup. Among those scoring at the maximum, 47 percent, or nearly twice the percentage as those scoring at the minimum, did so. If we control for a range of different demographics that might also predict what type of vehicle a person chooses, the effect of authoritarianism remains statistically significant ($p<.001$). Although the CCES did not ask a question about driving hybrids, we suspect that drivers of these vehicles are disproportionately people scoring low in authoritarianism.

with him. Those who score high in authoritarianism might have been inclined to think that this was a good idea long before September 11 because they tend not to trust people who are different from them. This example further illustrates that when threat is high, authoritarians and nonauthoritarians will act more alike than when threat is low.

Based on their respective expressed policy preferences in the 2000 campaign and their voting records when they were members of Congress, it seems reasonable to assume that Al Gore would score lower in authoritarianism than Vice President Dick Cheney. Had Gore been elected president in 2000, however, how different would his first impulse have been to September 11 when threat was overwhelmingly high? Would his first step have been to affirm his commitment to civil liberties, as the positive interaction between authoritarianism and threat suggests? This seems unlikely to us. Instead, we suspect that taking steps to ensure the safety of the nation would have been Gore's top priority.

As such, Gore probably would have given more serious consideration to initiatives like warrantless wiretapping than he would have had the attack not taken place. Although differences in Gore's and Cheney's preferences probably would have persisted (for example, Gore has stated that he would not have invaded Iraq), we suspect their respective preferences on trade-offs between civil liberties and security and the general use of force would have been closer in 2002 than they were in 2000. Indeed, it is probably instructive to recall that it was Franklin Roosevelt, a political leader who almost surely scored relatively low in authoritarianism, who thought it necessary to intern Japanese-Americans in special camps after the attack on Pearl Harbor.

In sum, in the face of a grave objective threat, authoritarians' preferences probably won't change too much because they feel relatively threatened by the world as a condition of their cognitive and emotional style. Hence the people to observe through changing threat conditions are those who score lower in authoritarianism. Those scoring lower in authoritarianism will likely adopt preferences more like those of authoritarians than they would under "normal" circumstances. What good, one might ask, are high-minded principles if you are dead?

Our thinking works in both directions. Assume that no terrorist attacks take place in the United States for many years. Perceived threat from terrorism ought to drop, especially among those who score lower in authoritarianism. Rather than continuing to be occupied with personal security, nonauthoritarians will be more likely to adopt, for example, a more pro–civil liberties position because the conditions that caused them to rely more on instinct and hence adopt more pro-security preferences have passed. Among those who score high in authoritarianism, perceptions of threat are likely to remain high and drop more slowly than for those who score low. In other words, perceptions of threat will ebb asymmetrically. As a result, the effect of authoritarianism in shaping preferences will increase. The preferences of authoritarians and nonauthoritarians will come to differ by a lot.

WHY PREVIOUS ANALYSIS SUGGESTS A POSITIVE INTERACTION

It is not as though scholars who have explored the relationship between threat and authoritarianism and found a positive interaction did sloppy work. A number of factors are potentially at play, both individually and in combination, to produce such an outcome. Some relate to survey-based analysis, specifically, and others to experiments.

In survey analysis, scholars have used many different measures of threat, some of which seem better than others. Although similar critiques could be leveled against a range of measures, we concentrate here on Stenner's because her treatment is among the most recent and is certainly the most comprehensive and powerful. Stenner (2005) distinguishes between garden variety threats, which she argues are often not important, and threats to the "normative order," which she argues are critically important. These normative threats are threats to "some system of openness and sameness that makes 'us' an 'us': some demarcation of people, authorities, institutions, values, and norms that for some folks at some point defines who 'we' are, and what 'we' believe in" (Stenner 2005, 17).

We have no quibble with her conceptual definition. Less clear is whether Stenner's measure of threat in the context of her *survey work* taps the concept.[4] Here we stress survey work because our expectations regarding survey work and experimental work are importantly different. Specifically, Stenner uses a scale of equally weighted items composed of the following four pieces: relative evaluations of presidential candidates, perceptions of distance between the respondent and both political parties, perceived belief divergence between "typical Americans" and "members of Congress," and perceived ideological distance between the respondent and "typical Americans." Feldman and Stenner (1997) also sometimes find a positive interaction between threat and authoritarianism but do so most often when their measure of threat is perceived ideological distance from major political actors. These seem to us excellent measures of political alienation but not really of normative threat. There are plenty of good reasons to think that the interaction between alienation and authoritarianism might be negative, which is likely why Stenner (2005) finds the pattern of results that she does. But it is probably unwise to infer too much about the sign on the interaction between perceived threat and authoritarianism from an analysis using this particular measure of threat.

When scholars introduce threatening conditions in the lab, they tend to use manipulations that ought to threaten those scoring high in authoritarianism disproportionately. But is a threat really a threat if it is not likely to be threatening to many of the subjects in the experiment? We suspect that such stimulus allows scholars to assess how susceptible to specific kinds of threats people are based on their level of authoritarianism. Changes in the dependent variable

---

[4] We leave aside Stenner's (2005) experimental work here, for which her manipulations are very clever and well implemented. It is clear that the survey and experimental worlds are different on this question. Surveys are able to determine only whether perceived threat exists after an uncontrolled set of circumstances unfolds in the real world.

are sure to be larger for authoritarians because they are more inclined to feel threatened by the manipulation. But it does not allow scholars to assess what effect threat actually has in conditioning the effect of authoritarianism. It might be the case that those scoring high in authoritarianism are more susceptible to threat, but it is not clear what effect authoritarianism will have when people who score low and high in authoritarianism both perceive threat.

Consider an experiment that focuses on gay rights in which subjects are presented with videotapes of gay men kissing. Since gays and lesbians are, as a baseline, more threatening to authoritarians than to nonauthoritarians, such a threat manipulation will show polarization between the groups because, on average, authoritarians will be threatened by the manipulation than nonauthoritarians. But what of the nonauthoritarians who actually perceive threat from the manipulation? Although there will be fewer of them than among those scoring high in authoritarianism, we suspect that, like authoritarians, their opinions about gay rights will grow more negative than if they did not see the videotape. What is missing, then, from these experimental manipulations is whether people actually feel threatened by the threat.

In that sense, our understanding of situationism departs from that of others (notably Feldman and Stenner 1997; Feldman 2003; Stenner 2005). They operate from the assumption that the most and the least authoritarian do not differ unless authoritarianism is activated by some threat. Perhaps this is possible in a vacuum, but we find it implausible in the real world. The results marshaled to support this contention tend to come from student samples with very small numbers of cases, results that we have been unable to replicate in our own efforts with either student samples or with representative national samples. As we detailed in Chapter 3, authoritarianism is moderately to highly correlated with a range of variables even without the manipulation of some threat condition in advance of asking the questions. One might argue that simply asking questions about normatively threatening objects is threat enough to activate authoritarianism. If so, though, what conditions in the real world would not be threatening? It is our belief that the world is generally a threatening place for those scoring high in authoritarianism and much less so for those scoring lower in authoritarianism.

To recap, although we believe threat is important in understanding the dynamic effect of authoritarianism, we will demonstrate that it works differently in the real world than has been shown by psychologists using experimental methods. Rather than assuming a threat is threatening, we rely on people's reports of how threatened they actually feel. And when we do, we find that the opinions of those scoring low in authoritarianism but who perceive significant threat come to mirror the opinions of those who score high in authoritarianism.

SOME DESCRIPTIVE EVIDENCE

If our thinking is correct, we ought to see increasing percentages of people backing, for instance, safety and security over civil liberties during a threatening time. People scoring very high in authoritarianism might be less concerned with abstractions like civil liberties under most circumstances, but people scoring lower in authoritarianism might swell the percentage of people willing to forgo certain civil liberty protections when threat is high (see also Mueller 1988). After 9/11, for instance, a much higher percentage of people across the distribution of authoritarianism would, we expect, perceive significant threat from world terrorism.

Starting in 1999, the First Amendment Center at Vanderbilt University started to ask a question to random cross-sections of Americans. After explaining the purpose of the First Amendment, the survey asked respondents whether "the First Amendment goes too far in the rights it guarantees." In the two years before the 9/11 attacks, only 28 and 22 percent of Americans, respectively, thought that the First Amendment went too far. At the end of 2001, however, the percentage jumped to 39 percent, nearly double the reading in 2000. And in 2002, with Americans living with constant updates about terror threat levels from the news media, the percentage of people who thought the First Amendment went too far peaked at 49 percent. As September 11 became a more distant memory and as people became accustomed to living with terrorism, public opinion began to turn. By 2003, only 34 percent thought the First Amendment went too far, and in 2004, only about 30 percent did, a percentage statistically indistinguishable from the percentage recorded in 1999.[5]

The First Amendment Center's findings are not anomalous. Starting in September 2001, the Pew Foundation for the People and the Press debuted a question that asked respondents, "In order to curb terrorism in this country, do you think it will be necessary for the average person to give up some civil liberties or not?" Sixty-one percent of an understandably shaken public said yes in a survey taken just two weeks after the attacks. By June 2002, that percentage had fallen to 46 percent, and in July 2004, only 38 percent said yes.

Similarly, whether people thought the government had "gone too far in restricting civil liberties" follows a similar pattern. Princeton Research Associates in collaboration with *Newsweek* asked this question six times between September 2001 and August 2002, and the Gallup Organization used the question in November 2003. Right after the 9/11 attacks, the percentage who thought the government had gone too far was in the single digits. Two years later, more than a quarter of the public expressed concern that the government was going to far in restricting civil liberties.

Finally, CBS News, at several points in time, asked people whether they were more concerned about the government failing to make anti-terrorist laws strong enough or whether government laws would excessively restrict civil liberties. The first reading from CBS was taken in December 2001, and 43 percent expressed more concern that the laws would not be strong enough while 45 percent expressed more concern about civil liberties. In the most recent survey, which was taken in November 2006, only 36 percent were concerned that the

[5] First Amendment Center's 2004 Report, p. 1.

laws would not be strong enough, while a slim majority (51 percent) expressed more concern about civil liberties.

The results here tell a story consistent with the theory we explicated above. The surge then decline in perceived threat increased then decreased the number of people willing to trade off civil liberties for security. Since those scoring high in authoritarianism are likely to feel more threatened than nonauthoritarians under typical circumstances, it is more likely that those moving the distribution are people who scored closer to the bottom of the authoritarianism scale.

TESTING THE HYPOTHESIS

To test our hypothesis, we replicate the regression models we estimated in Chapter 5, but we add an interaction between our measures of perceived threat and authoritarianism in each of the models. Recall that we included measures of threat in all these models because we (rightly) thought that perceptions of threat would affect support for things like gay rights, the use of force rather than diplomacy, and trade-offs between civil liberties and security.

Of course, the threat one might perceive from gays and lesbians is different from that which one perceives from terrorism, so we use a different measure of threat in each. In the gay rights models, the item we used to tap threat asked respondents whether and how strongly they agreed or disagreed with the following statement: "the newer lifestyles are contributing to the breakdown of our society." In the force versus diplomacy models and the security versus civil liberties models, the item we used asked respondents to place themselves on a 4-point scale ranging from "very worried" to "not worried at all" in response to the following question: "How worried are you that you personally might become a victim of a terrorist attack?"

Gay Rights

The results of the gay rights regression models, including the interactive terms, appear in Table 6.1. In discussing the results, we will focus solely on the effects of authoritarianism and threat because we discussed the effects of the other variables in the last chapter. The addition of the interactive terms did not much affect the estimates for the other variables in the models.

In terms of both sign and, for the most part, significance, the results consistently follow expectations. Authoritarianism has a very large effect when people perceive less threat. Contrary to the scholarly conventional wisdom, however, we find that authoritarianism's effect diminishes as people perceive increasing threat from "newer lifestyles." The results also suggest that perceived threat from newer lifestyles has an effect on these dependent variables, but, also counter to conventional wisdom, we find its effect is strongest among those who score lowest in authoritarianism.

In all four equations, the so-called main effect for authoritarianism is statistically significant and substantively quite large. The negative sign suggests

TABLE 6.1. *Support for Gay Rights Agenda Items as a Function of Authoritarianism, Symbolic Attitudes, Perceived Threat, and Social Characteristics, 2004, Logistic Regression Estimates*

Variable	Gay Adoption Param. Est. *(Std. Err.)*	Employment Protections Param. Est. *(Std. Err.)*	Gay Marriage Param. Est. *(Std. Err.)*	Gays in the Military Param. Est. *(Std. Err.)*
Intercept	3.419***	4.481***	3.897***	3.619***
	(0.545)	(0.657)	(0.535)	(0.714)
Authoritarianism	−3.127***	−3.017***	−2.178***	−1.882*
	(0.751)	(0.869)	(0.701)	(0.965)
Perceived Threat from "Newer Lifestyles"	−3.242***	−2.398**	−3.011***	−2.463**
	(0.718)	(0.829)	(0.691)	(0.911)
Authoritarianism* Perceived Threat	2.835**	2.713**	1.979*	1.747
	(1.053)	(1.149)	(1.077)	(1.260)
Race (African American)	−0.509*	0.350	−0.336	0.178
	(0.256)	(0.267)	(0.293)	(0.285)
Moral Traditionalism	−1.661***	−0.476	−1.768***	−0.991**
	(0.361)	(0.354)	(0.417)	(0.386)
Party Identification	−0.737**	−0.798**	−0.745*	−0.660*
	(0.287)	(0.296)	(0.326)	(0.323)
Ideological Self-Placement	−0.273	−1.013*	−1.765***	−0.500
	(0.490)	(0.501)	(0.551)	(0.539)
Female	0.673***	0.254	0.233	0.901***
	(0.165)	(0.169)	(0.185)	(0.186)
Income	0.237	0.467	−0.273	1.214***
	(0.276)	(0.293)	(0.308)	(0.328)
Education	1.164***	0.440	1.333***	0.644*
	(0.327)	(0.341)	(0.372)	(0.372)
Age	−0.791*	−0.735*	−1.498***	−0.251
	(0.357)	(0.368)	(0.406)	(0.395)
Attend Church at Least Weekly	−0.617**	−0.335*	−0.385	−0.368*
	(0.204)	(0.191)	(0.252)	(0.205)
Evangelical	−0.163	−0.708***	−0.889***	−0.576**
	(0.218)	(0.215)	(0.262)	(0.230)
Mainline Protestant	−0.046	−0.049	−0.402	0.139
	(0.262)	(0.274)	(0.295)	(0.317)
Catholic	0.494*	0.289	−0.025	0.052
	(0.214)	(0.233)	(0.230)	(0.251)
Cox and Snell R^2	0.288	0.165	0.344	0.153
Number of Cases	926	926	904	926

*p<.05, **p<.01, ***p<.001, one-tailed tests
Param. Est. = parameter estimate; Std. Err. = standard error
Source: American National Election Study, 2004

that those who are more authoritarian are significantly less likely to support gay rights than people who score low on the authoritarianism scale when perceived threat from a gay lifestyle is low (that is, when perceived threat is equal to 0). But the oppositely signed and most often statistically significant effect on the interaction between authoritarianism and perceived threat suggests that the magnitude of authoritarianism's negative effect on support for gay rights decreases as the perceived threat from "the newer lifestyles" increases. In other words, when respondents express feeling high levels of threat, knowing whether a person is authoritarian or not provides no guidance as to whether he or she supports various gay rights initiatives. But when they express feeling little to moderate threat, authoritarianism explains a lot.

We show graphically in Figure 6.2 how this interaction manifests itself in real terms. Although we could have used any of the items to show the pattern, we use adoption by gays because the issue has captured a good deal of attention and the results are particularly sharp. Since the model is estimated using logistic regression, we must use an algorithm to derive predicted probabilities that people support gay adoption, similar to the one explained in Chapter 5. To make the estimates substantively interpretable, we simulate a "typical" respondent and vary the values of both threat and authoritarianism. To simulate a typical respondent, we fix the variables measured on interval or ordinal scales, such as income, education, party identification, moral traditionalism, and ideology, at their sample means. We fix the dummy variables at specific values. Specifically, our simulation captures the predicted opinion of a non-African American, female, regular churchgoing, mainline Protestant.

Several features of Figure 6.2 are noteworthy. First, authoritarianism has no effect when threat is at its maximum, which is manifested in the flat line at

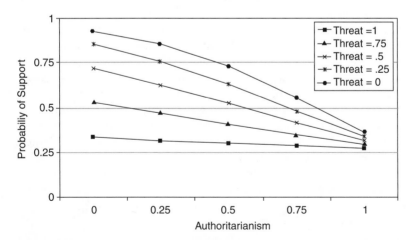

FIGURE 6.2. The Effect of Authoritarianism on Support for Gay Adoption at Various Levels of Perceived Threat, 2004

the bottom of the figure labeled "Threat = 1." If someone is threatened by the "newer lifestyles," that person's probability of supporting gay marriage, other things held constant, is about 0.30 no matter whether she scored at the high, middle, or low point on the authoritarianism scale. Since we would classify someone with a predicted probability below .5 as not supporting gay adoption, this result is a nice check on the reliability of our model. It is reassuring that it predicts people who feel substantial threat from newer lifestyles as opposing gay adoption.

Second, it is noteworthy that no matter how much or how little threat the most authoritarian respondents feel, their probability of supporting gay adoption is statistically the same. This is captured as the tightly clustered figure entries above the point where authoritarianism equals 1 on the x-axis. And third, it is those who score toward the minimum of the authoritarianism scale who show the most variation in their response to threat. This is indicated by the dispersed points above where authoritarianism equals 0 on the x-axis. When nonauthoritarians feel a lot of threat, their preferences are indistinguishable from those who score high in authoritarianism. Conversely, when people who score low in authoritarianism feel little to no threat, their preferences are enormously different from both authoritarians and nonauthoritarians who feel substantial threat. This is captured in the fanning out of predicted probabilities that run down the left side of the figure.

Even inside the extremes, authoritarianism can have a marked effect on preferences, provided perceptions of threat are low to moderate. For example, when people are only moderately threatened by "newer lifestyles" (Threat = .5), the predicted probability of someone supporting gay marriage increases from .316 among the most authoritarian to .718 among the least authoritarian, which represents a .402 point change in predicted probability. It is worth noting that the sample mean for the threat item is just above .5, making this a particularly relevant simulation. The result is substantively important as well. Based on our predicted probabilities, we would categorize those "typical" respondents who scored at or near the maximum of the authoritarianism scale as opposing gay adoption since their predicted probability of support is below .5. For those scoring at or near the minimum, however, we would categorize them as supporting gay adoption since their predicted probability of support is well above .5. When perceived threat is at its midpoint, then, authoritarianism can be decisive in explaining support or opposition to gay rights.

Again, consistent with expectations, the effect of authoritarianism is largest when threat is at a minimum, not at its maximum as some scholarship suggests. When people feel no threat from "newer lifestyles," the effect of authoritarianism is enormous. In moving from maximum to minimum authoritarianism, the probability of support for gay adoption increases from .361 to .928, more than a 50 percent change in probability. Again it is a substantively relevant change, with those scoring at the maximum in authoritarianism scoring below a predicted probability of .5 and those scoring lower in authoritarianism comfortably above .5.

We can also use this simulation to test whether certain issues are likely to cause polarization or convergence in public opinion. When perceived threat and authoritarianism are positively correlated, as we would expect to be the case most of the time given that those who score high in authoritarianism have a disposition that is sensitive to threat, it will cause polarization. People who score high in both authoritarianism and perceived threat will produce predicted probabilities that are in the lower right corner of Figure 6.2. Conversely, a positive correlation suggests that those who score low in authoritarianism will tend to score low in perceived threat. This profile will, on average, produce predicted probabilities in the top left of Figure 6.2.

For gay adoption, this is, indeed, the case. In the 2004 National Election Study (NES), the correlation between authoritarianism and the "newer lifestyles" item is .31, which is very strong for survey data. To put this correlation in more concrete terms, the average perceived threat among those who scored 0 in authoritarianism was .335, and it was .530 among people who scored at .25. Our simulation predicts that, other things being equal, these two profiles would be pro–gay adoption. The average perceived threat from "newer lifestyles" among those who scored at .75 was .711, and among those who scored at the maximum, it was .713. Our simulation suggests that, other things being equal, these two profiles will be anti–gay adoption. The result is polarization of opinion.

But consider how much less polarized opinions would have been had the relationship between authoritarianism and threat remained what it was in 1992. That year, the average threat perceived by those who scored either .75 or 1 in authoritarianism was about .75, which is almost the same as it was in 2004. Among those who scored at either 0 or .25, however, the average levels of threat were .482 and .612, respectively, which is significantly higher than in 2004. Our simulation would predict that many of the people scoring in the lower authoritarianism categories would have been classified as anti–gay adoption because they felt substantial threat from gays and lesbians, much like those who scored high in authoritarianism. Because threat is less strongly correlated with authoritarianism in 1992 than it is in 2004, we would predict more convergence on gay adoption. And, of course, that is exactly what the pattern has been with gay adoption over time. In the early 1990s, nearly everyone was opposed – an example of opinion convergence. In 2004, opinion was pulling apart – an example of opinion polarization.

Perceived Threat from Terrorism and Support for Civil Liberties

The interaction we show between authoritarianism and threat is not a function of the data we analyzed, the measure of threat we used, or the time that the survey was taken. To demonstrate this, we replicate our approach using a series of dependent variables that tap support for limitations on civil liberties. Our expectations are the same. Authoritarianism ought to have no effect when perceived threat is high; the opinions of nonauthoritarians who are frightened for their safety will mirror those of authoritarians who by disposition tend to feel this way. As perceived threat drops, however, we ought to see authoritarianism shaping preferences in an increasingly powerful fashion, with those scoring high in authoritarianism significantly more inclined to favor limitations to civil liberties.

Recall from the prior chapter that the NES neither asked people to assess how much threat they felt from terrorism nor asked people questions about civil liberties. Hence we again turn to the variables we examined last chapter from the 2006 Cooperative Congressional Election Study (CCES). Specifically, we asked people whether they (1) supported using wiretaps without a warrant, (2) supported using video cameras to monitor people in public places, (3) thought people ought to refrain from criticizing the president during the war on terror, and (4) thought the media ought to keep secrets from the public that might be relevant to fighting the war on terrorism.

We showed in the last chapter that those who score high in authoritarianism provide the government more latitude in infringing on civil liberties than do nonauthoritarians. We believe, however, that its effect ought to be conditioned by how much threat people perceive from terrorism. The results appear in Table 6.2. Again, they follow expectations. For all four models, the so-called main effect of authoritarianism is positive and significant. This indicates that when people "are not worried at all" that they will be personally affected by terrorism, authoritarianism has a large and positive effect on support for limiting civil liberties. When threat is low, those scoring high in authoritarianism are much more likely to support things like warrantless wiretaps and using video cameras to monitor public places than those who score low in authoritarianism. Similarly, those scoring high in authoritarianism are more likely to oppose criticizing the president about his efforts to fight the war on terror, and they are more inclined to support the media withholding stories that might affect the terror fight.

As was also the case for the gay rights items, we find the expected interaction between perceived threat from terrorism and authoritarianism carrying a sign that is opposite that of the so-called main effect. Moreover, this interaction is statistically significant in three of the four models. This suggests that, as perceived threat increases, the effect of authoritarianism decreases. Hence, when threat is low, how authoritarian a person is provides us a powerful explanation for a person's opinions about limiting civil liberties. But when threat is at its maximum, those who score low and high in authoritarianism are statistically indistinguishable from each other.

We again turn to a simulation to illustrate the effect of the interaction on support for, in this case, allowing wiretapping without a warrant. We fix party identification, ideology, and education and their sample means, and we fix race such that we simulate the opinions of a non-African American. We then allow threat, authoritarianism, and its interaction to vary across their ranges. The predicted probabilities of supporting wiretapping without a warrant appear in Figure 6.3.

The figure is strikingly similar to the one before. When people say they are "very worried" about being affected by terrorism personally, authoritarianism

TABLE 6.2. *Civil Liberties Agenda Items as a Function of Authoritarianism, Symbolic Attitudes, Perceived Threat, and Social Characteristics, 2004, Logistic Regression Estimates*

Variable	Support Wiretaps without a Warrant Param. Est. (Std. Err.)	Support Video Cameras in Public Places Param. Est. (Std. Err.)	Oppose Criticizing the President on Terrorism Param. Est. (Std. Err.)	Support Media Keeping Secrets on Terror Fight Param. Est. (Std. Err.)
Intercept	−4.566*** (0.412)	−0.759** (0.276)	−4.483*** (0.473)	−3.035*** (0.353)
Authoritarianism	1.992*** (0.459)	1.536*** (0.372)	1.956*** (0.528)	2.464*** (0.435)
Perceived Threat from Terrorism	2.759*** (0.626)	1.683*** (0.535)	2.039** (0.764)	2.551*** (0.601)
Authoritarianism* Perceived Threat	−2.110* (0.993)	−1.514** (0.894)	−2.258* (1.099)	−1.055 (1.059)
Race (Black)	−0.082 (0.323)	0.288 (0.289)	−0.265 (0.470)	0.376 (0.293)
Party Identification	3.064*** (0.331)	0.261 (0.297)	1.741*** (0.351)	2.062*** (0.340)
Ideological Self-Placement	2.873*** (0.500)	0.855* (0.413)	2.180*** (0.516)	2.190*** (0.478)
Education	−0.182 (0.346)	0.201 (0.294)	−1.135** (0.378)	−0.363 (0.336)
Cox and Snell R^2	0.394	0.074	0.199	0.324
Number of Cases	915	911	912	905

*p<.05, **p<.01, ***p<.001, one-tailed tests
Param. Est. = parameter estimate; Std. Err. = standard error

Source: CCES, 2006

has no effect. Our model suggests that the predicted probability for all respondents, regardless of where they fall on the authoritarianism scale, is about .75, which is solidly in favor of allowing wiretapping without a warrant. In addition, it does not really matter how much or how little threat is felt by those who score high on the authoritarianism scale; they tend to favor wiretapping regardless as the tightly clustered right-most panel shows. We should add that although the predicted probabilities are slightly further apart for those scoring at the maximum of the authoritarianism scale in this case than they were for gay rights, the differences are not statistically significant. And finally, we find the conditional effect of threat to be largest among those who score lowest in authoritarianism. For example, the predicted probability of supporting warrantless wiretapping among those who score lowest on the authoritarianism

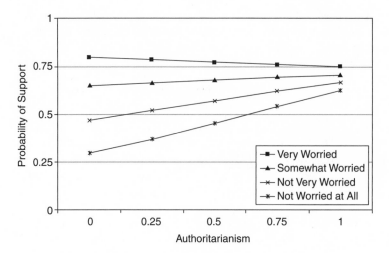

FIGURE 6.3. The Effect of Authoritarianism on Support for Wiretapping without Warrants at Various Levels of Perceived Threat, 2004

scale and are "very worried" about being affected by a terrorist attack is about .77. The predicted probability for those low in authoritarianism who are "not worried at all" about terrorism is less than .30, roughly a 50 percentage point difference.

The effect of authoritarianism is also substantial when perceived threat from terrorism is moderate. Among those who report being "not very worried," the predicted probability of those who score at authoritarianism's minimum supporting warrantless wiretaps is .336. Since that is less than .5, we would classify this "typical" respondent as opposed. In contrast, the predicted probability of someone who scores at the authoritarianism maximum is .649, which is about 30 percentage points higher. Since this typical respondent's predicted probability is greater than .5 we would classify this person as supportive of the practice.

As for gay rights, these results can also help us understand whether and under what circumstances polarization or convergence occurs in public opinion. The public is much less polarized on limitations to civil liberties than on things like gay adoption and gay marriage. Our models suggest that the relationship we have uncovered between threat and authoritarianism contributes to the difference. Whereas the correlation between authoritarianism and threat from "newer lifestyles" was more than .3, the correlation between authoritarianism and being personally affected by a terrorist attack is about half that. Put another way, the most and least authoritarian differed in their perceived threat by nearly 40 percentage points in our measure of perceived threat in the gay rights domain. In the civil liberties domain, the difference is only about 15 percentage points. If those differences widen, then it will produce an increase in polarization, other things being equal. If, however, we see another terrorist attack against the United States, we suspect that any differences we see in perceived threat between authoritarians and nonauthoritarians would shrink, maybe even disappear. This would lead to a convergence of preferences in the public toward the side of more limitations to civil liberties.

Disposition toward Force and Diplomacy

The last set of dependent variables we examined in the last chapter involved the use of force. Specifically, we asked people (1) whether the United States ought to follow its national interests or account for the preferences of its allies, (2) whether they thought the use of force or diplomacy was a more formidable weapon in the fight against terrorism, and (3) whether the Iraq war was a mistake.

Again, we include the interaction between authoritarianism and threat on the right-hand side of the models we estimated last chapter. And, as for the other domains, the results, which appear in Table 6.3, are generally as expected. In all three cases, we find that the so-called main effect for authoritarianism is positive and significant, suggesting that when threat is at its minimum, those who score high in authoritarianism prefer force over diplomacy more than do those who score low in authoritarianism. In two of the three cases, the interaction between authoritarianism and threat carries the expected negative sign and is statistically significant. This means that as threat increases, the effect of authoritarianism decreases.

In Figure 6.4, we demonstrate the shape of this interaction graphically, using a preference for force over diplomacy in the fight against terrorism as the illustration. As before, the predicted probabilities for our "typical" respondent who scores high in authoritarianism cluster together, which indicates that perceived threat does not affect those who score high in authoritarianism. And although the line for "very worried" seems to indicate that those who score low in authoritarianism but are highly threatened are even more likely to choose force, this is just a statistical artifact. These differences are, as in the previous two issue domains, not statistically significant.

Instead, we find statistically significant differences among people who score low in authoritarianism, depending upon how much threat they perceive from terrorism. Those who provide either 0 or 1 authoritarian answers to the child-rearing battery produce predicted probabilities well below .5 if they are either "not very worried" or "not worried at all" about terrorism affecting them personally, which means our model would classify them as favoring diplomacy over force. Our model predicts, however, that those scoring in the two low authoritarian categories will favor force over diplomacy if they feel either "somewhat worried" or "very worried." Again, we find that those scoring low in authoritarianism are the people to watch across different levels of perceived threat. This, of course, suggests that when threat is high across categories of authoritarianism, opinions will converge toward the strength over diplomacy position. But when perceived threat drops, as

TABLE 6.3. *Attitudes on the Use of Force as a Function of Authoritarianism, Symbolic Attitudes, and Social Characteristics, 2006 Logistic Regression Estimates*

Variable	Iraq War Was Not a Mistake Param. Est. (Std. Err.)	Follow National Interest vs. Allies Param. Est. (Std. Err.)	Better to Rely on Strength opposed to Diplomacy Param. Est. (Std. Err.)
Intercept	−4.761*** (0.444)	−3.432*** (0.374)	−4.751*** (0.422)
Authoritarianism	2.022*** (0.505)	0.937* (0.438)	1.743*** (0.471)
Perceived Threat from Terrorism	3.314*** (0.677)	0.270 (0.668)	3.247*** (0.648)
Authoritarianism* Perceived Threat from Terrorism	−3.265*** (1.076)	0.636 (0.986)	−2.621** (1.016)
Race (African American)	−0.173 (0.389)	0.158 (0.342)	−1.634*** (0.445)
Party Identification	4.334*** (0.381)	1.574*** (0.332)	2.614*** (0.329)
Ideological Self-Placement	2.440*** (0.533)	1.766*** (0.462)	3.167*** (0.515)
Education	−1.123** (0.376)	−0.307 (0.325)	0.167 (0.347)
Cox and Snell R²	0.456	0.176	0.394
Number of Cases	915	910	909

*p<.05, **p<.01, ***p<.001, one-tailed tests
Param. Est. = parameter estimate; Std. Err. = standard error

Source: CCES, 2006

has happened with September 11 receding deeper into memory, we get a polarization of opinion in this issue domain as well.

Approval of President Bush

Perhaps the best example of the convergence and polarization of opinion over the early years of the twenty-first century involve evaluations of George W. Bush. In the months after the September 11 terrorist attacks, he achieved approval levels higher than those ever achieved by a president, peaking at over 90 percent. He maintained extraordinarily high approval for well over a year after the attacks. At the time of the 2002 midterm elections, for example,

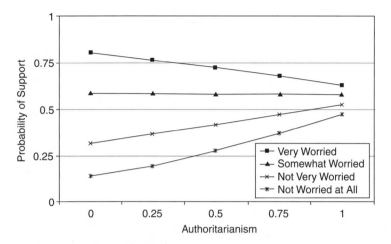

FIGURE 6.4. The Effect of Authoritarianism on Preferring Strength over Diplomacy, at Various Levels of Perceived Threat, 2006

his approval was above 70 percent, which many believe contributed to the Republicans' historic wins that year (see Hetherington and Nelson 2003).

Only two years later, Bush became the least popular president ever returned to office, with an approval rating below 50 percent in November 2004. Things, for the most part, only went downhill from there. By the time of our CCES survey in November 2006, his approval rating was in the low 30s, which is where it remained throughout the balance of his administration. Of course, many things contributed to the president's weakening approval ratings, including his administration's handling of Hurricane Katrina in New Orleans and the rest of the Gulf coast, an increasingly unpopular war in Iraq, weakness in some quarters of the economy, and the usual downturn in popularity that a president experiences during his second term. We believe, however, that the drop in perceived threat from terrorism and its interaction with authoritarianism is an important part of understanding the dynamics of Bush's approval ratings as well.

To build our case, we first turn to the 2000–2002 portion of the National Election Studies' 2000–2004 panel study. Although the authoritarianism battery was not asked in 2002, it was asked in 2000 to more than 700 people who were reinterviewed by the NES in both 2002 and 2004. Consistent with other survey organizations, the NES found that Bush had the approval of 69 percent of Americans in 2002. The difference between authoritarians and nonauthoritarians was marked, which we would have expected given the types of issues on the agenda in 2002. Those who scored at the scale's maximum provided Bush much higher scores than those who scored at the minimum, with a spread of just under 25 percentage points across the range of authoritarianism.

By 2004, Bush's approval rating among panel respondents dropped to 55 percent. More important, the difference between the most and least authoritarian increased to more than 30 percentage points. While approval dropped across all categories of the authoritarianism index, it dropped most precipitously among those toward the minimum of the scale. This pattern of change is consistent with our theory. In 2002, more Americans were feeling more threat from terrorism than they were in 2004. With threat higher across all categories of authoritarianism, it ought to lead to a convergence of preferences – in this case, approval of President Bush. As threat decreases, it ought to do so asymmetrically, with those scoring low in authoritarianism feeling less threatened more quickly than those scoring high. This would produce polarization in Bush's job approval numbers.

To test whether the interaction between threat and authoritarianism exists for presidential approval, we must turn again to the CCES since the NES failed to ask how threatened people felt by terrorism. Fortunately, we can specify a model of presidential approval using CCES data that would be almost identical to any model we could specify using the NES. Our dependent variable is whether respondents approved of the job George W. Bush was doing as president. To explain variation in responses, we start with our four-item authoritarianism battery, the perceived threat posed by terrorism item that we used in the civil liberties and use of force models above, and the interaction between the two. To make our estimates of these variables' effects more secure, we also provide controls for a range of political and demographic variables, including party identification, race, retrospective evaluations of the national economy, whether or not the United States should begin to withdraw troops from Iraq, race, gender, age, education, and income.

The results of the analysis appear in Table 6.4. The explanatory variables produce signs and levels of significance as they should. Republicans, conservatives, and those who think the national economy has gotten better over the last year are more inclined to approve of Bush. Those who want to withdraw from Iraq, African Americans, and the best educated are less inclined to approve of the president.

Most important for our purposes, we again find the familiar negative interaction between threat and authoritarianism. The positive and significant effect for the so-called main effect of authoritarianism means that when threat is at its minimum, people who score higher in authoritarianism are significantly more positive toward Bush than people who score lower. But the oppositely signed interaction between authoritarianism and threat means that as threat increases, the effect of authoritarianism decreases.

We show the effect graphically in Figure 6.5. Since we used logistic regression to estimate the model, we again need to fix the variables that are not part of the interaction at theoretically interesting values and vary the components of the interaction to simulate changes in predicted probabilities. In this case, we fix all the ordinal and interval scale variables at their means. We fix the dummy variables, such that our simulation predicts the opinions of nonblack women who are opposed to withdrawing from Iraq.

TABLE 6.4. *Approval of George W. Bush as a Function of Authoritarianism, Threat, Its Interaction, Political Predispositions and Social Characteristics, 2006 Logistic Regression Estimates*

Variable	Parameter Estimate (Standard Error)
Intercept	−7.002***
	(0.965)
Authoritarianism	2.301**
	(0.849)
Perception of Threat from Terrorism	2.736**
	(1.132)
Authoritarianism* Perception of Threat from Terrorism	−3.028*
	(1.729)
Partisanship	2.543***
	(0.560)
Ideology	4.580***
	(0.858)
Retrospective Economic Evaluations	4.980***
	(0.681)
Should Withdraw from Iraq	−1.378***
	(0.307)
Education	0.907**
	(0.315)
Gender (Female)	−5.603
	(3.148)
Race (African American)	−2.293***
	(0.728)
Income	−0.561
	(0.645)
Age	−0.039
	(0.722)
Cox and Snell Psuedo R^2	0.60
Number of Cases	759

*p<.05, **p<.01, ***p<.001, one-tailed tests
Source: CCES, 2006

As before, our model predicts that both people who report being "very worried" about terrorism affecting them personally and those who score high in authoritarianism show little variation in their evaluations of President Bush. We see the familiar flat line representing the "very worried" category and the clustering together of predicted probabilities in the high authoritarian categories. As threat levels drop to either "not very worried" or "not worried at all" about being personally affected by terrorism, however, the effect of authoritarianism

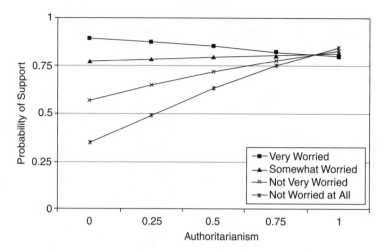

FIGURE 6.5. The Effect of Authoritarianism on the Probability of Approving of President Bush, at Various Levels of Perceived Threat, 2006

is large. For example, among those who score at the minimum of the authoritarianism scale, perceived threat has nearly a 50 percentage point effect on the probability of approving of the president.

In sum, President Bush's approval ratings dropped for any number of reasons. But one feature of the decay in approval that is interesting to us is that it occurred disproportionately among those who scored low in authoritarianism. This is particularly remarkable because those scoring low in authoritarianism were already substantially less likely to approve of the president than those scoring high. The reason for the asymmetry here appears to be a change in perceptions of threat. As September 11 continued to recede deeper into people's memories, those who score low in authoritarianism started to approve less. Whereas their preferences converged with those scoring high in authoritarianism right after 9/11, those preferences polarized years later.

CONCLUSION

Throughout this chapter, we have demonstrated time and again that when preferences on issues are structured by authoritarianism, an interaction exists between authoritarianism and perceived threat. Importantly, the sign we consistently find on the interaction is the reverse of the new scholarly conventional wisdom. We show that perceived threat narrows the differences between those who score high and low in authoritarianism. These results square well with political reality. Increased threat often increases the *number* of people supporting policies or candidates that promise to impose more order. People who score high in authoritarianism already tend to support such initiatives. It is the changing preferences of those who score lower in authoritarianism but who feel significant threat from political circumstances at a particular point in time that explain changes over time.

Understanding this relationship can also explain why issues can cause either convergence or polarization. When threat is fairly evenly felt across levels of authoritarianism, as was the case for gay rights in the early 1990s or right after the September 11 terrorist attacks, convergence is the result. When people who score low in authoritarianism perceive significant threat, their preferences are often much like those of people who score high in authoritarianism. When threat is perceived asymmetrically across the authoritarianism distribution, polarization ensues. This is the case with gay rights in the early 2000s. Perceived threat from "newer lifestyles" has dropped, but not across the board. As a result, those who score low in authoritarianism now have much different preferences about gay rights. If we are correct in our hypothesis that authoritarianism now cleaves party preferences as well, this is an important part of the story of mass party sorting. It also suggests that if people continue to feel less threatened by gays and lesbians and if the United States is able to keep terrorism at bay, it will lead to increased sorting over time on issues in which authoritarianism explains preferences, other things being equal.

Although we have focused throughout this chapter on the scholarly implications of our findings, there are obvious electoral implications as well. This chapter helps to explain why, at least lately, Republicans seem to benefit by raising the specter of threat, especially as it relates to terrorism. In making this observation, we do not mean to suggest that this is a cynical strategy; terrorists have proven that they can cause the United States significant damage. The important point is that if threat is broadly perceived, people across levels of authoritarianism will tend to adopt more conservative preferences on issues that are structured in part by authoritarianism. This will advantage Republican candidates. But if people feel relatively safe from a terrorist threat, their preferences on these issues will move in a more liberal direction, advantaging Democratic candidates.

In making these observations, we do not mean to suggest that threat is only the currency of conservatives. Liberals use threat of economic insecurity, in particular, to their advantage with regularity. Conservatives do not make reference to grandmothers too poor to pay for prescription medication or having to skip meals because Social Security benefits might be reduced under privatization "schemes." Those were campaign themes forwarded by Democratic presidential nominee Al Gore in 2000. We do not focus on these particular threats because preferences about Social Security and Medicare are not structured by authoritarianism, but it is not that they are unimportant. They are important, yet are beyond the scope of our study.[6]

---

[6] One might wonder why these types of threats do not cause a rush toward conservative leaders who are viewed by the more authoritarian as the proper authorities. Our sense is that the conservative solution to economic unease is not particularly muscular, relying instead on the hidden hand of free markets. This is likely unattractive to the more order-minded authoritarians who are looking for more clarity and less ambiguity than an abstraction like free markets can provide.

7

Evidence of Worldview Evolution

On May 15, 2007, a crowded field of Republican presidential hopefuls gathered in South Carolina for the second in a series of debates. An all-Republican affair roughly eight months before the first primary contest should attract only the most committed and ideologically extreme people. Although ideologically unrepresentative, this base is critically important, since candidates have to appeal to it first to gain the nomination. After the nomination is secure, candidates can tack their way back toward the middle where the swing voters, who decide elections, tend to reside.

Candidates, armed with polls and consultants, calibrate their responses to capitalize on the opinion environment. The audience reaction to these responses during the debates can provide a window on activist opinion. Several exchanges suggested that authoritarian-themed rhetoric resonated well with the Republican base. The clearest indications occurred when moderator Brit Hume asked candidates how they would respond to the following hypothetical scenario:

HUME: "The questions in this round will be premised on a fictional, but we think plausible scenario involving terrorism and the response to it. Here is the premise: Three shopping centers near major U.S. cities have been hit by suicide bombers. Hundreds are dead, thousands injured. A fourth attack has been averted when the attackers were captured off the Florida coast and taken to Guantanamo Bay, where they are being questioned. U.S. intelligence believes that another larger attack is planned and could come at any time.

Former New York City Mayor and hero of September 11, Rudy Giuliani, received the loudest applause of the evening for his response.

MR. GIULIANI: In the hypothetical that you gave me, which assumes that we know there's going to be another attack and these people know about it, I would tell the people who had to do the interrogation to use every method they could think of. It shouldn't be torture, but every method they can think of –

MR. HUME: Waterboarding?

MR. GIULIANI: – and I would – and I would – well, I'd say every method they could think of, and I would support them in doing that because I've seen what – (interrupted by applause) – I've seen what can happen when you make a mistake about this, and I don't want to see another 3,000 people dead in New York or any place else.

Waterboarding is a controversial interrogation technique, which originated during the Spanish Inquisition, in which a person is laid on his back, has his head covered, and has watered poured over his nose and mouth to simulate drowning. A growing range of intelligence officers, war veterans, and military judges regard it as torture. The U.S. State Department refers to interrogation techniques that involve submersion in water to be torture.

Earlier in the debate, John McCain, a former prisoner of war during his service in Vietnam, responded to the same question by saying "The use of torture – we could never gain as much we would gain from that torture as we lose in world opinion. We do not torture people." Unlike Mayor Giuliani, he received a chilly reception from the audience.

In our part of the 2006 CCES survey, we asked questions about people's attitudes about torture, in general, not waterboarding, specifically.

We're going to read you a pair of statements about the issue of prisoner rights. Please tell us which statement comes closer to your own point of view.

Statement A: Terrorists pose a grave danger to American civilians and are not the same as sovereign nations. Therefore, the United States should ignore the Geneva Conventions on the treatment of prisoners and reserve the right to torture them in fighting the War on Terrorism.

Statement B: The United States must maintain its moral authority as a world leader. Even though terrorists do not follow traditional rules of war, it is important that the U.S. continue to follow the Geneva Conventions on the treatment of prisoners and not torture them in fighting the War on Terrorism.

In our sample, people who scored at the maximum of the authoritarianism scale were more than twice as likely as those who scored at the minimum to choose Statement A. This suggests that preferences about torture are structured at least in part by authoritarianism as well. This comports well with findings presented in Chapter 5 in which preferences for security over force and opinions on the war on terror are structured by authoritarianism.

What is interesting is that this structuring, for which we found ample evidence in Chapter 5, has clearly taken a partisan bent even though President Bush has been adamant that the United States does not use torture. Although only a little over 30 percent of the entire sample endorsed the pro-torture position, more than half of self-identified Republicans did. And among people who identified themselves as "strong Republicans," the people who likely made up a disproportionate share of the audience at the South Carolina debate, the percentage who endorsed Statement A was over 60 percent. Little wonder Giuliani's position was more popular than McCain's.

Similar rhetoric was on display when candidates discussed the U.S. detention facility at Guantanamo Bay, Cuba. American officials originally set up the
facility so that people termed "enemy combatants" could be housed on what
is technically non-American soil.[1] If brought to the United States and housed
in the federal prison system, such prisoners would be accorded habeas corpus
rights and access to lawyers. Bush administration officials have argued that
such rights would undermine their ability to obtain information that could aid
U.S. efforts in combating terrorist threats.

Not everyone agrees with the administration's position. Critics include
President Bush's first secretary of state, Colin Powell. He told Tim Russert on
Meet the Press that the Guantanamo Bay facility should be closed because it
was having an adverse impact on American's image abroad. Specifically, Powell
suggested that "if it were up to me I would close Guantanamo not tomorrow
but this afternoon ... and I would not let any of those people go. I would simply move them to the United States and put them into our federal legal system."
As a retired government official, Powell was clearly not attempting to appeal to
the Republican electoral base.

In contrast, presidential hopeful Mitt Romney was. When the former
Massachusetts Governor and 2008 Republican hopeful had his turn at Hume's
hypothetical scenario, he argued that Powell had it all wrong.

MR. ROMNEY: You said the person's going to be in Guantanamo. I'm glad they're at
Guantanamo. I don't want them on our soil. I want them on Guantanamo, where they
don't get the access to lawyers they get when they're on our soil. I don't want them in
our prisons. I want them there.

Some people have said, we ought to close Guantanamo. My view is, we ought to double Guantanamo. We ought to make sure that the terrorists – (applause) – and there's no
question but that in a setting like that where you have a ticking bomb that the president
of the United States – not the CIA interrogator, the president of the United States – has
to make the call. And enhanced interrogation techniques, yes.

Alongside the ovation Giuliani received for his willingness to employ waterboarding, Romney's call for two Guantanamos drew the largest ovation of the
night.

Two things are noteworthy about these responses. First, Giuliani and
Romney were not fringe candidates. At the time of the debate in South
Carolina, they were the two front-runners for the Republican nomination.[2]

---

[1] On June 12, 2008, the Supreme Court ruled unconstitutional the portion of the Military
Commissions Act that denied Guantanamo Bay detainees the right to appeal their detention
before federal courts. Writing in dissent, Justice Antonin Scalia decried the ruling by saying that "it
will almost certainly cause more Americans to be killed." Republican presidential nominee John
McCain declared the ruling "one of the worst in the history of this country" (Greenhouse 2008).

[2] Of course, both were later eliminated, but not because of their position on torture. Giuliani's fortunes deteriorated after the primary season started because his campaign chose a poor strategy
of ignoring the early nomination contests. Romney's change of position on social issues rendered
him untrustworthy in the eyes of evangelicals who went with Mike Huckabee instead.

Second, the substantial applause that each received for endorsing waterboarding and a facility designed to circumvent the protection of civil liberties, respectively, is suggestive of a significant sympathy for a worldview consistent with authoritarianism.

Although one might be tempted to argue that the ultimate winner of the Republican nomination battle, John McCain, was the one candidate who voiced his opposition to torture in the South Carolina debate, it is significant that McCain's position evolved as the nomination process ground forward. On February 13, 2008, the U.S. Senate passed the Intelligence Authorization Act of 2008, mostly along party lines. McCain voted against that act, explaining that he did so because of an amendment that would have required the CIA to restrict itself only to interrogation techniques deemed acceptable under the Army Field Manual. The Army Field Manual specifically bans torture, and McCain himself has stated that waterboarding is a form of torture.

Why would McCain, a former prisoner of war himself who was tortured during his many years as a prisoner of war in Vietnam, change his position? His problems with the party's ideological base were surely part of the calculation. As McCain began to separate himself from the Republican field in early February 2008, important voices in the conservative movement, including talk radio host Rush Limbaugh and best-selling author Ann Coulter, began to express serious doubts about him. In fact, Coulter even suggested that she would vote for Hillary Clinton over McCain. McCain clearly needed to make certain concessions. We are not alone in making this inference. The *Los Angeles Times* noted the day after the vote that "McCain led earlier efforts in the Senate to ban cruel treatment of prisoners, and has denounced waterboarding in presidential debates. But preserving the CIA's ability to employ so-called enhanced interrogation methods has broad support in the party's conservative base."[3]

Importantly, the Democratic presidential candidates in 2008 have taken a much different tack in their efforts to appeal to a primary constituency that is disproportionately nonauthoritarian these days. In stark contrast to Romney's call for two Guantanamos, Barack Obama said, "[The United States] will be ready to show the world that we are not a country that ships prisoners in the dead of night to be tortured in far off countries. That we are not a country that runs prisons which lock people away without ever telling them why they are there or what they are charged with."[4]

Three days later, at a Senate Armed Services Committee meeting, Hillary Clinton, the Democratic front-runner in the polls at the time, sounded like Colin Powell, not Mitt Romney or Rudy Giuliani. Clinton said, "Guantanamo has become associated in the eyes of the world with a discredited administration policy of abuse, secrecy, and contempt for the rule of law. Rather than keeping us more secure, keeping Guantanamo open is harming our national interests. It compromises our long-term military and strategic interests, and

[3] Greg Miller, "Senate OKs Limits" (2008).
[4] In his speech to the Council on Global Affairs in April of 2007.

it impairs our standing overseas. I have certainly concluded that we should address any security issues on what to do with the remaining detainees, and then close it once and for all."

We do not wish to succumb to the temptation of focusing solely on issues in which the authoritarian position seems so extreme, as in the case for torture. The increasingly nonauthoritarian base of the Democratic Party constrains Democratic elites in certain ways, too. Positioning the party on the war in Iraq provides one example. With the exception of Ron Paul, all of the Republican presidential hopefuls in 2008 endorsed President Bush's plan for a significant troop buildup in early 2007. The so-called surge of 30,000 more troops seemed risky to support in January 2007, when President Bush initially proposed it, but it has had a range of salutary effects in Iraq. Although a political solution to the nation's problems was not yet at hand as the presidential candidates sought their parties' nominations, life for ordinary Iraqis was clearly improving as violence in the country plummeted. One measure of success was the substantial increase in Iraqi refugees returning to their country in late 2007 and early 2008.

Despite the success of the surge, all the major Democratic contenders not only opposed the troop increase but favored often aggressive plans of complete withdrawal from Iraq. John Edwards proposed bringing all American troops home within nine or ten months of taking office, and Barack Obama suggested the process should end within sixteen months. Hillary Clinton provoked the wrath of many on the left because her phased withdrawal plan would take several years to complete rather than several months, no matter what the consequences of a precipitous American departure might be. Our CCES sample explains why. Among Democrats who scored at the minimum of the authoritarianism scale, 90 percent favored withdrawal.

Although such contrasts are clear on a range of issues beyond torture, Guantanamo, and the war in Iraq, we use these illustrations to make clear that Republican and Democratic elites are taking opposing positions on authoritarian-structured issues prominent in the political dialogue. Other scholars have shown that these contrasts extend to race, gay rights, and several other issues for which preferences are structured in part by authoritarianism as well. In this chapter, we demonstrate that the result has been what we call a worldview evolution in which mass level party choices are now significantly affected by how authoritarian a person is.

FROM ISSUE EVOLUTION TO WORLDVIEW EVOLUTION

The notion of issue evolution, initially developed by Carmines and Stimson (1981, 1986, 1989), outlines a plausible means by which issues emerge as central to political debates and in the process divide the parties. They argue that "most issues most of the time lie dormant" and therefore do not make an impact with the public or on the political system (Carmines and Stimson 1986, 902). Every so often, however, an issue that evokes a strong emotional response emerges and has the power to redefine the lines of political conflict. Importantly, changes in elite behavior are at the core of this understanding of political change, and they drive mass partisan response. For the mass response to occur, the public must recognize a difference in the positions of the parties on the new issue and come to care about that difference.

The issue evolution framework is relevant to our work for two reasons. First, scholars have produced ample evidence that the necessary polarization of opinion on the elite level has already taken place on a range of issues in which authoritarianism structures opinions – namely, race (Carmines and Stimson 1989), criminal rights (Sniderman et al. 1991), feminism (Wolbrecht 2000), and gay rights (Lindaman and Haider-Markel 2002). Our discussion about torture, the rights of enemy combatants, and the war in Iraq make clear that the distinctions extend to these areas as well. Importantly, scholars have shown that the mass response to this elite polarization had already occurred in certain areas (e.g., race and feminism), and we have shown in Chapter 5 that the same process has more recently occurred for gay rights, the disposition toward force and Iraq, and preferences for trade-offs between civil liberties and security. Second, all these issues have been of interest to scholars in the past specifically because of their ability to evoke a strong emotional response.

If an issue evolution creates a new and enduring cleavage line between the parties, our notion of a worldview evolution creates a widening and deepening of that cleavage. The issues that cause the mutation from issue evolution to worldview evolution might be considered, to use Carmines and Stimson's term, *organic extensions*. Such issues fit into the niche that already exists. Although Carmines and Stimson (1989) did not treat organic extensions as particularly consequential, this is likely because the New Deal party system was ascendant prior to the race-based issue evolution. Whether to increase federal aid for education in the 1960s, which reinforced existing New Deal conflicts, was not an issue potent enough to stir great passion.

Organic extensions to the race-based party system wrought in the 1960s ought to be different. The issue evolution occurred, in part, because race was a visceral issue. Issues that reinforce this cleavage will tend to involve other gut-level considerations with the capacity to stir especially strong passions. We have demonstrated that preferences on many of these new, reinforcing issues can, like race, be explained by knowing how authoritarian a person is. Indeed, this is why these issues have "worked" for political operatives in much the same way race did.

THE FIRST STEP: VOTING BEHAVIOR

Since party identification is a deeply held psychological attachment to a centrally important political group, changes in it are slow to come. For example, even though the party system evolved from one structured by the New Deal to one structured by race and the civil rights movement in the 1960s (Carmines and Stimson 1989), it took another twenty years for durable changes in party identification to take root, particularly in the South (Green, Palmquist, and Schickler 2002). Many who lived through this tumultuous period found it difficult to identify themselves with the party of Lincoln even though their sensibilities on race matched those of the contemporary Republican Party.

Even if party identification did not change quickly, voting behavior did. The first rumblings of a realignment in southern voting behavior, if not identification, occurred in 1952 when Dwight Eisenhower won Virginia, Tennessee, and Florida and then added Louisiana to these three in 1956. In 1964, anti-integration forces delivered Barry Goldwater, the GOP nominee, five southern states, the only states that he won nationally other than his native Arizona. Former Georgia governor, Jimmy Carter, nearly swept the region in 1976 for the Democrats, but in 1980, Ronald Reagan dominated Carter in the incumbent's home region, with Carter only hanging on to Georgia. Even so, most southern whites continued to think about themselves as Democrats well into the 1980s (Green, Palmquist, and Schickler 2002).

We expect to find a similar chronology for authoritarianism. Changes in party identification might take time to occur, but such changes ought to be presaged by changes in voting behavior. It is not as though gay rights and the proper response to terrorism are the only issues that might divide the more authoritarian from the less authoritarian. Given that Republican and Democratic elites were taking clear positions on issues like race, rights, feminism, and an assortment of "culture wars" issues for years, we expect to find some indication of worldview evolution emerging in presidential voting well before the beginning of the twenty-first century.

This might manifest itself in two ways. First, it seems likely that authoritarianism might create an asymmetry to whether Republicans or Democrats decided to vote or stay home. Specifically, as the Republican position on issues for which preferences are structured by authoritarianism became friendlier to those who score high and as the Democrats took a clear and opposing position, Democrats who score high in authoritarianism might become less likely to participate in elections than Republicans who score high. Second, among those who turn out to vote, authoritarianism ought to do more to explain vote choice as more issues on the authoritarian dimension become more salient. Indeed, the use of these issues in election contests is apparently designed to attract swing voters. Hillygus and Shields (2008) show that Democrats are particularly vulnerable to them because a significant number of Democratic partisans do not share their party's position on things like race, gay rights, and the like. In the short run, these issue appeals may attract them to the Republican candidate. In the long run, these voters will be the prime candidates for party identification change.

Vote or Abstain

It is well established that those scoring high in authoritarianism tend to feel alienated from many things, including politics. As a result, they tend to vote at much lower rates. Table 7.1, which tracks voter turnout among Republican

TABLE 7.1. *Authoritarianism and Voter Turnout – 1992, 2000, 2004, Nonblack Voters, Leaners Included as Partisans*

Authoritarianism	1992		2000		2004	
	Republicans	Democrats	Republicans	Democrats	Republicans	Democrats
0	89	93	81	90	86	93
0.25	89	88	85	85	89	88
0.5	81	86	84	80	89	76
0.75	80	75	79	75	90	70
1	65	63	79	56	73	56
Overall	80	79	82	77	86	77

Source: American National Election Studies, 1992, 2000, 2004

and Democrats broken down by the number of authoritarian responses they provide to the child-rearing battery, provides further support for this finding. We confine this analysis and those that follow in this chapter to nonblack respondents. African Americans are, in fact, the most authoritarian racial group in the United States by far.[5] Yet, for obvious historical reasons, they remain an overwhelmingly Democratic group (see also Bartels 2006 in focusing on nonblacks). Although it is plausible to think that the Republican issue agenda might be attractive to African Americans in the future, they are a group that is clearly tethered to the Democratic Party for now.

For the three years for which we have data on authoritarianism – 1992, 2000, and 2004 – those nonblacks who score at the scale's maximum are significantly less participatory, regardless of party. For example, roughly 80 percent of Republicans and Democrats claimed to have voted overall, yet only about 65 percent of those scoring at the maximum of the authoritarianism battery did. The 1992 data are particularly important for our purposes because they show that those scoring high in authoritarianism regardless of party were about equally likely to say they voted (65% of Republicans and 63% of Democrats).

After 1992, however, an interesting, and we argue predictable, new dynamic developed. As the Republicans adopted a larger number of issue positions friendly to those with an authoritarian worldview and Democrats took the other side, self-identified nonblack Democrats who score high in authoritarianism began to turn out at lower rates while self-identified Republicans who score high in authoritarianism started to vote at higher rates. Specifically, the voting rate among Republicans who scored at the maximum of the authoritarianism index increased from 65 percent in 1992 to well over 70 percent in both 2000 and 2004. For Democrats, the percentage of reported voters fell from 63 percent in 1992 to 56 percent in both 2000 and 2004.

---

[5] The mean authoritarianism score for blacks is .75 in 2004. For nonblacks it is .55.

Among those who scored at .75 in authoritarianism, the change in behavior was stark between 2000 and 2004, specifically. Among Democrats, self-reported turnout among this group dropped by five percentage points, from 75 to 70. Among Republicans, self-reported turnout surged from 79 to 90 percent. We conclude from this pattern of results that Republicans who score high in authoritarianism, typically a politically disaffected group, feel more enthusiasm about politics because of the recent tack of the Republican Party. Democrats with a similarly authoritarian worldview feel the reverse because their party no longer reflects their preferences particularly well.

Presidential Vote Choice

In addition to guiding decisions about voter turnout, we suspect authoritarianism will have started to guide decisions about vote choice by the 1990s. Table 7.2 provides the evidence. In the table, we present the mean authoritarianism score among people who voted for major party presidential candidates over the three elections for which we have data on authoritarianism: 1992, 2000, and 2004. We also track the degree to which people who defected from their party identification in voting differ from those whose voting was consistent with their party identification. To the degree that differences between defectors and loyal partisans exist, it suggests that partisan changes might soon be in the offing.

Our data reveal some evidence of such a pattern with authoritarianism. In 1992, there was a modest, although statistically significant difference, in the authoritarianism of George H. W. Bush voters and Bill Clinton voters, with Bush voters scoring about eight percentage points higher in authoritarianism. It is also worth noting that in a GOP campaign kicked off in some respects by Pat Buchanan's fiery culture war speech at the Republican National Convention, authoritarianism among Democrats who voted for Bush was about thirteen percentage points higher than authoritarianism among Democrats who voted for Clinton.

Between 1992 and 2000, the difference in authoritarianism between Republican and Democratic presidential voters increased by nearly 50 percent from 8 to about 12 percentage points. Once again we see authoritarianism driving defections among Democrats, with the mean among those who voted for Gore significantly lower than the mean among those who voted for George W. Bush in 2000. This time, Republicans who defected from Bush were also about 14 points less authoritarian than Republicans who stayed loyal to Bush.

We find the largest differences in authoritarianism between major party presidential candidate voters in 2004. Bush voters scored 14.5 percentage points higher in authoritarianism than Kerry voters. In 2004, however, we see a return to the asymmetry in party defections we observed in 1992. Specifically, Democrats who defected to Bush were about 15 points higher in authoritarianism than Democrats who stayed loyal to Kerry. There was no difference in authoritarianism between Republicans who defected or remained loyal.

TABLE 7.2. *Mean Authoritarianism and Presidential Vote Choice – 1992, 2000, 2004, Nonblack Voters, Leaners Included as Partisans*

	1992	2000	2004
Loyal Democrat	.502	.493	.436
Defecting Democrat	.636	.620	.583
Difference	.134	.127	.147
Loyal Republican	.583	.611	.592
Defecting Republican	.526	.469	.580
Difference	.057	.142	.012
All Republican Presidential Voters	.590	.613	.589
All Democratic Presidential Voters	.505	.491	.454
Difference	.085	.122	.145

Source: American National Election Studies, 1992, 2000, 2004

In our view, the generally asymmetric pattern to defections suggests the success of the Republicans' campaign strategy. The Bush campaign's micro-targeting efforts were mostly directed at cross-pressured voters, those who identify as Democrats but have policy preferences that run counter to that party's elites (Hillygus and Shields 2008). Since the issues on which most Democrats were cross-pressured were authoritarian issues, such as gay rights and combating terrorism, evidence that Republicans had successfully peeled off such voters would be a large gap in authoritarianism between loyal and defecting Democrats, exactly what we find. On gay rights and dealing with terrorism, specifically, Democratic elites have been much less aggressive in using these issues to peel away nonauthoritarians who identify with the GOP, probably (rightly) fearing that they would risk repelling more authoritarian Democrats.

Voting at the Senatorial Level

Presidential voting might not reflect general trends because the characteristics of specific candidates and themes of specific campaigns can play a vital role. The pattern of results above might reflect a particular set of candidacies. Examining results at the Senate level can help mitigate this concern. Senate elections offer a broad sample of candidates and campaigns across contexts. To the extent that authoritarianism seems to structure vote choice at this level, too, we would be more confident about our findings at the presidential level. Again, using race as a parallel, many anti-civil rights Democrats, who had voted for Republicans from Goldwater to Reagan, continued to vote down the ballot for Democrats because these candidates were generally less pro-civil rights than the party's standard-bearers. Race-based voting filtered down to lower levels as older Democratic members of Congress retired.

TABLE 7.3. *Mean Authoritarianism and Senate Vote Choice – 1992, 2000, 2004, 2006 Nonblack Voters*

	1992	2000	2004	2006
Loyal Democrat	.491	.485	.407	.343
Defecting Democrat	.553	.572	.595	.517
Difference	.062	.087	.188	.174
Loyal Republican	.569	.601	.622	.594
Defecting Republican	.564	.534	.599	.448
Difference	.005	.067	.023	.146
All Republican Senate Voters	.562	.589	.596	.594
All Democratic Senate Voters	.501	.496	.454	.364
Difference	.061	.093	.142	.230

Source: American National Election Studies, 1992, 2000, 2004; CCES 2006

In Table 7.3, we replicate the presidential analysis for Senate vote choice. The Senate results follow a similar pattern, but they depart in ways that even more aptly fit our theory. In 1992, Republicans voting for a Senate candidate were slightly more authoritarian than Democratic Senate voters, but even less so than at the presidential level. Similarly, Democrats who defected from their party's candidate were also only slightly more authoritarian than Democrats who voted for their party's candidate. The story was basically the same in 2000, although the difference in authoritarianism between Republican and Democratic voters increased to some degree.

In 2004, however, we see a fundamental change in the relationship. Whereas the difference in authoritarianism between Republican and Democratic voters was 9 percentage points in 2000, it increased to just over 14 percentage points in 2004. Even more dramatic, however, was the nearly 19 percentage point difference between Democrats who stayed loyal to the Democratic Senate candidate and Democrats who defected to the Republican candidate. We read this as further evidence of a winning Republican electoral strategy.

The results from our part of the 2006 CCES study, which we referenced in Chapter 5, also support the worldview evolution hypothesis. The authoritarianism difference between Republican and Democratic voters reached its maximum at 23 percentage points. Moreover, authoritarianism seems to be at the heart of both Republican and Democratic defections. Loyal Democrats were 17 percentage points less authoritarian than Democratic defectors, and, in this case, Republican defectors were about 15 percentage points less authoritarian than loyal Republicans. This is the only year in which the decision of Republicans to stay loyal to or defect from their party's candidate was influenced by authoritarianism.

A new attitude structuring vote choice can often be a harbinger of a change in the ingredients of party identification. This is the pattern of results we find in the turnout and vote choice analyses. We should add that the results for defections in the later year are particularly impressive, if we are correct that party identification is now, in part, structured by authoritarianism. If people are already sorted into the correct party on this cleavage, it decreases the percentage whose party and authoritarianism are poorly matched. The fact that the results seem to sharpen in these later years is particularly impressive. We turn next to examining whether party identification is indeed now a function of authoritarianism as well.

EXPLAINING PARTISANSHIP

To test whether authoritarianism now structures party identification, we estimate a regression model explaining party identification at several points over time. Again, we focus on nonblack respondents. Specifically, we regress the 7-point partisanship scale on the range of social characteristics, including education, age, income, gender, race (whether or not the respondent is Hispanic), religious denomination, and church attendance, along with authoritarianism. In addition, we take into account the traditional left-right dimension in American politics. Hence we also include the respondent's preference for how much the government ought to spend on a range of programs.[6] In addition, we control for moral traditionalism to account for the traditional component of modern conservatism.

We feel strongly that authoritarianism is causally prior to partisanship. Indeed, some research suggests that it may be an inherited trait (Altemeyer 1996). Although theory is sometimes undermined by measurement, we believe that is unlikely in this case. One great advantage of the authoritarianism battery is that it asks about child-rearing preferences, which are not a specific part of the political dialogue. Moreover, if we assume simultaneity and estimate an instrument for party identification using two-stage least squares, it is not significant in a model explaining authoritarianism.[7] If we find a significant effect for authoritarianism, it suggests that causation flows only from it to party identification, not the other way around.

---

[6] We calculate this as the mean score of people's spending preferences on three issues: public schools, Social Security, and child care. These are the three issues that the NES asked in all three election studies that we would not expect authoritarianism to affect. Although the 7-point scale questions are also attractive, the NES only asked them to a half-sample in 2000, while the other half-sample received branching items in phone interviews.

[7] The model that we specified for authoritarianism using 2004 NES data controlled for gender, ethnicity, income, education, age, church attendance, and a belief in biblical inerrancy, in addition to the party identification instrument. We created the party identification instrument using the following variables: religious denomination (dummy variables for Protestants, Catholics, and Jews), moral traditionalism, economic evaluations, preferences for government spending, opinions on tax cuts, the death penalty, Social Security privatization, school vouchers, and the Iraq war as well as racial resentment. Of course, the party identification instrument also included each of the exogenous regressors in the authoritarianism equation.

RESULTS

The NES has only irregularly asked the authoritarianism battery that we use in our analysis, so our inquiry necessarily focuses on three election studies: 1992, 2000, and 2004. We are also able to make some use of a fourth study, the 2006 NES Pilot Study. In 2006, the NES conducted 675 interviews with people who participated in the 2004 NES. Although the NES did not ask its authoritarianism battery in 2006, these questions were asked in 2004. Provided responses to these items are reliable over time, we can use the 2004 responses to explain variance in partisanship as measured in 2006. Unfortunately, the NES asked only a random half sample its partisanship questions, so our analysis of 2006 data includes fewer than 300 cases. Hence we must be very conservative about the conclusions we draw from these data. To the extent that we find significant relationships, however, it does suggest that they are particularly robust given the small number of cases.

The results from our models appear in Table 7.4. Most important for our purposes is the changing effect of authoritarianism. In 1992 the effect of authoritarianism did not even approach conventional levels of statistical significance. By 2000, the effect of authoritarianism had increased such that it brushed up against the boundary of statistical significance, but its magnitude was not substantively very large at .055. This estimate means that in moving from least to most authoritarian in 2000, our model predicts that a person's party identification would move about 5 percentage points in a Republican direction on average.

Of course, the importance of issues like gay rights, the role of Christian fundamentalists in politics, the war in Iraq, and the trade-offs required by the war on terrorism increased exponentially after 2000. As a result, we should – and do – find that the effect of authoritarianism increased dramatically. In fact, its parameter estimate more than triples in the four years between 2000 and 2004. Since all the variables are mapped onto (0,1) intervals, these effects can be interpreted easily. In 2004, when one moves from least to most authoritarian, placement on the party identification scale moves in a Republican direction by .169 points, or something about one-sixth of the scale's range. Of course, such a change represents a full point on the NES's partisanship scale, a substantively significant effect to say the least.

It is not just that this increase in effect is impressive considered alone. Its effect relative to other variables is at least as impressive. Although class as measured by income has become an increasingly important predictor of party identification (Stonecash 2000), the effect of authoritarianism goes from being less than half that of income in 2000 to being larger in 2004, other things being equal. Indeed, authoritarianism's effect in 2004 is larger than all the demographic variables in the model.

We do not mean to suggest that authoritarianism has rendered unimportant the traditional cleavage that divides into parties those who prefer smaller government that spends less and those who prefer larger government that spends

TABLE 7.4. *Partisanship as a Function of Authoritarianism, Support for Government Spending, Principled Conservatism, and Social Characteristics, 1992, 2000. 2004, Nonblack Respondents*

Variable	1992 Param. Est. (Std. Err.)	2000 Param. Est. (Std. Err.)	2004 Param. Est. (Std. Err.)	2006 Param. Est. (Std. Err.)
Intercept	0.653*** (0.044)	0.590*** (0.059)	0.501*** (0.065)	0.362** (0.129)
Authoritarianism	0.045 (0.028)	0.055 (0.036)	0.169*** (0.044)	0.366*** (0.092)
Support for Government Spending	−0.305*** (0.038)	−0.350*** (0.043)	−0.290*** (0.059)	−0.313** (0.115)
Moral Traditionalism	0.252*** (0.032)	0.231*** (0.036)	0.354*** (0.047)	0.172* (0.092)
Female	−0.013 (0.016)	−0.025 (0.019)	−0.053* (0.023)	−0.114* (0.047)
Race (Hispanic)	−0.005 (0.030)	−0.023 (0.044)	−0.081* (0.045)	−0.132 (0.099)
Income	0.155*** (0.029)	0.119*** (0.033)	0.115** (0.038)	0.293*** (0.080)
Education (Some College)	0.047** (0.020)	0.037 (0.023)	0.027 (0.029)	0.088 (0.061)
Education (College)	0.082*** (0.024)	0.035 (0.028)	0.024 (0.034)	0.067 (0.074)
Education (Graduate School)	0.023 (0.032)	−0.004 (0.036)	−0.023 (0.040)	0.042 (0.084)
Age	0.112 (0.150)	−0.231 (0.166)	−0.133** (0.052)	−0.216* (0.109)
Attend Church at Least Weekly	−0.215 (0.155)	0.035 (0.193)	0.010 (0.029)	0.053 (0.060)
Mainline Protestant	0.032 (0.018)	0.038 (0.024)	0.042 (0.036)	−0.052 (0.097)
Evangelical Protestant	0.058** (0.017)	0.040 (0.028)	0.051 (0.034)	0.010 (0.068)
Catholic	0.012 (0.020)	0.047 (0.027)	−0.019 (0.029)	0.005 (0.059)
South	−0.053*** (0.022)	−0.005 (0.025)	0.048* (0.027)	0.022 (0.059)
Adjusted R^2	0.16	0.21	0.19	0.20
Number of Cases	1638	1148	795	249

*p<.05, **p<.01, ***p<.001, one-tailed tests
Param. Est. = parameter estimate; Std. Err. = standard error
Source: American National Election Studies, 1992, 2000, 2004

more. Indeed, between 1992 and 2004, preferences for government spending consistently exerts a larger effect than authoritarianism. Even in 2004, with authoritarianism's effect increasing dramatically, the effect of preferences for government spending is nearly twice that of our variable of interest. However, the effect of authoritarianism was less than one-sixth that of preferences for government spending in 2000. By 2004, the effect of authoritarianism was little more than one-half smaller, a remarkable change in four years.

The results from 2006 appear in the last column in Table 7.4. Again, we reiterate the need to be conservative in our interpretation of results because of the small sample size and the nature of the data collection.[8] With those caveats in mind, the results for authoritarianism are remarkable. Despite the fact that all the independent variables, including authoritarianism, are measured in 2004 while party identification is measured in 2006, the effect of authoritarianism in the 2006 model is more than double what it was in the 2004 model when both variables were measured at roughly the same time.[9] Although the standard errors are too large to make too much of it, authoritarianism actually has a larger estimated effect than any other variable in the model, including preferences for government spending and moral traditionalism. It is not as though these variables are not important in 2006. In fact, their effects are roughly what they were in 2000 and 2004. The important change is that the effect of authoritarianism has grown so much larger.

We believe the pattern of these results squares well with our theory and the results presented in the previous two chapters. It is first important to have issues for which preferences are structured by authoritarianism find their way to the issue agenda. This process has been building over time. With the introduction of terrorism on the U.S. homeland, the war in Iraq, and the increased importance of gay rights, it appears that the political dialogue became saturated with such issues by 2004. It is also likely that the increased effect of authoritarianism between 2004 and 2006 is the result of decreasing levels of threat people feel from both terrorism and gays and lesbians. Unfortunately, this hypothesis is impossible to test using NES data because the NES did not ask how threatened people felt by terrorism at all and only asked how threatened people felt by gays and lesbians only in 2004.[10] We suspect that those

---

[8] Although we employ a range of statistical controls, we still use the panel weight for the multivariate analysis. This has the effect of actually decreasing the estimate for authoritarianism slightly and increasing the effect of income greatly.

[9] Indeed the simple correlation between authoritarianism and partisanship measured in 2004 among nonblack respondents was .17, which is relatively strong for survey data. But the correlation between authoritarianism measured in 2004 and partisanship measured in 2006 is a much stronger .25.

[10] Our CCES data provide us some indication that the negative interaction between authoritarianism and threat holds for partisanship as well. Although we cannot estimate a fully specified model of party identification because too many variables, such as moral traditionalism, are not available, we could estimate one that included most of the demographic controls. If we use the threat from terrorism measure to tap threat, we do uncover the familiar negative interaction between threat and authoritarianism.

scoring lower in authoritarianism felt more threat from these things in 2004 than in 2006 for fairly obvious reasons. On terrorism, the country was two more years removed from September 11. And on feelings about gays, the trend in threat since the 1980s has been decreasing. If we are correct that the negative interaction between threat and authoritarianism exists, the preferences of those scoring lower in authoritarianism would move to the left as a result while those scoring high in authoritarianism would remain about the same. Other things being equal, that would lead to a polarization of opinion and with it, a greater effect for authoritarianism.

Analysis of Panel Data

As a further test, we can also use panel data to test whether authoritarianism is structuring *change* in party identification among individuals. Panel data are rare in the social sciences, but they can be very useful. In regular cross-sectional data, different samples are taken for each reading, so none of the respondents are actually the same people. Panel data are different in that the same people are asked the same questions at multiple points in time. Hence it allows researchers to track how a cross-section of the same individuals behaves over time.

In Table 7.5, we present the average party identification score among those who responded to both the 2000 and 2004 waves of the American National Election Studies 2000, 2002, and 2004 panel study. Party identification is coded from 1 to 7, anchored by strong Democrat at the minimum of the scale and strong Republican at the maximum. Hence, negative differences between two readings of party identification, which appear in the last column, suggest that people are moving toward the Democrats in the period in question. Of course, positive differences suggest movement toward the Republicans.

The results, for the most part, conform to expectations. Consistent with the results in the multivariate model, it is worth noting the increasingly strong linear relationship between authoritarianism and party identification. The average difference between those scoring at the minimum of the authoritarianism scale and those scoring at the maximum increases from under a point in 2000 to 1.3 points in 2004. This increase is statistically significant at conventional levels of significance. More important for our purposes, we see the expected directional change occurring in all categories. For those who score either 0 or .25, we find negative signs, suggesting movement toward the Democrats. Among those scoring .75 or 1, we see positive signs, indicating movement toward the Republicans.

We should make clear that these changes in individual categories are small, and only those at the extremes of the scale graze statistical significance. But it is important to realize that we are tracking change over time in party identification, which is by far the most stable of political attitudes (see, e.g., Campbell et al. 1960; Krosnick 1991), and the time frame we are constrained by is only four years. Hence, the pattern of change across categories is probably more important in this case than the raw magnitude of the change over time.

TABLE 7.5. *Change in Partisanship among Panel Respondents by Authoritarianism, 2000–2004*

Authoritarianism	Mean Party Identification in 2000	Mean Party Identification in 2004	Difference (2004–2000)
0	3.57	3.36	−0.21
0.25	4.12	4.05	−0.07
0.5	3.88	3.92	0.04
0.75	4.12	4.25	0.13
1	4.41	4.66	0.25

Source: National Election Studies, 2000–2004 Panel Study

AN APPARENT ASYMMETRY

The conventional scholarly wisdom about authoritarianism would suggest that changes in the relative attractiveness of the Republican and Democratic parties under the contemporary conditions might reflect more authoritarian individuals abandoning the Democratic Party because they view it as too weak to cope with internal and external threats. The data we presented earlier in the chapter seem to suggest this as it relates to voting behavior. And our panel analysis provides some evidence for this thinking as well.

Most theories, however, are silent on what nonauthoritarians might do in response to this new environment. Our theory of political change suggests that nonauthoritarians might also be an important group to watch. Indeed, the panel data on change in party identification suggest that this is the case, as we see those scoring low in authoritarianism moving toward the Democrats. Another way to examine the question is to examine people's feelings about the parties over time rather than just their identification with the parties.

Fortunately, the NES regularly asks Americans to rate both major parties on what they call a feeling thermometer. People are asked to rate people or groups on a scale from 0 to 100 degrees, where 0 to 49 means they feel negatively, 51 to 100 means they feel positively, and 50 means they feel neither positively nor negatively. Included among these groups are "the Republican Party" and "the Democratic Party." Unfortunately, the NES did not ask these questions to the panel respondents in 2004. Hence, we will have to compare the results from the two cross-sections that participated in the 2000 and 2004 NES surveys, respectively. We focus on these two years because the marked increase in authoritarianism's effect on party identification occurred between these two presidential election years.

We first segment our sample by party identification. The conventional scholarly wisdom about authoritarianism would suggest that self-identified Republicans, who are increasingly authoritarian, would increasingly rally around their own party and against the other, which would manifest itself as a higher Republican mean and a lower Democratic mean among Republican

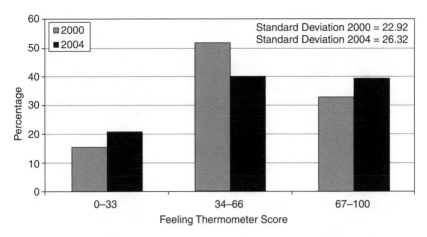

FIGURE 7.1. Relative Polarization in Feelings about the Republican Party, Nonblacks, 2000 versus 2004

identifiers. This story is only half correct. We find that among Republicans, opinions about the Democratic Party remained constant between 2000 and 2004. It is true, however, that in 2004, Republicans' evaluation of the Republican Party increased by a statistically significant 3 degrees.

Evaluations by Democratic partisans, who became decreasingly authoritarian over the period, have changed as well. While Democrats' evaluations of their own party have remained constant, their evaluations of the Republican Party have dropped significantly. In 2000, the mean score that Democrats gave the Republican Party was 42.26 degrees. In 2004, it was only 37.72 degrees, a statistically significant drop of about 4.5 degrees. Taking these results together with the analysis of Republican identifiers, the difference between how Republicans feel about the Republican Party and how Democrats feel about it increased by more than 7.5 degrees between 2000 and 2004, which is a substantively important change.

This increase in the relative polarization of opinion about the Republican Party is reflected in Figure 7.1. To be clear, we do not argue that this is a picture of popular polarization. Such a picture would feature two peaks at the poles of the distribution with few people providing answers in the middle. Still, we do find a marked increase in respondents scoring the Republican Party in the lower and upper thirds of the thermometer. In 2000, better than 50 percent of Americans scored the party in the middle third, but only about 40 percent did in 2004. The percentage of people scoring the Republicans in the lower third of the thermometer increased by more than a third, from 15 to 21 percent. We also find a 6 percentage point increase in the percentage of Americans providing responses in the warmest third of the distribution. Moreover, given that Republicans like their party more in 2004 than 2000 and Democrats like it

TABLE 7.6. *Change in Feelings about the Republican Party by Authoritarianism, 2004 versus 2000*

Authoritarianism	Mean Feeling Thermometer – Republican Party 2000	Mean Feeling Thermometer – Republican Party 2004	Difference
0	44.73	37.54	–7.19
0.25	50.39	50.33	–0.06
0.5	55.20	55.90	0.70
0.75	57.99	61.77	3.78
I	58.25	61.89	3.64

Source: American National Election Studies, 2000, 2004

less, it is not surprising to see a large increase in the standard deviation from 22.92 to 26.32.

Our central interest is how people's levels of authoritarianism affected their evaluations. Again we focus on responses to the Republican thermometer because there was no change in the Democratic thermometer over time. Specifically, we compare how feelings about the Republican Party changed between 2000 and 2004 at various levels of authoritarianism. The results appear in Table 7.6. Consistent with the scholarly conventional wisdom about authoritarianism, we find significant increases in positive affect among those who score .75 or 1 in authoritarianism. Both these groups move from a mean in the high 50s to one in the low 60s. But it is those who score 0 in authoritarianism whose evaluations change the most. The mean for this group in 2000 was 44.73 degrees, but it dropped dramatically to 37.54 degrees in 2004, which is more than a 7 point drop.

Explaining the Polarization in Feelings about the Republican Party

Why would nonauthoritarians take such a dim view of the Republican Party in 2004? One way to gain insight on this question is to test what is on people's minds when they are asked to evaluate the Republican Party. To do this, we compare the correlations between people's answers to the Republican Party feeling thermometer and their answers to feeling thermometers for a number of groups in society. Our approach follows Miller, Wlezien, and Hildreth (1991), who performed a similar analysis in their effort to explain the Democrats' sagging fortunes in the 1980s. They found that the correlations between the Democratic Party thermometer and feelings about controversial groups like feminists and black militants had increased dramatically while the correlation between the Democratic Party thermometer and universally embraced groups like the working class had decreased.

We find a similar transformation in the minds of nonauthoritarians with respect to the Republican Party when we compare the correlation between nonauthoritarians' feeling thermometer scores for the Republican Party and a wide range of feeling thermometers for social groups, political groups, and political institutions in 2004 with the same correlations in 2000. In most cases, the correlations that were strong in 2000 were about equally strong in 2004. For example, the correlation between the Republican Party and "conservatives" was .52 in 2000 and .51 in 2004. Similarly, the correlation between the Republican Party and the military was .43 in 2000 and .42 in 2004.

The correlation between the Republican Party and Christian fundamentalists, however, skyrocketed. In 2000, the correlation was a moderately strong .26. In 2004, it had nearly doubled to .51. This suggests that, when nonauthoritarians are thinking about the Republican Party, they are inclined to have Christian fundamentalists on their mind. As we noted in Chapter 5, this change is important because Christian fundamentalists are a deeply and increasingly unpopular group among nonauthoritarians. Between 2000 and 2004, the mean Christian fundamentalists feeling thermometer score for people who provided no authoritarian responses to the four-item battery of questions dropped from 35.48 degrees to 29.46 degrees.

Of even greater consequence, nonauthoritarians felt more coldly by far toward this group than *every single one* of the more than thirty groups that the NES asked about in 2004. The next closest was "Big Business," with a mean just over 42. Of course, if these nonauthoritarians have Christian fundamentalists on their mind when asked to evaluate the Republican Party, they are going to provide the Republican Party much lower marks than they would if they were thinking about any other group in American public life.[11] This provides further evidence that those at the bottom of the authoritarianism scale are centrally responsible for increased perceptions of polarization in American political life.

THE FUTURE OF PARTISAN POLARIZATION ON AUTHORITARIAN ISSUES

These findings about the relationship between authoritarianism and party identification have important implications for the scholarly debate on party polarization. It follows from Fiorina's argument that less polarizing cues from political elites will lead to less polarization along party lines on the issues of the day. In that sense, it is relevant that George W. Bush and John Kerry really were polar opposites in the 2004 presidential campaign, a traditional Texas conservative squaring off against a typical Massachusetts liberal. Indeed, Fiorina and

---

[11] It is possible that the apparent polarizing effect on feelings about the Republican Party are driven by another variable. To guard against this concern, we estimated a multivariate model similar to the one we estimated for partisanship above, but this time using the Republican Party feeling thermometer as the dependent variable. Our model provides controls for other potential causes of affect for the Republican Party. As we expected, the effect of authoritarianism more than doubles between 2000 and 2004 from 7.321 to 16.526, ceteris paribus.

Levendusky (2006) rightly note that the evidence Abramowitz (2008) finds for increased party polarization is driven disproportionately by data gathered in 2004. Moreover, citing data gathered from the late 1980s through the early 2000s by the Pew Foundation, Fiorina (2006) argues that even these increased differences are not very large, with the average difference between Republican and Democratic attitudes about 15 percentage points in 2003. Adding more fuel to Fiorina's argument, the Pew Center's most recent update in 2007 shows these differences holding steady at around 14 percentage points.

The implications we draw for the future of polarization are at odds with Fiorina's. We do not dispute that partisans are, in large part, reacting to the stimuli they receive from their elites. But one important consequence of this is that authoritarianism has become an important new ingredient in party identification in early twenty-first-century America, suggesting that people have internalized party differences on issues that are structured in part by authoritarianism. This has been the case for the traditional left-right dimension for decades, which means that the sorting process on this dimension is much further along. Since it is relatively new for the authoritarian dimension, it ought to lead to a deepening of party differences on these issues at least for the foreseeable future, other things being equal.

The fact that the Pew data do not suggest such a deepening of party differences between 2003 and 2007 seems to undermine our argument. However, it is important to recall that our argument does not imply increased polarization on all issues. Instead it implies that we ought to see greater polarization only on issues that are structured in part by authoritarianism. By aggregating all the issues into one construct, the Pew researchers miss this potential line of variation. Moreover, they also include measure of efficacy and trust in their analysis, which are conceptually distinct from issue preferences. We drop these from our analysis. Hence, the reason that party differences overall might not have increased between 2003 and 2007 is that on many issues the party differences have decreased or remained roughly the same. This would offset any increase in the party differences on authoritarianism-structured issues.

To test our hypothesis, we reanalyzed the Pew data, comparing the party differences in 2003 with those in 2007. We focus on change between these two years because our analysis above demonstrates that authoritarianism became an increasingly important ingredient in party identification during this time frame. As those scoring high in authoritarianism increasingly sorted themselves into the Republican Party and those scoring low into the Democratic Party, the average differences between partisans on these issues ought to rise.

In terms of measurement, our analysis departs slightly from Pew's and Fiorina's use of these data. For all the items, people were read a series of statements and asked to place themselves in one of four response categories: completely agree, mostly agree, mostly disagree, and completely disagree. Although it is rarely a good idea to discard information, we collapse these 4-point scales into a dichotomous measure of agreement or disagreement. Certainly the distance between completely and mostly agree is substantially smaller than the distance between mostly agree and mostly disagree. Hence treating these variables as an interval scale and calculating a mean difference between groups makes little sense. Moreover, we believe that some people by disposition might be more or less likely to categorize themselves as "completely" rather than "mostly" in agreement or disagreement whether or not differences in people's attitudes really exist.

Table 7.7 presents our results. The top half of the table includes items for which preferences are plausibly structured by authoritarianism. The bottom half includes items in which we would not expect authoritarianism to play a role. Unfortunately, we cannot know for sure because Pew did not ask the battery of questions to measure authoritarianism in its surveys. The first two columns present the percentage difference in preference between self-identified Republicans and Democrats in 2003 and 2007, respectively. The last column is the difference between the years. A positive difference suggests that party differences grew between the two years, and a negative difference suggests that party differences shrank. As before, we confine our analysis to nonblack respondents.

The results conform largely to expectations. On the issues for which authoritarianism likely structures preferences, we find mostly positive signs and, given the short time frame, substantively large differences. Of the fourteen items, ten reveal increases in the difference between Republicans and Democrats of 5 or more percentage points. This is generally true across the authoritarian concerns from difference (sexual orientation, immigration) to civil liberties to a preference for force. For example, we find a 5 percentage point increase in whether school boards should fire gay teachers, a 9 point increase in whether newcomers threaten traditional American customs, a 17 point increase in whether the police should be able to conduct a search of a known drug dealer without a court order, and 6 point increase in whether strength is the best way to ensure peace. We should add that not all the differences grow, with matters involving African Americans generally holding steady. In most cases, however, we are encouraged to find the expected pattern.

For preferences and values that we would not expect to be structured by authoritarianism, the story is quite a lot different. Of these fourteen items, none of the differences increased by as much as 5 percentage points. Three items showed 4 percentage point increases, which grazes conventional levels of statistical significance. When differences between 2003 and 2007 were large, all suggested a narrowing rather than a widening. Self-identified Republicans and Democrats in 2007 were much closer together on government regulation of business and the federal government's role in policy making. These two items, which saw double-digit decreases between 2003 and 2007, are central to understanding the traditional New Deal cleavage.

Overall, the average difference on the fourteen authoritarian structured issues increased from about 15 points to about 20, roughly a 5 percentage point change, which is statistically significant. For the traditional issues, the average difference across all issues held relatively steady, dropping from about 22.5 points to about 20.5, which is a statistically insignificant change. It is

TABLE 7.7. *Differences between Partisans on Authoritarian-Structured versus Traditional Issues, 2003 and 2007, Nonblack Respondents*

	2003	2007	2007–2003
Authoritarian-Structured Values and Preferences			
School Boards Should Fire Gay Teachers	16	21	5
Police Should Be Able to Search Known Drug Dealer without Court Order	1	18	17
Have Old-Fashioned Values about Family and Marriage	20	20	0
There Are Clear Guidelines about Good and Evil	12	19	7
Free Speech Should Not Extend to Neo-Nazis and Other Extremists	7	12	5
Books with Dangerous Ideas Should Be Banned from School Libraries	4	9	5
Concerned Gov't Is Gathering too Much Info about People like Me	21	25	4
Newcomers Threaten Traditional American Customs	11	20	9
Improve Position of Blacks even Providing Preferences	28	25	−3
Should Do More to Restrict People Coming into the Country	8	13	5
Discrimination against Blacks Is Rare	7	15	8
Hasn't Been Much Improvement in the Position of Blacks in US	28	25	−3
Best Way to Ensure Peace Is through Strength	29	35	6
Willing to Fight for Country, whether It Is Right or Wrong	17	25	8
Mean Change	14.9	20.1	5.2
Traditional Political Values and Preferences			
Businesses Strike Fair Balance between Profits and Public Interest	17	20	3
Too Much Power Concentrated in a Few Big Companies	24	21	−3
Businesses Make Too Much Profit	28	22	−6
Unions Are Necessary to Protect Working People	24	26	2
Often Worry about the Chances of Nuclear War	16	7	−9
Today Rich Are Getting Richer, Poor Poorer	36	35	−1
I Often Don't Have Enough Money to Make Ends Meet	17	18	1
I Think the Tax System Is Unfair to People like Me	8	12	4

TABLE 7.7. *(continued)*

	2003	2007	2007–2003
Poor Have Become Too Dependent on Government Assistance Programs	23	27	4
Government Must Take Care of Those Who Can't Care for Themselves	22	23	1
Government Should Help More Needy People Even if It Means More Debt	32	36	4
Government Should Guarantee All Enough to Eat and Place to Sleep	36	36	0
Government Regulation of Business Does More Harm than Good	17	3	–14
Federal Gov't Should Run ONLY Things that Can't Be Run at Local Level	16	4	–12
Mean Change	22.5	20.6	–1.9

Source: Pew Research Center for the People and the Press Values Study, 1987–2007

noteworthy that in 2007, Republicans and Democrats were about as divided on the authoritarian issues as they were on the traditional issues. In 2003, the cleavage was significantly deeper on the traditional issues than on the issues where preferences are structured by authoritarianism, further evidence of the increased importance of authoritarianism in understanding what divides Republicans from Democrats.

One could argue that some of these items from the Pew survey are not sufficiently concrete for us to be confident that politically relevant sorting is taking place on the hot-button issues that politicians actually talk about. However, we uncover the same pattern of results as it relates to perhaps the most divisive of cultural issues in the early twenty-first century: gay marriage. Starting in October 2004, various survey houses have asked respondents to place themselves in one of three categories: supporting the legality of gay marriage, supporting civil unions, and opposing both. The October 2004 survey, which was conducted by the *Los Angeles Times*, found that, among nonblacks, Republicans were 22 percentage points less likely to support legal gay marriages than Democrats and 20 percentage points more likely to oppose both gay marriage and civil unions. By April 2005, according to a survey taken by ABC News and the *Washington Post*, those differences had both grown to 24 percentage points. Most recently, *Newsweek* in conjunction with Princeton Research Associates asked the same question in March 2007. By then, Republicans were fully 31 percentage points less likely to support gay marriage and 29 percentage points more likely to oppose both. To put it another way, party differences on the question of same-sex marriage have deepened by 9 percentage points between late 2004, in the midst of a presidential election that highlighted the issue, and early 2007. To us, this is a remarkable change over such a short period of time.

In sum, in understanding party differences in the electorate, it is important to disaggregate them by issue type. On traditional New Deal–style issues, differences between partisans did not grow between 2003 and 2007. On issues structured by authoritarianism, they did. Now that authoritarianism is an important dividing line between Republicans and Democrats, we expect these differences to at least persist and perhaps deepen until one party or the other moderates its position on these matters, something we have seen little inclination for even in the presidential candidacy of the relatively moderate Senator John McCain.

CONCLUSION

We provide strong evidence that attention to authoritarianism in the study of American political behavior provides great benefits. Consistent with the issue evolution framework, a coalitional reconfiguration of the parties is in the works, with authoritarians increasingly gravitating toward the Republican Party and nonauthoritarians increasingly gravitating toward the Democratic. This first manifested itself in voter turnout and vote choice and later in party identification. As Carmines and Stimson (1989) note, the consequence of such an evolution need not be an increase in aggregate support for one party (although it can). Thus, if scholars are looking for evidence of a tectonic realignment as opposed to the less dramatic impact of evolution-driven change, they miss "the effects of erosion and drift ... even though the end result can be at least as substantial" (Adams 1997, 735). This is consistent with our own findings – there has been no aggregate increase in authoritarianism and only a modest increase in Republican identification during the period of our study.

The parties, however, have sorted more clearly along authoritarian/nonauthoritarian lines, with substantial consequences for understanding the nature of the political divide. For example, the increased importance of authoritarianism on partisanship coincides with a period when people are more strongly tied to their party than in previous decades. The test-retest correlation between partisanship as measured in 2002 and partisanship measured in 2004 is significantly higher than that taken from previous panel studies conducted by the NES. In the 1974–76 panel, the test-retest correlation was .72. In the 1990–92 panel, it increased to .80. In the 2002–04 panel, it increased even further to .88. We believe that the centrality of a worldview like authoritarianism is an important part of why people are more strongly tied to their party.

In addition, it helps us understand the issues that elites decide to highlight. We do not mean to suggest that all Republicans are authoritarian and all Democrats are not, but it is certainly true that party elites seem to recognize that sorting has occurred on this dimension. In 2006, as the solidity of President Bush's support waned among conservatives, Republicans turned to a steady diet of issues that seem to us to be structured by authoritarianism. These efforts included the introduction of constitutional amendments to ban flag burning and gay marriage, postponing the extension of the Voting Rights Act due to concerns about multilingual ballots, discussing English as the nation's official language, congressional resolutions resisting withdrawal from Iraq, and a security-first approach to illegal immigration that would feature hundreds of miles of fences between the United States and Mexico. In 2008, Democratic presidential hopefuls responded in ways that would be attractive to their decreasingly authoritarian base of support. None of the candidates supported a continued presence in Iraq, often favoring instead timetables for precipitous withdrawal. All the major candidates criticized the use of waterboarding and the detention facility at Guantamamo Bay. And all expressed a good deal of support for the gay rights agenda even if they stopped short of endorsing gay marriage specifically.

Finally, our results are significant because they suggest that the growing polarization in American politics may reflect fundamental dispositional orientations. It further suggests that polarization may be persistent and sustain an increasingly intense and acrimonious political divide. Our results suggest that the differences between authoritarians and nonauthoritarians explain an important piece of that conflict which, in turn, has become increasingly central to the nature of political conflict more generally in America today.

8

Immigration: A Reinforcing Cleavage that Now Constrains the Republican Party (GOP)

In the early twenty-first century, immigration reform, as has periodically been the case, clawed its way onto the national issue agenda. One explanation for its reemergence is simple reality. An estimated forty-seven million foreign-born individuals now reside in the United States, and while no precise figures are possible, it is typically estimated that roughly a quarter are in the country illegally. Significantly, illegal immigration has increased dramatically since the early 1990s, with an estimated ten million illegal immigrants arriving between 1990 and 2005 (Pew Hispanic Center 2005). In fact, the undocumented represent the fastest growing portion of the immigrant population.

There are political realities also at play. Over half of all immigrants come from Mexico, and, combined with immigrants from elsewhere in Latin America, Hispanics now comprise a majority of the foreign-born population in the United States (Pew Hispanic Center 2008). Even though many of these immigrants are in the country illegally, children born to them are, by law, U.S. citizens. This makes both legal and illegal immigrants politically relevant. As of 2007, Latino Americans had surpassed African Americans as the largest racial or ethnic minority in America.[1] Therefore, politicians stand to reap a harvest of new voters if they can appeal successfully to this group (Judis and Teixeira 2002). At the same time, however, such gains might come at the cost of existing supporters, something the Democrats experienced when whites fled the party with the enactment of the Voting Rights Act of 1965, as we discussed in Chapter 4.

The impact of immigration on party competition is complicated by the fact that as an issue it encompasses so many layers. As a cross-cutting issue that has

---

[1] Despite their larger numbers in the population, there are still many fewer eligible Hispanic voters than African American ones. For example, while Hispanics accounted for 50 percent of population growth between 2000 and 2004, they accounted for only 10 percent of new voters. One consequence of the lag between immigration and citizenship is that Hispanics' impact on electoral politics is likely to be more deeply felt in the years ahead (Schaller 2006, 179).

historically divided the parties at the elite level internally as much as externally (Tichenor 1994; Monogan 2007), it has traditionally produced only small differences among mass partisans (Citrin et al. 1997; Monogan 2007). In recent years, however, we find strong evidence of mass-level party sorting on the issue, with Republicans taking the anti-immigration position and Democrats a more pro-immigration position. Whether elites are leading public opinion, as is usually the case, or following it is not altogether clear.

The nature of the immigration issue in the early years of the twenty-first century illustrates larger dynamics in the process of worldview evolution. Led by George W. Bush and his chief political strategist, Karl Rove, elite elements in the Republican Party hoped to chart a moderate course on the issue to further their efforts to attract Latino support. The party base at the mass level, which we have demonstrated is increasingly authoritarian, combined with more nativist elements at the elite level to stymie Bush's efforts in 2006. In that sense, the worldview evolution that has been shaped by issues like race, civil liberties, gender equality, gay rights, and the war on terrorism apparently constrained moderate party elites from pursuing a vote-maximizing strategy. Given that Latinos are the fastest growing minority group in the United States, with particularly large populations in the most electorally competitive parts of the country, the worldview evolution that has generally served Republicans so well over the past forty years increasingly has the potential to harm their future electoral prospects.

In this chapter, we provide a brief sketch of the recent history of the pattern of immigration. Next we detail how party positions have evolved, which has affected the types of laws that have been passed and the subsequent flows of immigration. Although the parties have generally been relatively indistinct on this issue until recently, that is no longer the case. We provide evidence suggesting that as worldview evolution has taken root, mass preferences on immigration have widened by a lot. Finally, we demonstrate that attitudes on immigration are also structured by authoritarianism, suggesting that the evolution of the mass base of the Republican Party has likely had important consequences for elite behavior on the issue.

A BRIEF RECENT HISTORY

Since the 1970s, new immigrants to the United States have been disproportionately nonwhite, hailing from Asia, Latin America, and the Caribbean. Along with a surge in legal immigration, the 1970s and 1980s also saw a dramatic increase in illegal immigration, which ultimately required a legislative remedy. In response, Congress produced two major pieces of legislation – the Immigration Reform and Control Act of 1986 (IRCA) and the Immigration Act of 1990. Noteworthy about both pieces of legislation is that despite public opinion in favor of restricting illegal immigration at the time (Espenshade and Calhoun 1993), both had the opposite effect. Indeed, the ICRA dealt with illegal immigration by, in a sense, making it legal, granting legal status to nearly three million people who were in the country illegally (for a review, see Tichenor 1994).

A key dynamic during the process of hammering out the provisions of these two acts were the significant internal ideological divisions within both liberal and conservative circles, which required significant cross-party cooperation to ensure final passage. On the liberal side, there was strong support for protecting nonwhite immigrants, especially through efforts to strengthen antidiscrimination provisions. At the same time, other liberals wanted to restrict temporary migrant labor both because they believed the population could be easily exploited and because it could undercut American jobs. Consequently, liberals rejected so-called bracero programs that had previously supplied American business with significant pools of cheap, seasonal labor.

Conservatives were similarly split. For some, support for immigration was primarily driven by a pro-business agenda to secure a cheap source of labor. But other conservatives, whose central concerns were more cultural in nature, opposed immigration on grounds that it would lead to increases in multicultural education, bilingualism, and ultimately, pressure to increase spending on social welfare programs (Tichenor 1994). The Reagan and Bush administrations played largely secondary roles in the passage of both pieces of legislation, with their preferences for pro-business policies decisive in their respective support for both acts. In accommodating liberals to ensure the legislation's passage, however, Republican strategists also saw an opportunity to cultivate the growing bloc of Hispanic voters by granting amnesty for some who were in the country illegally.

As both legal and illegal immigration increased dramatically in the 1990s, the issue began to take on a more rancorous political tone. Nowhere was this more evident than in the intense debate stoked by California's Proposition 187, a ballot measure in 1994 intended to deny social service benefits to the American-born offspring of illegal immigrants. As a relatively moderate Republican senator from California in the 1980s, Pete Wilson had adopted pro-immigration positions on most issues. But as governor in 1994, Wilson apparently decided his reelection prospects would benefit more from cracking down on illegal immigration and supporting Proposition 187. Wilson was right in the short run, as evidenced by his 15 percentage point trouncing of Kathleen Brown in the gubernatorial race (Nicholson 2005). In the long run, however, the coalition of racial minorities who were angered by the anti-immigrant campaign in 1994 has combined with liberals to make it difficult for Republicans to win in California since. Only celebrity candidate Arnold Schwarzenegger (an immigrant!) has been able to win either a gubernatorial or senatorial race between 1994 and 2008 for the California GOP. In fact, Republicans managed to win only four of twenty-four statewide elections over this period.[2]

The Republicans' national platform in 1996 sharpened the party's rhetoric about immigration, drifting toward the culturally conservative side of the party.

---

[2] "A GOP Farm Team for California Office," by Phil Willon, *Los Angeles Times*, April 18, 2007.

Specifically, it criticized Bill Clinton for having opposed Proposition 187 and for failing to enact policies that matched his tough rhetoric on the issue.[3] After securing the Republican nomination for president in 1996, Senator Bob Dole (R-Kan.) employed ads that accused Clinton of coddling illegal immigrants (Burns and Gimpel 2000). Although ultimately unsuccessful, Republicans in both the House and Senate pushed for limitations to both legal and illegal immigration (Gimpel and Edwards 1999).

The public outcry against illegal immigration appeared to put the Democrats on the defensive. In 1992, the party's platform included a perfunctory statement about immigration.[4] In 1996, however, the platform, while making the obligatory nod toward our "nation of immigrants," included tough talk about illegal immigration:

Today's Democratic party also believes we must remain a nation of laws. We cannot tolerate illegal immigration and we must stop it. For years before Bill Clinton became President, Washington talked tough but failed to act. In 1992, our borders might as well not have existed. The border was under-patrolled, and what patrols there were, were under-equipped. Drugs flowed freely. Illegal immigration was rampant. Criminal immigrants, deported after committing crimes in America, returned the very next day to commit crimes again.

President Clinton is making our border a place where the law is respected and drugs and illegal immigrants are turned away. We have increased the Border Patrol by over 40 percent; in El Paso, our Border Patrol agents are so close together they can see each other. Last year alone, the Clinton Administration removed thousands of illegal workers from jobs across the country. Just since January of 1995, we have arrested more than 1,700 criminal aliens and prosecuted them on federal felony charges because they returned to America after having been deported.

With the Democrats moving to the right on the issue along with the Republicans, elite signals were not sufficiently clear to bring about significant partisan sorting on the issue at the mass level (see Citrin et al. 1997; Burns and Gimpel 2000, for evidence). This would continue to be the case for nearly another decade. In an analysis of House votes on immigration between 1989 and 2004, Democrats were consistently more pro-immigrant than Republicans, but not dramatically so. As a result, party differences in public opinion were similarly muted (Monogan 2007).

Immigration Politics in the Early Twenty-First Century

Latino voting behavior is relatively easy to understand, at least on the surface. With the exception of Hispanics of Cuban descent, they tend to vote

[3] California Democrat Dianne Feinstein, running for the Senate in 1994, often spoke out against illegal immigration during her campaign against the wealthy conservative Michael Huffington. However, Feinstein ultimately came out against proposition 187.

[4] All party platforms were accessed through the American Presidency Project at the University of California at Santa Barbara: http://www.presidency.ucsb.edu/platforms.php.

Democratic, generally by a ratio of about two to one. Democratic dominance likely comes from two sources. First, since the issue evolution of the 1960s, the Democratic Party has been significantly more supportive of racial and ethnic minorities than have the Republicans. At various times, this has extended to both African Americans and Latino Americans, as with Bobby Kennedy's strong support in 1968 of Cesar Chavez's farm workers' strike. Second, the Democrats' relatively greater support for government solutions to economic problems provides more benefits to people lower on the socioeconomic ladder. Since Latinos tend to achieve lower levels of education and income, they tend to benefit more from redistributive government programs, which also makes the Democratic Party a more welcome home (Martinez 2000). While we do not mean to suggest that Latinos from Mexico behave politically the same as those from places like Puerto Rico and Central America, our general point is that most Latinos vote Democratic.

As the percentage of Latinos in the United States continued to grow, the prospect of a second, large strongly anti-Republican voting bloc became a real concern. With Republicans already uncompetitive with African Americans, who make up about 13 percent of the U.S. population, they could not afford to lose in overwhelming numbers to another similarly sized minority population. Perhaps it took a political operation that cut its teeth in a state bordering Mexico to show just how important Latino voters might be to the future of the Republican Party. Hailing from Texas where they had enjoyed great success attracting Latino voters, George W. Bush and his most trusted political operative, Karl Rove, took steps to nationalize this success. In 2000, this took the form of speaking Spanish on the stump, holding bilingual town meetings in certain states, advertising on Spanish language radio stations, and appealing to this largely Catholic group by stressing conservative stands on social issues. Although Bush won only 35 percent of the Latino vote, it represented a substantial increase from Dole's showing in 1996 (Leal et al. 2005).

As president, George W. Bush set in motion in early 2004 an ambitious immigration reform plan that would help deal with the burgeoning problem of undocumented workers in the United States while at the same time allowing the Republican Party to compete for Latino voters in what was expected to be a very close reelection fight. Specifically, the Bush plan offered legal status to the millions of immigrants in the country illegally, provided they registered as temporary workers. To qualify, undocumented workers had to have a job or a promise of one, and they needed to pay a one-time fee to participate. Once enrolled, they could travel between the United States and their country of origin without fear of being denied reentry or being deported, provided they continued to be employed and did not break the law.

Although the plan was tagged as amnesty for illegal immigrants by critics, Bush denied this because the plan did not put undocumented workers automatically on a path to citizenship. The approach favored by Bush and other supporters has generally been referred to as comprehensive immigration reform because it emphasizes greater law enforcement efforts and some form of guest worker program, and it attempts to provide a path to citizenship. In the 2004 elections, thanks to his long-standing cultivation of Latino voters, a savvy GOP operation in Spanish-speaking communities, and his immigration reform approach, Bush captured, according to exit polls, 44 percent of the Latino vote. Although subsequent analysis suggested that this percentage was probably inflated (Leal et al. 2005), his showing still suggested a marked increase from the 35 percent he received in 2000. At the time, it seemed reasonable to expect that being identified with the passage of a Latino-friendly immigration law would surely, over time, edge that percentage higher and create a durable following, especially among first-generation immigrants.

After securing reelection, Bush made immigration reform a top priority of his second administration, even trumpeting his plan in his 2005 State of the Union address. But tension within the Republican Party emerged with new force almost as soon as his second term began. In the spring of 2005, while the Senate was considering comprehensive immigration reform, House Republican leaders were amending new Iraq spending legislation with tough new immigration restrictions. In December, the House passed a measure that framed the problem of illegal immigration almost exclusively as a law enforcement problem, proposing a 700-mile fence along the Mexican border and calling for further crackdowns on providing any services to unauthorized immigrants, including children. Better than 90 percent of House Republicans voted in favor of the measure, while more than 80 percent of Democrats voted against it. It took until March 2006 for the Senate, which was more hospitable than the House to Bush's approach, to pass a version of his plan, but with very little Republican support. In an effort to salvage his initiative, Bush gave a prime time national address in May of that year to push the House and Senate to reconcile their difference on a comprehensive immigration reform bill.

In addition to Bush's lack of popularity, the evidence suggests that the process of worldview evolution came to stand in the way of his preferred solution to immigration reform. The increasingly authoritarian character of the party's base would be unlikely to embrace the plight of nonwhite immigrants, especially those who were in the country illegally. Members of the House of Representatives, with their smaller and more homogenous constituencies, were likely more sensitive to such influences. And facing the prospect of losing their majority status, they determined that their electoral fortunes would be better served by get-tough-on-immigrant measures that seemed to excite the base than the comprehensive approach championed by Bush.

A special election in the summer of 2006 seemed to provide the GOP with some evidence for their position. Republican Brian Bilbray retained the San Diego district formerly held by Representative Randy "Duke" Cunningham (R-Calif.) in a race against Francine Busby, who had run a strong race against Cunningham in 2004. Although Cunningham's district was a solidly Republican one, Democrats had high hopes of a pickup here because Cunningham had been forced from office earlier in 2006 after a bribery conviction. Amid allegations of vote fraud, Bilbray triumphed by four points. Most commentators credited his success in this border district to his decision to run against Bush's immigration plan.

Public Opinion on Immigration

Although public opinion data on immigration showed little polarization between Democrats and Republicans through 2004 (Monogan 2007; see also Citrin et al. 1997; Burns and Gimpel 2000), things began to change after that. The timing coincides with the development of an authoritarian cleavage in party identification, which we detailed in Chapter Seven. This is true in terms of both preferences about immigration and the intensity of those preferences. As for intensity, a May 2007 CBS News-New York Times poll asked respondents which of a range of domestic issues the president and Congress should concentrate on: reducing taxes, making health insurance available to all Americans, strengthening immigration laws, or promoting traditional values. Among Democrats, only 12 percent named strengthening immigration laws as the most pressing concern. In contrast, fully 40 percent of Republicans did. Moreover, those who cared about strengthening immigration laws had a much more negative view of immigration and immigrants than those who identified other topics (Frankovic 2007).

Differences between the attitudes of mass partisans have widened recently as well. The National Election Study (NES) has not consistently asked many questions about either illegal immigration or immigration. But among the two that have been asked a minimum of four separate years, interparty differences were larger in 2004 than any other year. For example, in 1992, the mean Republican response to the NES "illegal immigrant" feeling thermometer was about 6 degrees cooler than the average Democratic response. In 2004, the difference in party means had nearly doubled to 11 degrees. The NES has also regularly asked whether immigration rates should increase, decrease, or stay about the same. As recently as 2000, there was no difference between Republicans and Democrats, with 42 percent of each favoring a decrease in immigration. In 2004, however, self-identified Republicans were 8 points more supportive of decreasing immigration.

Of course, the sorting of the parties along authoritarian lines ought to deepen such differences, as those who are more authoritarian find a home in the Republican Party and those who are less so find a home in the Democratic Party. Although the NES did not ask any items on immigration in its 2006 pilot study, CNN asked people in mid-2007 whether they supported building a 700-mile border fence between the United States and Mexico to control illegal immigration. On this question, at least, interparty differences are very large. Fully 60 percent of self-identified Republicans backed the plan. Only 32 percent of Democrats did. In the AmericasBarometer by LAPOP, we asked whether people agreed that the government ought to provide social services to foreigners. About 40 percent of Democrats agreed, about 40 percent disagreed, and 20 percent professed that they had no opinion. Among Republicans, however, only 9 percent agreed, a whopping 84 percent disagreed, and 7 percent said they had no opinion.

Sorting on the mass level during this period apparently had a profound effect on decisions made by political elites. For example, the Republican presidential debates leading up to the 2008 nomination process sometimes focused on how tough the contenders would be on immigration. On November 28, 2007, the two leading contenders at that time, Rudy Giuliani and Mitt Romney, traded insults about which was softer on illegal immigration. Giuliani accused Romney of running a "sanctuary mansion" because of the latter's use of undocumented workers as domestic help. In response, Romney attacked Giuliani for "coddling" illegal immigrants while mayor of New York by extending health services to some of them. Notably, at the conclusion of the debate, Congressman Tom Tancredo (R-Col.), a fringe candidate who staked his campaign on his anti-immigration positions, exclaimed, "All I've heard is people trying to out-Tancredo Tancredo" (*Boston Globe,* November 29, 2007).

Perhaps most noteworthy is the evolution of eventual nominee John McCain's position on the issue. After having long favored comprehensive reform legislation, which included the Bush-backed compromise in the Senate that he co-sponsored with Ted Kennedy (D-Mass.), McCain moved to the right as the primaries progressed, and in a Republican debate on January 30, he claimed he would vote against the legislation he once co-sponsored. In its place, he advocated a solution that featured a primary reliance on a law enforcement approach to the problem. Broadly speaking, we suspect that the worldview evolution based on race, rights, feminism, gay rights, and the war on terrorism we have detailed throughout the book has caused Republican Party leaders to gravitate toward a position much more consistent with authoritarian preferences on immigration at a time when the issue has emerged as a truly national one.

The noteworthy feature of this change is that the impetus for the party's direction appears to have been significantly bottom up rather than top down. Though issue evolution posits that the process begins as an elite-initiated one, it also surmises that once party clarity on the issue in question is well established, it may be that party elites are beholden to their constituents' now strongly held views on the issue in question. If we are right about worldview evolution, this outcome is predictable, provided preferences in this issue domain are structured, as we expect, by authoritarianism. Republican leaders now feel pressure to adopt positions on immigration that, while perhaps perilous to their ability to attract Hispanic voters in the future, is a necessary response to its base, whose concerns are being clarified and stoked by a steady media drumbeat from well-placed anti-immigrant spokesmen and an increasingly firmly rooted authoritarian worldview on key issues.

AUTHORITARIANISM AND PREFERENCES ON IMMIGRATION

Are more authoritarian attitudes connected with more negative feelings about immigration and immigrants, both legal and illegal? Thanks to data we have collected recently, we can do more than merely compile indirect evidence of the relationship between authoritarianism and these views. Specifically, in 2006, we asked as part of our CCES survey a series of questions about immigration.

Here are several pairs of statements about the issue of immigration. For each pair, please tell us which statement comes closer to your own point of view – even if neither is exactly right:

STATEMENT A. Immigration is an economic benefit to the United States because immigrant workers fill jobs in America that citizens either do not want or cannot do.

STATEMENT B. Immigration is an economic threat to the United States because immigrant workers take jobs that would otherwise be filled by American citizens.

STATEMENT A. The United States should be a country with a basic American culture and values that immigrants take on when they come here

STATEMENT B. The United States should be a country made up of many cultures and values that change as new people come here.

STATEMENT A. Illegal immigrants are lawbreakers, plain and simple, and Congress needs to pass laws that make them pay for breaking the law.

STATEMENT B. Illegal immigrants often come to the United States to make a better life for their families. Even if they technically violate the law, we need to give them some way of making it here.

In addition, the common content to the 2006 CCES included a question about a path to citizenship for illegal immigrants. Specifically, the question read:

Another issue is illegal immigration. One plan considered by the Senate would offer illegal immigrants who already live in the U.S. more opportunities to become legal citizens. Some politicians argue that people who have worked hard in jobs that the economy depends on should be offered the chance to live here legally. Other politicians argue that the plan is an amnesty that rewards people who have broken the law. What do you think? If you were faced with this decision, would you vote for or against this proposal?

On all these questions, those scoring higher in authoritarianism were much less positive toward immigration and immigrants than those who scored lower. We present descriptive statistics for these items, broken down by authoritarianism, in Table 8.1. For ease of presentation, we compare those who scored at the minimum, midpoint, and maximum of the authoritarianism scale. We exclude respondents who classified themselves as Latino/Hispanic. For all four items, those who score highest in authoritarianism are better than 30 percentage points less supportive of immigration than those who score lowest in authoritarianism. In three of the cases, the differences approach or exceed 40 percentage points.

For example, more than 80 percent of those scoring at the maximum of the authoritarianism scale viewed illegal immigrants as lawbreakers, "plain and simple." Less than 40 percent of those scoring low in authoritarianism endorsed that statement, believing instead that illegal immigrants had come to the United States to make a better life for their families. Whereas 77 percent of

TABLE 8.1. *Percentage Favoring Position Unfavorable to Immigrants or Illegal Immigrants*

	Immigration Is a Threat to American Economy	Immigrants Should Adopt American Culture	Illegal Immigrants are Lawbreakers, Plain and Simple	Against Path to Citizenship for Illegal Immigrants
Minimum Authoritarianism	28	50	38	37
Midpoint Authoritarianism	58	76	66	69
Maximum Authoritarianism	67	83	82	77
Difference (Maximum – Minimum)	39	33	44	40

Source: CCES, 2006

those scoring highest in authoritarianism opposed a path to citizenship for illegal immigrants, only 37 percent of those scoring lowest did. Those scoring high and low in authoritarianism were in more agreement about culture. Although the word "illegal" was not used in this question, which might account for some of the difference, fully 50 percent of those scoring at the minimum of the authoritarianism scale favored the statement suggesting that immigrants should adopt the American culture and its values. While 83 percent of those scoring highest did, the difference across the range of authoritarianism was 33 percentage points, which was the least for the four items. It is worth noting that the inclusion of the term *illegal* does not seem to affect the gap profoundly. When asked whether they thought immigration was an economic threat or an economic benefit, without the term *illegal* attached, those scoring highest and lowest produced a 39 percentage point gap. Only 28 percent of those scoring lowest viewed immigration as an economic threat, compared with two-thirds of those who scored highest in authoritarianism.

Multivariate Tests

Of course, a central part of our argument throughout the book has been that authoritarianism has come to be an important determinant of party identification. It could be, then, that the bivariate relationships we present in Table 8.1 are spurious. Perhaps it is really party identification, or some other variable correlated with authoritarianism, that is driving the relationship. To guard against such a possibility, we estimate a set of logistic regression models designed to take into account a range of competing considerations. Specifically, we include statistical controls for partisanship, ideology, and a host of demographic factors,

TABLE 8.2. *Immigration Items as a Function of Authoritarianism, Symbolic Attitudes, and Social Characteristics, 2004, Logistic Regression Estimates*

Variable	Immigration Is a Threat to American Economy Param. Est. (Std. Err.)	Immigrants Should Adopt American Culture Param. Est. (Std. Err.)	Illegal Immigrants Are Lawbreakers, Plain and Simple Param. Est. (Std. Err.)	Opposed to Path to Citizenship for Illegal Immigrants Param. Est. (Std. Err.)
Intercept	−1.293** (0.422)	−2.335*** (0.495)	−0.408 (0.431)	−1.786*** (0.382)
Authoritarianism	0.900** (0.314)	1.854*** (0.390)	1.004** (0.333)	0.982*** (0.293)
Party Identification	0.727*** (0.389)	1.379** (0.476)	1.417*** (0.419)	0.733* (0.346)
Ideology	1.184* (0.531)	1.795** (0.630)	0.967* (0.567)	1.779*** (0.496)
Race (Black)	0.148 (0.323)	0.402 (0.379)	−0.009 (0.341)	0.089 (0.292)
Education	0.989** (0.376)	−0.212 (0.449)	1.183*** (0.398)	−0.415 (0.348)
Female	0.508** (0.201)	0.137 (0.237)	−0.159 (0.212)	0.359* (0.181)
Income	0.000 (0.032)	0.082* (0.038)	−0.035 (0.034)	0.046 (0.029)
Age	0.826* (0.488)	1.207* (0.583)	0.758 (0.520)	0.864* (0.449)
Cox and Snell R^2	0.127	0.198	0.166	0.136
Number of Cases	929	929	929	905

*p<.05, **p<.01, ***p<.001, one-tailed tests
Param. Est. = parameter estimate; Std. Err. = standard error

Source: CCES, 2006

including education, income, gender, age, and being an African American. The results appear in Table 8.2.

Most important for our purposes, authoritarianism is positively signed and statistically significant in all these models. Since authoritarianism carries a parameter estimate most often about three times its standard error, we can be particularly confident that the effect is real. It is also noteworthy that the effect of party identification is also consistently significant. This suggests that, other things being equal, Republicans and Democrats are now sorted in this issue domain.

To provide a sense of the magnitude of the effect, we simulate changes in predicted probabilities for a "typical" respondent at various levels of authoritarianism. For our typical respondent, we choose a white woman who is at the sample mean of all the other characteristics accounted for in the model.

Even controlling for other opinions, the magnitude of authoritarianism's effect is sizeable. For example, we find particularly large differences in preferences for immigrants adopting American culture. For our typical respondent, the predicted probability that he or she endorses the pro-American culture view is .596 if we fix authoritarianism at its minimum and all other variables at their respective means. That predicted probability jumps to .904 if we fix authoritarianism at its maximum, a .308 point difference. Authoritarianism also has a large effect on whether people see illegal immigrants as lawbreakers. Again taking our typical respondent and fixing authoritarianism at its minimum, the predicted probability of perceiving illegal immigrants as lawbreakers, pure and simple, is .771. But if we fix authoritarianism at its maximum, the predicted probability is much higher at .902 – a difference of .131. The results follow a similar pattern for the other two dependent variables.

The effect of partisanship is also noteworthy given the fact that congressional Republicans in 2006 often adopted a more strongly anti-immigration position than the one promoted by President Bush. Our model explains why. In 2006, Republican legislators were struggling to maintain support from their rock-ribbed base supporters. This group includes many people who are self-identified conservative Republicans. And this group was, other things being equal, staunchly anti-immigration in 2006. If we replicate the simulation we performed above, this time fixing authoritarianism at its mean, partisanship such that it represents a "weak Republican," and ideology such that it represents a "conservative," the need for Republican candidates to move to the right to hold their base is obvious. The predicted probability that this "typical" conservative Republican took the anti-immigrant position was .918 on immigrants adopting the culture and .927 on whether immigrants were lawbreakers. The predicted probability for the other two issues also approached 1.

In sum, these results follow the expected pattern. We find that attitudes about immigration, both legal and illegal, are strongly a function of authoritarianism. Although the Bush administration wanted to chart a more moderate course on the issue to attract Latino voters, especially starting in the second term, the new nature of the Republicans' electoral coalition made that impossible. Although it would have no doubt been difficult to win a legislative victory on this issue under any circumstances, the fact that the Republican base is increasingly made of up people scoring high in authoritarianism rendered the initiative impossible to carry out.

CONCLUSION

In the end, House Republicans never attempted to reconcile their differences on immigration reform with the Senate in 2006, effectively killing the president's initiative. The party at the elite level has seemed to gravitate toward a position on immigration more consistent with its party's base since the package's demise. This is true even of erstwhile strong supporters of immigration reform including 2008 Republican standard-bearer John McCain, as noted above. Especially noteworthy is that McCain, as with his position against torture, most clearly repudiated his earlier support for comprehensive reform *after* he had all but secured the nomination as he continued his efforts to mollify the party's base. It is worth noting, however, that McCain did return to a more moderate position on immigration in July 2008, speaking to the National Council of La Raza, a large and vocal pro-Latino interest group.

McCain's evolution on the issue notwithstanding, taking a hard line law and order position on immigration will apparently come at a cost for Republicans. Support among Latino voters dropped to an estimated 30 percent in the 2006 midterm elections, at least 10 points below Bush's level of support from this group in 2004 and maybe more. Exit polls from the 2008 presidential elections suggest that Obama carried Hispanics by a two to one margin. States with substantial Latino populations like New Mexico, Colorado, and Nevada, which have traditionally been Republican strongholds, have been moving toward the Democratic column, and Obama won them all decisively in November 2008. Moreover, five of the six senators from these states will be Democrats in the 111th Congress. Both Colorado and New Mexico have Democratic governors as well.

In Chapter 4, we discussed the distinction between programmatic and symbolic issues and suggested that it was more fruitful to conceive of most issues as comprising both dimensions rather than categorizing some issues as programmatic and others as symbolic. Immigration, complex as it is, is a good example of an issue that should be viewed not as "easy" or "hard" but as comprising multidimensional frames, including race, economics, culture, budgetary, crime, labor, and border/national security. What is especially relevant from our perspective is the degree to which the debate about immigration in America is apparently being increasingly framed around its more symbolically laden and emotionally charged aspects.

Much of the debate in the 1990s, especially in the Proposition 187 fight in California in 1994, focused on the provision of social services. And some of the highest profile media personalities to focus on the issues, including Lou Dobbs and Bill O'Reilly, have certainly targeted issues like jobs and immigrants' tendency to drain public coffers. However, their widely viewed cable news programs, as well as anti-immigration frames more generally, have increasingly focused on hot-button issues like illegal immigrants' criminality, *reconquista*,[5]

---

[5] *Reconquista* is the claim that many Mexicans believe the American Southwest was improperly taken from Mexico in the nineteenth century and have a secret plan to reconquer it. According to one media study, Dobbs has mentioned this notion on his show nine times since 2006. Michelle Malkin, among the most popular conservative bloggers, with a daily audience of nearly 200,000 readers, was a guest-host on *The O'Reilly Factor* until 2007. In one such appearance in 2006,

the related NAFTA super-highway and North American Union,[6] and a supposed outbreak of leprosy in America attributable to illegal immigrants – as well as on the broader threats to our society. The combination of growing elite polarization on immigration policy and the increasingly emotionally charged and symbolically focused aspects of public debate about the issue readily map onto the existing worldview evolution we describe. In this way, the issue evolution of immigration squares well with our findings on the relationship between authoritarianism and immigration and the consequences of that relationship for deepening the larger worldview divide.

she referred to pro-immigrant rallies as "hundreds of thousands of lawbreakers coming out and … really pushing a very radical, extremist reconquista agenda" (Waldman 2008, 14). O'Reilly has also mentioned the idea on his show.

[6] The NAFTA superhighway and North American Union beliefs both posit that there are plans to fully integrate Mexico, Canada, and the United States into a single, supra-national entity that would, according to an article that appeared on Ron Paul's Web site, "represent another step toward the abolition of national sovereignty altogether" (Waldman 2008, 1).

9

What the 2008 Democratic Nomination Struggle Reveals about Party Polarization

By 2006, journalists and even some political scientists had become comfortable with the term *polarization* to describe competition between the parties in the United States. In 2008, however, they started to use the term to describe conflict between two Democrats, Barack Obama and Hillary Clinton, who were vying for the party's presidential nomination. For example, in detailing how long-time political allies in the Boston area had suddenly found themselves at odds, Bella English wrote in the *Boston Globe,* "That the contest has come to this has both energized and polarized the candidates' supporters."[1] In a March 28 opinion column, Scot Lehigh expressed concern about "new findings from Gallup [that] show the peril that looms as the contest becomes more polarized."[2] In *USA Today*, national beat writer Susan Page suggested that "the controversy over inflammatory words by Obama's former pastor, Jeremiah Wright, polarized the electorate."[3] And, perhaps most helpful from our perspective, Perry Bacon and Anne Kornblut wrote in the *Washington Post*, "Clinton's last chance for a big upset is Oregon, where she will go on Thursday, but she faces an uphill climb among an electorate that one of her aides described as 'demographically polarized.'"[4]

It was a bruising race unlike any other nomination battle since voters started to play a more direct role in candidate selection in 1972. This partly owed to the length of the contest. Starting in the 1990s, both parties made concerted efforts to frontload primary elections, so the strongest candidate could emerge early and allow the party adequate time to heal its wounds. With an unprecedented twenty-two contests scheduled on February 5, Democratic operatives

---

[1] "The Diversity Bloc Is Divided: Women Democrats Maneuvering an Unprecedented Rift," Bella English, *Boston Globe*, p. A1.

[2] "A Superdelegate Solution," Scot Lehigh, *Boston Globe,* p. A11.

[3] "Key Demographics Hold for Candidates." Susan Page, *USA Today*, p. A1.

[4] "Clinton Aides Doubtful about Future," Perry Bacon Jr. and Anne E. Kornblut *Washington Post.*, p. A7.

in 2008 had good reason to expect that one candidate would have things wrapped up by early March at the latest with the smart money on Clinton. That failed to happen. As the process wore on into May with no clear winner, feelings grew particularly raw. It was not uncommon to hear Obama's supporters charge Clinton and her supporters with racism, nor was it uncommon to hear Clinton's supporters charge Obama and his supporters with misogyny.

The reason the Obama-Clinton case is important is because it represents a clear case of "polarization" without ideological or issue differences. According to Poole and Rosenthal's DW-NOMINATE scores, the two candidates are essentially ideologically indistinguishable based on their voting records in Congress.[5] Their policy thrust as presidential candidates was remarkably similar as well. Both presented relatively generous health care plans, although Clinton's was somewhat more so. Both suggested that they opposed, at least in part, the North American Free Trade Agreement (NAFTA), a bugaboo for organized labor. Both opposed continuing the war in Iraq, although Obama's timetable for withdrawal was somewhat faster than Clinton's. Both opposed the shape of the Bush tax cuts from 2001, and both offered big tax increases for very high-end wage earners to help pay for programs that would benefit working- and middle-class Americans. Both offered support for gay rights and both opposed the use of torture in fighting the war on terrorism.

We suspect that the divisions that caused journalists to invoke the term *polarization* had to do with something more deeply felt in individuals than issue preferences or ideological commitments. Rather than a distance apart that is easy to measure, it is a feeling inside that is hard to measure. The evidence we present below suggests that authoritarianism was a central factor in defining the Democratic primary conflict just as it has become in defining interparty conflict in the early twenty-first century.

We begin this chapter by drawing parallels between certain characteristics of the interparty conflicts in 2000 and 2004 and the Democrats' intraparty conflict in 2008. Having shown that authoritarianism came to cleave party preferences in the former period, we believe that the similarly sticky preferences for candidates in both periods might suggest that authoritarianism played a similar role in 2008. We then detail the candidates' characteristics and campaigns, which we suspect played a role in making authoritarianism relevant. We next turn to an analysis of the electorate. Like their favored candidates, Obama and Clinton supporters agreed on most issues. Jackman and Vavreck (2008), however, find clear differences on racial resentment and immigration preferences. And through an original survey, we find significant differences in attitudes among supporters of each candidate toward torture and political tolerance as well as those on immigration. Of course, the data we have presented

---

[5] One arguable exception is foreign policy. Obama, not yet in the Senate, opposed the resolution authorizing force against Iraq in 2002. Clinton supported it. More generally, Clinton adopted a tougher stance toward U.S. adversaries, notably Iran, but the apparent passion of their supporters seemed to go well beyond this particular policy difference.

throughout the book suggest that preferences on race, immigration, torture, and tolerance are all powerfully structured by authoritarianism. These findings are particularly noteworthy because the candidates did not stake out differing positions on any of these matters, suggesting a more deeply felt symbolic basis for the differences in support rather than a programmatic basis.

In testing the relationship between authoritarianism and candidate support in the 2008 Democratic nomination contest, we find that authoritarianism is a much more powerful predictor of candidate preference than any of the stock journalistic accounts. Given the lack of ideological differences between Obama and Clinton, it suggests that both this conflict and perhaps the inter-party conflicts of the early twenty-first century are polarized about something other than issues. We believe the increased importance of a worldview that weaves together a range of issue preferences is the basis of that polarization and provides contemporary politics with an extra dose of heat.

STICKY PREFERENCES

One characteristic of a political system deeply divided is when voters' prefer-ences appear resistant to change even in the face of intense stimulus designed to cause change. Indeed, this appears to be at least one reason that an elec-toral system can earn the description polarized. Presidential elections in the early twenty-first century, at least in the aggregate, possess this characteristic. Consider the differences between the statewide outcomes in 2000 and 2004. Only three states switched from one party to the other. New Mexico and Iowa, which went very narrowly for Gore in 2000, went very narrowly for Bush in 2004. New Hampshire, the one Republican holdout in the Northeast in 2000, went for Kerry, who hailed from neighboring Massachusetts, in 2004. Although Bush won higher percentages in some states in 2004 than 2000, they were most often not battleground states in which serious campaigning took place, and the differences were usually quite small.

Further indication of the stickiness of outcomes between 2000 and 2004 can be drawn from specific battleground states where party strategies differed from one year to the next but where outcomes remained almost the same. In 2000, the Gore campaign decided in early October that it would not be able to win Ohio and diverted resources that had originally been intended for Ohio to states like Pennsylvania and Florida where they thought they had a better shot. According to the independent watchdog group, Democracy in Action, Bush and Cheney visited the state about twice as many times as Gore and his running mate Joe Lieberman did during the fall campaign, which should affect outcomes significantly (Shaw 1999). Furthermore, Vice President Gore made his last trip to the state on October 4, and Lieberman last visited the state in September. By contrast, Bush held a major rally in Ohio just two weeks before the election, and Cheney made multiple visits in October. Bush won Ohio by 3.5 percent, much closer than one might have expected given that Gore pulled his resources out a month before the contest while Bush continued to campaign hard.

In 2004, the Kerry campaign decided that Ohio would be ground zero in determining the outcome of the election and, accordingly, spent heavily in the state. In addition, independent groups sympathetic to the Democratic presidential nominee, such as Americans Coming Together and Moveon.org, dumped enormous resources into get-out-the-vote efforts, especially in cities like Cleveland and Columbus. The Bush campaign again committed significant resources to Ohio. In stark contrast to 2000, the Democratic nominee did not pull the plug early in Ohio in 2004, with Kerry visiting the state more than he did any other state in the campaign and about half again as often as President Bush did. If the campaign mattered, Kerry should have narrowed the gap substantially on Bush. Instead, Kerry's efforts had shockingly little effect, with Bush winning this time by 2.1 percent.

Enhanced efforts by the Bush campaign in 2004 in certain states produced similarly negligible effects. From the earliest days of the Bush administration, his campaign team targeted Pennsylvania as a state they might be able to swing from blue to red. During his first term, Bush visited the state twenty-nine times, more than any other state. During the campaign itself, the Bush team spent much more heavily in 2004 than it had in 2000, while the Democratic nominee committed similar resources each time. Despite Bush's efforts, the outcome was, like Ohio's, almost identical to the result in 2000, with Gore winning by 4.2 percentage points in 2000 and Kerry winning by 2.5 percentage points in 2004. Campaigning and advertising clearly did little to change many hearts and minds, instead apparently reinforcing existing preferences. A stickiness of preferences ought to be a central characteristic of a political universe cleaved by a worldview.[6]

Fiorina et al. (2004) suggest an ideological explanation for the stickiness. He concludes that recent campaigns ought to make little difference because people realize that they are being asked to choose between very liberal Democrats (Gore and Kerry) on the one hand and a very conservative Republican (Bush) on the other. Leaving aside that Bush in the 2000 campaign attempted to run as a "compassionate conservative," "a uniter not a divider," the logic, in a Downsian (1957) sense, is sound; polarized choices make for polarized voting behavior. A moderately conservative person might not be entirely happy with a staunch conservative like Bush, but in terms of issue distance, Bush is still a better alternative than a solid liberal like Kerry (see Rabinowitz and McDonald 1989). We agree that this explanation carries significant merit. Yet the experience of 2008 suggests something more complicated is at work as well.

---

[6] It is true that Obama's campaign efforts appeared to pay significant dividends in November 2008, particularly in his stunning wins in North Carolina and Indiana, two long-time Republican strongholds. A variety of factors, including the historically effective campaign operation and the exploding financial crisis probably each played a role in loosening the electoral map to some degree. The larger point about the doggedness of political battle lines still holds, a point we take up in more detail in the Epilogue.

Interestingly, the 2008 race for the Democratic nomination revealed voting behavior similar to that in the 2000 and 2004 general elections, even though the two candidates who survived until the end of the process, Barack Obama and Hillary Clinton, have produced remarkably similar voting records during their time in the Senate. Although much of this book has been devoted to demonstrating how *inter*party conflict has changed in response to the growing importance of authoritarianism as a cleavage line between the parties, it appears to be true that *intra*party conflict within the parties can be affected, too, at least under certain circumstances. At first blush, it seems somewhat surprising that such intraparty conflict would take place within the Democratic Party because it is increasingly identified with the less authoritarian side of political disputes involving authoritarian issues. However, the nature of the Democratic coalition, combined with the presence of an African American candidate, appears to have produced such an outcome.

WHY AUTHORITARIANISM IN THE DEMOCRATIC PRIMARY?

Race, a central authoritarian concern, clearly played an important role in the contest, but Obama's candidacy brought into play considerations more complex than race alone. Obama might be perceived by many not so much black as exotic. His mother is a white Kansan, but his father was not an African American – rather, an African from Kenya. Even his name, Barack Hussein Obama, screams difference, a point that led to a whispering campaign among both Republicans and Democrats that suggested he was a Muslim, not a Christian.[7] He did not grow up in a traditional two-parent household, either. His father left the family early in Obama's life, and his mother and grandparents raised him in places as atypical as Indonesia and Hawaii. The literature on authoritarianism would suggest that such a dizzying array of differences would adversely affect the way the more authoritarian would evaluate him.

One indication of such a dividing line is the deep racial polarization in voting that occurred throughout much of the 2008 primary season. Given that Obama is the strongest African American candidate in history, it is not surprising to find that he consistently carried 80 percent and sometimes more than 90 percent of the African American vote in state primaries. The literature is rife with examples of blacks' strong racial identity affecting voting preferences in subpresidential races (e.g., Bullock 1975, 1984; Abrajano, Nagler, and Alvarez 2005). Indeed, blacks' preferences for black political figures can be so strong that it can work against the material interests of African Americans. For example, African Americans were, in a set of experimental manipulations, as likely to take cues on issues from Clarence Thomas, even though his position

---

[7] During the Al Smith benefit dinner late in the campaign, Obama himself joked that "I got my middle name from someone who obviously didn't think I'd ever run for President."

on many racial policy questions was far to the right of those of most African Americans, as they were from Jesse Jackson (Kuklinski and Hurley 1994).

The voting behavior of nonblacks in the Democratic primaries is more of a puzzle, particularly within a party in which members generally claim to be more open to racial differences. After the contest winnowed the contestants to a two-person race after Super Tuesday, Hillary Clinton generally won at least 60 percent and sometimes as much as 70 percent of the nonblack vote. Since whites, in particular, almost always have white candidates to choose from, identity politics is a less compelling explanation for their voting behavior.

There is strong suggestive evidence that authoritarianism was a core reason for the voting behavior of nonblacks. Despite the interparty sorting on authoritarianism that we have detailed throughout the book, it is far from complete. As we noted at the beginning of Chapter 1, there are still plenty of Democrats who score high in authoritarianism and plenty of Republicans who score low. Disproportionately, the source of authoritarianism among nonblack Democrats can be found in the working class, with some of the earliest scholarly work on authoritarianism focused on its working-class roots (Lipset 1959; Lane 1962). Although the Rust Belt union constituency carries much less influence in the 2000s than it did decades before, it still makes up a significant share of the party faithful (Stanley and Niemi 2005). And it is in this part of the country, from Indiana in the West, wrapping to Massachusetts in the Northeast, that Clinton dominated Obama. In addition, although Obama won most southern states, he relied most heavily on black votes because whites, for the most part, provided low levels of support for his candidacy in this region.

Of course, there are always competing, or perhaps complementary, explanations for the split. Every major journalistic treatment of the race noted that Clinton ran best among older Democrats who were less well educated and earned lower incomes than Obama's white supporters. The story goes that if one were looking for Clinton voters, one might be best served to look in a bowling alley or a bar that does not sell much beer from micro-breweries. If one were looking for white Obama voters, one might be better off looking at a wine and cheese tasting or a coffeehouse. It is certainly clear that Obama would have been better served by avoiding all bowling alleys himself, after rolling a 37 in Altoona, Pennsylvania, the week before the primary there.

These journalistic accounts are borne out in the data. For example, in Pennsylvania where both candidates expended significant resources and Clinton won by about 10 percentage points, she won a whopping 75 percent of the vote among whites with a high school diploma or less. Among those with at least a college diploma, Clinton won a bare majority. According to a post-election analysis by CBS News, people from households making less than $50,000 were about 20 percentage points more likely to support Clinton than people from households making more than $50,000. These differences by education and income among whites were evident by varying degrees in the exit poll data from most other primary states as well. Of course, this meant that Clinton dominated in low-education, low-income states like West Virginia, while Obama did much better in higher education, high-income states like Maryland and Virginia, which, of course, border West Virginia.[8]

Campaign Behavior

The two campaigns' approaches both contributed to and solidified these divisions. Starting in March, 2008, after a relatively disappointing showing in the twenty-two Super Tuesday primary and caucus contests (where Clinton thought her campaign would dispatch all other competitors from the race) and a string of defeats in the succeeding month, the Clinton campaign's efforts seemed directed almost single-mindedly to appealing to the white working class, whether it was waxing nostalgic about her father teaching her to shoot a gun or slugging down a shot of Crown Royal at an Indiana bar. In more specific terms, Clinton's appeals along with those of her surrogates focused on race, Obama's religious identification, his lack of toughness, and his stuffy elitism. All are arguably considerations structured by authoritarianism.

Certainly not a racist herself, having compiled a laudatory record on race over her thirty years in public life, Clinton said some things that must have caused her some discomfort as the campaign wore on. Indeed, some commentators argued that several of these appeals may have crossed the line from good, tough politics to good old-fashioned George Wallace–era race baiting. To note one particularly notorious example, Clinton continued to argue after splitting the Indiana and North Carolina primaries on May 6 that Obama could not fashion a winning coalition in the general election against John McCain, the Republican nominee. In an interview with *USA Today*, Clinton cited an Associated Press analysis that, in Clinton's words, "found how Senator Obama's support among working, hard-working Americans, white Americans, is weakening." Of course, the implication was that white Americans were particularly hard-working folk while black Americans were, perhaps, not quite so much. At a very minimum, Clinton seemed to be arguing that African American support was less significant than white working-class support.

From the early days of the campaign, Clinton surrogates, most notably Bob Kerrey, a former governor and senator from Nebraska, said, in remarks published in the *Washington Post*, that Obama's middle name was Hussein, implying that he was a Muslim. Although surely Kerrey and others knew that Obama was a Christian, such efforts likely had the effect of appealing to authoritarians' more general concern about difference. At least anecdotally, this effort appeared at least somewhat successful, whether the evidence is drawn from a local newspaper in Hazleton, Pennsylvania (a local woman scoffed at the idea of voting for Obama, saying "I don't want to be a Muslim!"), or a bunco game in Brentwood, Tennessee (a local woman quarreled with fellow players about

---

[8] Both Maryland and Virginia have higher black populations than West Virginia as well. But in these two states, Obama did much better with low-education whites than he did in Appalachia.

Obama's religious affiliation, noting that "It was all part of Al Qaeda's plan to elect a Muslim president").

In addition to race and religion/ethnicity, the Clinton camp also repeatedly trumpeted its candidate's toughness and questioned Obama's. Especially veterans of past Democratic national campaigns wondered aloud whether Obama had the stuff to stand up to what they described as the Republican attack machine, which would surely expose all of Obama's weaknesses in the fall. In an interview with *Newsweek*, James Carville, a Clinton strategist and the campaign manager for Bill Clinton's successful 1992 presidential run, put the issue in the most succinct (and most coarse) terms, "If she gave him one of her *cojones*, they'd both have two."

Although it is unclear how the candidate herself felt about the implication that she has three testicles, Carville's point illustrated perfectly the campaign's charge that she was tough and he was not. As the campaign wore on, Clinton often characterized herself as a "fighter," which seemed a particularly compelling theme as she picked up primary wins late in the primary season despite the seeming inevitability of Obama's nomination. Her campaign worked relentlessly against long odds. The emphasis on toughness is potentially important to our thinking because it was one of the nine characteristics that Adorno et al. (1950) identified in the *Authoritarian Personality*.

Using a complementary line of attack, Clinton (Wellesley, Yale Law) charged that Obama was an "elitist," to which an Obama misstep opened the door. In a private appeal to fund-raisers in San Francisco in March 2008, Obama suggested working-class whites were "bitter" about consistently deteriorating economic outcomes and, as a result, retreated to considerations like God and guns, ground more fertile to Republicans, when voting. After Obama's comments leaked to the press through a blogger working for the Huffington Post Web site, the Clinton campaign pounced. Obama's gaffe allowed the Clinton campaign to portray his background as soft, leaving him out of touch with ordinary working people. How could a Columbia and Harvard Law School–educated man who worked as a law school professor at the University of Chicago understand why Rust Belt whites vote as they do?[9] Campaign professionals clearly seem to believe that tagging an opponent with the elitist label is potent. Bush used very much the same charge against Kerry in the 2004 general election, a charge that seemed to stick after Kerry was filmed wind surfing off the coast of Nantucket. In general, American voters seem to prefer decisive, commonsense doers to ruminating highfalutin' thinkers. And, as noted earlier, the general charge of elitism has been an often successful line of attack against liberal candidates back to the Eisenhower-Stevenson elections.

[9] Of course, like President Bush, who has degrees from Yale and Harvard, Senator Clinton has a similarly elite educational pedigree, as a graduate of Yale Law School. But, again, these factual realities notwithstanding, it is the symbolic labels that often prove most persuasive. And those symbolic labels can serve as especially appealing shortcuts to certain cognitive styles and worldviews.

Clinton's campaign was not alone in taking steps that might have created an authoritarian-based voting cleavage. Obama's approach to the election should have been particularly attractive to nonauthoritarians. While his preternaturally calm style might have suggested to those scoring high in authoritarianism that he was not tough or fiery enough to confront America's enemies, it was likely reassuring to those who scored low in authoritarianism, who are more inclined to value thought over emotion and talk and diplomacy over isolating opponents and using force. Whether it was talking about foreign affairs or race, Obama usually chose nuanced arguments rather than concrete ones. In response to his willingness to engage in dialogue with rogue countries like Iran and North Korea, he noted that campaigns are "not particularly good with nuance," a word that rarely sees the light of day in political campaigns. Similarly, when his campaign was in crisis after the inflammatory words of his pastor, the Reverend Wright, came to light, Obama did not, at first, definitively distance himself from his long-time friend and spiritual advisor. Instead, he gave a nuanced speech about how difficult race was as an issue, a point we take up in more detail in Chapter 10.

Finally, we suspect that the fact that Obama's speeches dealt more with abstract and lofty notions like hope, unity, and political reconciliation, while studiously avoiding divisive political messages and specific issue stances, was also attractive to those scoring low in authoritarianism. While Obama was certainly not the first major candidate to appeal to such notions, he may have been the first to do it while consistently using a measured, even-handed tone that at times actually celebrated subtlety and shades of gray. Obama, then, embodied a package that may have been especially appealing to less authoritarian voters.

HARD EVIDENCE

Data that we and others gathered through surveys conducted by Polimetrix at different times during the nomination process certainly seem suggestive that authoritarianism might have played a role in structuring preference formation. Jackman and Vavreck (2008) asked potential Democratic primary voters a battery of questions designed to tap racial resentment, which we described in Chapter 2. They found that Clinton's supporters possessed significantly more racial resentment than Obama supporters did. In addition, although they uncovered negligible differences between the two candidates' supporters on most specific policy attitudes, the one exception they revealed was on immigration. Among non-Latino whites, Clinton supporters were much more likely to favor jailing and deporting illegal immigrants than were Obama supporters. Like racial resentment, attitudes toward immigration engage people's tolerance for difference, which is central to differentiating the more authoritarian from the less authoritarian.

Although we did not ask questions about racial resentment in the AmericasBarometer by LAPOP survey, we asked three questions about immigration. The first asked people which of two views on immigration most closely approximated their own: "Immigrants do the jobs Americans do not want to do" or "Immigrants take jobs away from Americans." Since Latinos are the sources of most immigration these days, we limited our analysis to white, non-Hispanic respondents. Among white Obama supporters, only 31 percent said they thought immigrants took jobs. Among white Clinton supporters, fully 55 percent did. We also asked people to place themselves on a 5-point scale ranging from strongly agree to strongly disagree regarding whether they thought government should provide social services to foreigners. White Clinton supporters were 13 percentage points less likely to agree that government should provide these services than were white Obama supporters. Finally, we asked people to place themselves on a 7-point scale anchored by strongly agree and strongly disagree regarding whether national identification cards should be required. Although the mean score for both groups was on the "disagree" side of the midpoint, white Obama supporters were 17 percentage points more opposed than were white Clinton supporters. Such differences are remarkably large given that the candidates did not offer differing views on immigration during the campaign.

In addition to race and immigration, we uncover other important policy differences that further suggest the importance of authoritarianism in structuring support for either Obama or Clinton. In May 2008, the AmericasBarometer by LAPOP asked respondents which of the following statements they agreed more with:

"In order to protect us, when the CIA catches terrorists red-handed, it should be allowed to use torture to get information," or

"Even when the CIA catches terrorists red-handed, it should not be allowed to use torture to get information."

The results follow a familiar pattern. First, authoritarianism clearly structures preferences, with 56 percent of those scoring highest in authoritarianism endorsing torture compared with only 27 percent of those scoring lowest endorsing it. Second, we find a very large difference in the attitudes of Republicans and Democrats, with 77 percent of those who described themselves as strong Republicans endorsing the use of torture in this scenario and only 29 percent of those describing themselves as strong Democrats endorsing it. Third, and most important, we find that Clinton supporters differ significantly from Obama supporters, although neither group is particularly high on torturing terrorists. Among Clinton supporters, 41 percent say the CIA should be able to use torture. Among Obama supporters, only 27 percent do. Given that the statements made by Obama and Clinton revealed no policy differences between them on the issue, it is again noteworthy to find such a large gap between their supporters.

In addition, we find a significant difference between Obama and Clinton supporters in their levels of tolerance. The 2008 AmericasBarometer by LAPOP survey asked whether critics of the United States should be able to do things like run for office, appear on television, give speeches, and the like.

Respondents were asked to place themselves on 10-point scales, and we combined the different indicators of tolerance into a single scale and calculated the mean. Obama supporters scored high in tolerance, with a mean score of 7.86. Clinton supporters were significantly less tolerant, with a mean score of 6.73. Neither candidate took positions on these issues, so, to the extent that these means differ, it must be because of the dispositions of the individual respondents. Combined with the findings on immigration, racial resentment, and torture, these differences in tolerance suggest strongly that we ought to find differences between Obama and Clinton supporters in authoritarianism, which structures preferences on all these items.

Given all the suggestive evidence, we are not surprised to find a relationship between authoritarianism and candidate preference. Yet even we are somewhat surprised by just how strong the relationship is. We limit the analysis to nonblacks, and since the contest involved a fight for the Democratic nomination, we focus our analysis on self-identified Democrats and independents. The results appear in Table 9.1. Among those who provided zero authoritarian responses to the battery, only 24 percent expressed a preference for Clinton compared with 76 for Obama. Among those who provided four authoritarian responses, however, we find 69 percent Clinton supporters compared with 31 percent for Obama. Put another way, across the range of authoritarianism, the difference in candidate support is a whopping 45 percentage points. The relationship is linear across the distribution of authoritarianism as well. Those providing one authoritarian response to the child-rearing battery prefer Obama 58 to 42, while those who provide three authoritarian responses prefer Clinton by 61 to 39.

To put into perspective the effect of authoritarianism on structuring candidate preference in the 2008 Democratic nomination contest, consider the effect of ideology. According to exit poll data, Obama consistently received more support than Clinton from those who consider themselves more ideologically liberal. Indeed, this fact opened Obama up to the charge that his coalition of white liberals and African Americans was eerily similar to George McGovern's in 1972, a candidacy that was perhaps the weakest Democratic effort of the twentieth century (Judis 2008). Among those who identified themselves on a 5-point ideology scale as "very liberal," 60 percent favored Obama. Among those who identified themselves as "very conservative," the opposite pole of the scale, 42 percent supported Obama. This nearly 20 point difference is significant to be sure, but it is less than half as large as the difference across the range of authoritarianism.

That authoritarianism appears to be playing such a central role in decision making may provide a solution to a puzzle about the campaign for the Democratic nomination. Obama generally did poorly in states in which educational attainment is low. His difficulties with low-education voters in states like Kentucky and West Virginia, both overwhelmingly white states situated near the end of the primary election calendar, were well documented. The story, however, is more complicated than that. Although Clinton beat Obama two

TABLE 9.1. *Authoritarianism and Democratic Candidate Preference, Nonblack Respondents, 2008*

Number of Authoritarian Responses	Percentage for Obama	Percentage for Clinton
0	76	24
1	58	42
2	41	59
3	39	61
4	31	69
All	47	53

Source: AmericasBarometer by LAPOP, 2008

to one among low-education whites in Appalachia, Obama ran relatively better with this group elsewhere. In terms of race, Oregon does not seem like a great bet for Obama with an African American population of less than 5 percent. Yet, in a primary held the same day as the one in Kentucky, he defeated Clinton there by more than 10 percentage points. Even among low-education whites, Obama did reasonably well, securing the support of nearly 50 percent according to exit polls. How can Obama win some low-education whites and not others?

The reason is because not all whites who possess lower levels of educational attainment are the same. Although education and authoritarianism are negatively correlated, that correlation is far from perfect. There is a significant number of people who score relatively low in authoritarianism but who have not gone to college, though there are more who score high in authoritarianism. Of course, it is also true Clinton does better among college-educated whites in some places than others. Similarly, there is a significant number of college graduates who score high in authoritarianism, though there are more who score low in authoritarianism.

Table 9.2 captures these dynamics. Here we display the percentage of people who expressed a preference for Obama over Clinton broken down by both education (in the rows) and authoritarianism (in the columns). The data in the last column of numbers confirm what commentators have noted throughout the campaign: education matters. Our data show that 37 percent of nonblacks with a high school education or less supported Obama while 58 percent of those with at least a four-year college degree did, a 21 percentage point difference. For ease of presentation, we have collapsed our measure of authoritarianism into three categories, with those providing zero or one authoritarian responses to the child-rearing battery in the first column of numbers, those providing two authoritarian responses in the second column, and those providing three or four authoritarian responses in the third column. Even if we collapse the categories this way, the effect of authoritarianism is still remarkably clear, with 66 percent

TABLE 9.2. *Democratic Candidate Preference by Authoritarianism and Education, Nonblack Respondents, 2008*

	Low Authoritarian (0 or 1 authoritarian responses)	Middle Authoritarian (2 authoritarian responses)	High Authoritarian (3 or 4 authoritarian responses)	All
Education				
High School or Less	57	33	32	37
Some College	68	48	46	54
College or Graduate Degree	73	52	38	58
All	66	41	36	

Source: AmericasBarometer by LAPOP, 2008

of those scoring low in authoritarianism backing Obama and 36 percent scoring high in authoritarianism backing him, a 30 percentage point difference.

The entries in the table's interior deepen the picture helpfully. Obama's success depends mightily on authoritarianism even within education groups. Most people who do not go beyond a high school diploma fall in either the middle or high authoritarian groups and both provide only about a third of their support to Obama. Although we do not have enough data for a rigorous test, we suspect that levels of authoritarianism are higher in the places where Clinton has done best among whites, namely, the South and Appalachia. Although a rarer breed, about 22 percent of nonblacks who earned a high school degree or less score low in authoritarianism. Obama received 58 percent support among people in this group, which is about 25 points more than those who scored high or medium. Again, we do not have sufficient data to test the hypothesis, but we suspect low levels of authoritarianism even among the not well educated are likely more prevalent out west in places like Oregon.

Obama's strongest supporters are, as expected, people with college or graduate school education who score low in authoritarianism, with 73 percent preferring him over Clinton. Even among the college educated, however, Clinton wins a clear majority of those who score high in authoritarianism. Fortunately for Obama, about 50 percent of college-educated respondents fall into the low authoritarianism category while only about 25 percent fall into the high category. To provide a sense of how important authoritarianism is in conditioning the effect of education, low-education nonblacks who score low in authoritarianism are actually about 20 percentage points *more* likely to support Obama than are college-educated nonwhites who score high in authoritarianism. This is, of course, quite the opposite of the dominant journalistic narrative, which suggests that education plays the central role in understanding the voting behavior of whites. Instead, it appears to be authoritarianism.

TABLE 9.3. *Preference for Obama over Clinton as a Function of Authoritarianism, Ideology, and a Range of Democraphics, 2008, Self-Identified Democrats and Independents*

Variable	Parameter Estimate (Standard Error)
Intercept	0.995**
	(0.387)
Authoritarianism	−1.460***
	(0.305)
Income	0.000
	(0.026)
Ideology	−0.272
	(0.414)
Race (Hispanic)	0.393*
	(0.221)
Female	−0.578***
	(0.174)
Age	−0.015**
	(0.006)
Education	0.176**
	(0.062)
Cox and Snell Psuedo R²	0.124
Number of Cases	648

Source: AmericasBarometer by LAPOP, 2008

In the fight for the 2008 Democratic nomination, education was not the only critical dividing line among nonblacks. Indeed, with the remarkable success of a black candidate, it is easy to forget that no woman had ever been even remotely as close to securing a major party presidential nomination as Hillary Clinton was in 2008. Identity politics was surely at play for women as well, as major journalistic accounts have all made clear. In our sample, Clinton's support from women was very strong, with 54 percent expressing support for her. But, as with education, gender's effect is markedly different depending on how authoritarian a female respondent is. Among women who provided either three or four authoritarian responses to the child-rearing battery, more than seven in ten (72%) expressed support for Clinton compared with 28 percent for Obama. But among women who provided either zero or one authoritarian responses, it was Obama who dominated, winning nearly 60 percent (59%) of these women's support. Put another way, more authoritarian women were 31 percentage points more likely than less authoritarian women to support the female candidate. Authoritarianism appears to matter more than gender as well.

It is also possible to estimate a multivariate model of candidate preference, taking into account the whole range of potential explanations, from demographics like education, gender, age, race (being Hispanic), and income to attitudinal variables like ideology and authoritarianism. Since the choice between Obama and Clinton is binary, logistic regression is the most appropriate estimation technique. The results of this analysis appear in Table 9.3.

The effects of authoritarianism, gender, education, race, and age are all statistically significant and in the expected direction. That is, men, the better educated, younger voters, Hispanics, and the less authoritarian are all more inclined to prefer Obama over Clinton. In the multivariate context, the effects of income and ideology are not statistically significant.

We can calculate a first difference for each of the significant regressors to determine their effects across the range of their distributions. The results appear in the last column of the table. Using as a typical respondent, a non-Hispanic male who is average in all his other characteristic, our simulation shows that authoritarianism has the largest effect of all the variables in the model. For this typical respondent, his probability of voting for Obama if he scores at the maximum of authoritarianism is only .333. But if he scores at the minimum, his probability of preferring Obama jumps by 35 percentage points to .683. The first differences for education and age are both larger than .20, but they are not nearly as large as that for authoritarianism. This suggest that as far as understanding candidate preference in the 2008 nomination contest between Barack Obama and Hillary Clinton, there is no more powerful explanation than authoritarianism.

CONCLUSION

In this chapter, we have shown that politics can be polarized even when no issue differences exist between competitors. That is not to suggest that the large issue differences between George W. Bush and John Kerry did not lead to polarized assessments of the candidates and voting behavior. They surely did. But we are not as sure that the ideological gulf between them made people *feel* like the political system was polarized. Indeed no one talked about polarization when Ronald Reagan, the unquestioned leader of the contemporary conservative movement, faced off against Walter Mondale, a staunch liberal out of the Minnesota Farmer-Labor tradition of Hubert Humphrey, in 1984. These two were polar opposites, too, but no one thought the political system was polarized then.

We believe that these results involving an intraparty battle help support our main point about the nature and intensity of interparty competition, which we have made throughout this book. We suspect that one reason the primary election fight between Barack Obama and Hillary Clinton seemed so polarized was that support was powerfully structured by authoritarianism. Moreover, we suspect that this is also why people seemed so resistant to candidate appeals during the course of the primary fight. No matter how much Obama spent in states like Texas and Pennsylvania, it did not appear that he moved many voters his way. Similarly, it did not matter how many resources Clinton committed to North Carolina as she tried to save her candidacy. As was the case in the months leading up the Bush-Kerry contest, people had already made up their minds. We have demonstrated here that large issue differences between the candidates are clearly not a necessary condition to bring about this behavior. Choices structured by a worldview like authoritarianism are inclined to be sticky because people have deeply felt reasons for their preferences.

A New View of Polarization

Over the last generation, the major parties in Washington and, to a lesser extent, parties in the electorate have become more distinct from each other. The changes at the elite level have had a profound effect on changes at the mass level (Hetherington 2001; Levendusky forthcoming), just as most theories of public opinion would suggest (e.g., Key 1966; Zaller 1992). The clear signal now provided by the two parties in government is allowing more Americans to reflect the ideological and issue preferences of their party.

To many, the increasingly distinct nature of parties has caused the American political system to become polarized. The term *polarization* in a strict defini-tional sense captures what has been going on among political elites. Conservative Democrats and liberal Republicans have largely become a thing of the past (Rohde 1991), a process advanced significantly by the 2006 congressional elections. Although ordinary Americans profess to dislike the polarization in Washington, the political system is rigged such that it is nearly impossible to remove its most polar elements. Ideologically less moderate members tend to run in the safest of districts. To the extent that competition occurs in such districts, it is most likely to come in primary elections, which feature an ideo-logically extreme sample of voters from a district (Fiorina 2006). In that sense, elections themselves seem to be contributing to the polarization at the elite level.

Of course, even in this polarized time, some members of Congress are more moderate than others. Oftentimes legislators are moderate because their con-stituencies are ideologically balanced between conservatives and liberals, which means their elections will be competitive relative to those hailing from more ideologically homogenous districts. When a significant number of incumbents lose, as was the case in 2006 among Republicans, they tend to be dispropor-tionately moderate. As a result, 2006 witnessed far more Republican losses in places like New York, Connecticut, and Pennsylvania, which are in the most liberal region of the country, than in the South or the Great Plains, which are the most conservative. To the extent that southern Democrats and northeastern

Republicans once served to moderate their party caucuses, the last thirty years has seen the gradual erosion of this tendency.

Polarization of elites has not led to a polarization of opinion among mass partisans, at least in the strict definitional understanding of the word. Instead, these ordinary people have sorted themselves better into the correct party given their existing ideological proclivities (Fiorina 2006; Levendusky forthcoming). To be sure, the average distance between the average Republican and the average Democrat has increased significantly on an increasing number of issues, and mass partisans' opinions are more tightly constrained than before (Abramowitz and Saunders 2008), but opinions on the major issues of the day do not cluster nearer the ideological poles, as they now do in Congress.

Our understanding of what makes the American political system seem so polarized is more subtle than can be captured by measuring differences of means and changes in standard deviations alone. We have shown that on issues that are sure to stir great passion, the preferences of mass partisans have grown more distinct between the parties and homogenous among them. And, importantly, they are structured in large part by a common element, authoritarianism, which connects these sometimes disparate seeming issues.

In this concluding chapter, we will speculate about the implications of an authoritarianism-based political divide. First, we explore how commentators increasingly talk about the parties and their representatives, which we think is the result of this divide. We suggest that this is why the Republicans have become known as the Daddy Party and the Democrats as the Mommy Party. Second, we explore how our work bears on polarization, adopting a less strict definition of it. Most centrally, the visceral quality of the issues that are structured by authoritarianism is critical. But we also believe that a key source of what people perceive to be polarization results from the fact that those who score high and low in authoritarianism simply think about problems differently. Their moral reasoning is often incompatible. This makes it difficult for people on different sides of the political aisle to understand the other side, which undermines the search for common ground. Since these disagreements occur on visceral issues, they have the potential to produce very strong responses.

ON MANLINESS

Differences in interpreting how the world works go far beyond those of programmatic policy disagreements; they go to the heart of the worldview divide we have explicated. And this divide at a basic gut level is informing perceptions of the parties. George Lakoff's (1996) treatment of morality in contemporary American politics tracks helpfully with our analysis in this regard. He views liberalism and conservatism as comparably consistent frameworks for making sense of politics. Lakoff asserts that his schematic conceptions of liberalism and conservatism have increasingly developed into competing models of family. His conception of conservatism, which is premised on a "strict father morality," is closely related to our conception of authoritarianism.

Strict father morality asserts that we live in a dog-eat-dog world, and that coddling is not only a sign of personal weakness but also undermines the social fabric more generally by failing to teach people the skills necessary to survive in life in what is, ultimately, a zero-sum game. Obedience to authority is central to this outlook: straying from legitimate authority can undermine the moral order, unhinging a society's moorings, casting people into anarchy, lethargy, and laziness. Crucial to this worldview are the primacy of fatherly authority and the importance of a traditional family structure.

The other side of the divide is the nurturant parent. Although less well developed as an ideology according to Lakoff (1996), the things that liberals provide – health care, a social safety net, understanding when things go wrong – are consistent with the label. Of course, the descriptions are deeply gendered. Strict fathers are clearly men. Nurturant parents are apparently women.

We believe one manifestation of this frame for political conflict is the starkly gendered nature of contemporary political discourse. For example, in the first chapter, we noted Chris Matthews's characterization of the Republicans as the "Daddy Party" and the Democrats as the "Mommy Party," and Arnold Schwarzenegger's description of Democrats in the California legislature as "girlie men." Such gendered references comport well with the divide we describe.

When it comes to issues in which the public wants toughness, particularly when dealing with foreign threats, Democrats are in a difficult position. Even their resumés appear insufficient to overpower the public's overall view of a "feminine" party. Even though John Kerry was a decorated veteran and despite his call for increasing troop strength in Iraq and Afghanistan, he was widely perceived, as Democrats have generally tended to be since the 1980s, as soft on security matters. Kerry was seen as effeminate because of his poufy "French" hairdo, predilection for windsurfing, and use of big words. Similarly, Al Gore, who volunteered for service in Vietnam while his opponent in the 2000 election never left the United States during his apparently incomplete service, was widely perceived as something less than manly because he took fashion advice from a feminist. This prompted *New York Times* columnist Maureen Dowd to say of Gore that he was "practically lactating," especially when compared with the "charming, limber, cocky, fidgety" George W. Bush.[1] These perceptions apparently owe less to policy stances and background characteristics of the candidates and more to the worldview divide we have described.

Conversely, Bush was celebrated for his manliness, especially once he became president. Of course, Bush made policy choices and used rhetoric that was associated with toughness. Still, the commentary about him, beyond policy

---

[1] In fact, a recent study of Dowd's columns, by the liberal media watchdog Media Matters, revealed that Dowd, perhaps America's most widely quoted op-ed columnist, has frequently characterized Democratic candidates as feminine, with the notable exception of Hillary Clinton, whom Dowd has described as "in touch with her masculine side" and, following a hard-fought primary win in Indiana, as "the Man." (Media Matters 2008).

preferences, was often remarkable and suggestive of how he contrasted with Democratic leaders. Perhaps the most extreme example occurred on May 1, 2003. The president, attired in a fighter pilot suit, landed in a fighter jet on the deck of the USS Abraham Lincoln aircraft carrier and declared "Mission Accomplished" in the Iraq War. On MSNBC that night, the long-time political pundit and former Tip O'Neill aide Chris Matthews gushed about Bush's performance. "We are proud of our president. Americans love having a guy as president, a guy who has a little swagger, who's physical, who's not a complicated guy like Clinton, or even Dukakis or Mondale, all those guys, McGovern. They want a guy who's president" (Greenwald 2008, 140).

A few days later, Matthews asked former Nixon aide and long-time talk radio icon G. Gordon Liddy what he thought of the criticism of the president's appearance. Liddy said: "Well, I – in the first place, I think it's envy. I mean, after all, Al Gore had to go get some woman to tell him how to be a man. And here comes George Bush. You know, he's in his flight suit, he's striding across the deck, and he's wearing his parachute harness, you know – and I've worn those because I parachute – and it makes the best of his manly characteristic" (Greenwald 2008, 143).

Examples of such gendered ascriptions to distinguish Democrats and Republicans abound. Ann Coulter has, for example, opted for a variant of that theme by branding more than one Democratic candidate a "faggot," most notably 2004 vice presidential nominee John Edwards. Especially striking, when it came to the Democratic nomination battle in 2008, it was not only James Carville who questioned the manliness of Democratic candidates not named Hillary Clinton in the 2008 primary campaign. Talk radio giant Rush Limbaugh castigated the Democratic Party in similar terms, intoning: "I mean, where are the real men in the Democratic party? Where are the real men? Hillary Clinton's one of them. But, where are the others?"

Of course, Coulter, Liddy, and Limbaugh make up the most extreme elements of conservative commentary, but they are not fringe players, with tens of millions of combined readers and listeners. Nor is it is not just figures like this who employ such language. Susan Faludi catalogued a number of gendered knocks on Obama from prominent media elites. She wrote:

On MSNBC, Tucker Carlson called Mr. Obama "kind of a wuss"; Joe Scarborough, the morning TV talk show host, dubbed Mr. Obama's bowling style "prissy" and declared, "Americans want their president, if it's a man, to be a real man"; and Don Imus, the radio host ... dubbed Mr. Obama a "sissy boy."[2]

Finally, Maureen Dowd regularly ascribed to Hillary Clinton male-gendered characteristics while viewing other Democrats, notably Obama, as "feminine." Dowd characterized Obama's more conciliatory approach to foreign policy as "Obama [tapping] into his inner chick by turning the other cheek."

[2] Susan Faludi, "Think the Gender War Is Over? Think Again," *New York Times*, June 15, 2008.

Discussion of masculine or feminine attributes suggests that the worldview divide we describe has seeped deep into our political conversation. The frequent feminization of Democrats is not meant to flatter them. This is an arena in which Republicans have gained great advantage over the past generation or so in burnishing their credentials as the tough and credible party on national security. Although George W. Bush's approval ratings ranged from the high twenties to the mid thirties for most of the last three years of his administration and the Republican Party lost both their House and Senate majorities in 2006, the public continued to think highly of Republicans in this area. Specifically, when survey organizations have asked the public which party would do a better job with specific issues ranging from health care to the economy to the environment to terrorism, a plurality has consistently chosen the Democrats since 2005 on every issue except one – protecting the nation from terrorism. Moreover, even in the depths of the Republicans' struggles, their advantage on terrorism has most often been greater than 10 percentage points.

During the 2008 presidential campaign, Charlie Black, John McCain's campaign chairman, caused a stir when he suggested that a terrorist attack on the United States before the election would benefit his candidate. Black was almost certainly correct even though such an attack would have happened under the watch of Bush, a fellow Republican. Beyond Bush's resolute stand against terrorism and the absence of a foreign terrorist attack after September 11, 2001, we suspect a major reason for the Republicans' durable advantage in this area is that when people want protection from a bully, they are more likely to turn to their fathers than to their mothers.

ON POLARIZATION

When scholars and pundits forward explanations for what they term *polarization* on the mass level, ideology and issue stances usually play the central roles (Fiorina 2004; Abramowitz 2007). Objectively speaking, the parties in Washington are, in fact, more distant from one another than they have been in nearly 100 years (Poole, Rosenthal, and McCarty 2006). So, of course, that must have something to do with why people perceive that the political system is more polarized now than before and why journalists often suggest that the public is similarly polarized.

But we are not sure that an ideological or issue-based understanding of the question is the only way to proceed. Certainly the Obama-Clinton split that we detailed in the previous chapter suggests to us that polarized feelings about politics might go far beyond individual issue stances or even ideology. Moreover, we know from decades of behavioral research that few Americans are ideological. Indeed, many are completely "innocent of ideology" (McClosky 1964). And, on the discrete issues of the day, we have known for decades that people are not deeply wedded to their views. Although Converse's (1964) black-white model exaggerates the matter, it is still the case that too many Americans change their issue preferences from time 1 to time 2 to believe that these positions matter much to them. Perhaps, then, ideology and issues are not really the main places to look for evidence of polarization in ordinary Americans.

Indeed, we have a seemingly odd set of circumstances in contemporary American politics. Political elites are polarized on the issues, but ordinary Americans are only better sorted, not polarized (Fiorina et al. 2006), which suggests a large swath of the public ought to be dissatisfied with politics. Although we might expect staunch liberals and conservatives to be overjoyed by polarization in Washington, the roughly 50 percent of Americans who either think of themselves as moderate or who do not think of themselves in ideological terms ought to be turned off. This, however, has not been the case. On nearly every measure of electoral and nonelectoral participation, including voting, persuading others, and expressing interest in politics, moderates and the nonideological have come to participate at higher rates and feel better about the political process as the parties in Washington have become more polarized (Hetherington 2007). If issues were a big concern to these people, then we would expect them to express more anger that neither of the parties is representing them.

Perhaps it would be better to look back further in the causal chain and deeper inside people for indications of how they understand the world and how that maps onto politics. Of course, these considerations are harder to measure and stir more controversy, but this is the approach we have taken. When the political system is divided along authoritarian lines, it is divided, on one level or another, in terms of competing understandings of how the world works and what general approach to problem solving makes the most sense, as well as on fundamental questions of right and wrong.

As we detailed in Chapter 3, there are significant cognitive differences across the authoritarianism distribution. Most important, those who score high tend to view the world in more black and white terms, in which shades of gray ought to be avoided, not embraced. Those who score low tend to embrace those same shades of gray, believing that a black and white view of the world, Occam's razor notwithstanding, is problematically simplistic. As a result, those who score high in authoritarianism will have little patience for nonauthoritarians' hand-wringing tendency to ruminate over nuance and wash out legitimate distinctions in the swamp of relativism. Those who score low in authoritarianism will have little patience for what they perceive to be authoritarians' seeming inability to accommodate subtlety and complexity, to prefer a proverbial anvil to a forceps for even the most delicate and sensitive matters.

One last piece of evidence to suggest those who score high and low in authoritarianism see the world in fundamentally different ways can be found in the data we collected in May 2008 as part of the AmericasBarometer by LAPOP. Specifically, we asked the following question. "In today's world there is a struggle between good and evil. How much do you agree or disagree that such a struggle between good and evil exists?" Respondents were instructed to place themselves on a 7-point scale anchored by strongly disagree at one pole and strongly agree at the other. We thought this question captured well the fundamental competition between a tendency toward black and white thinking on one hand and shades-of-gray thinking on the other. Such understandings of the world, moreover, ought to have political implications.

First, it is worth noting that most Americans tend toward the black and white, consistent with the notion that authoritarianism, at least as we have measured it, is far from a "fringe" view in American political life. Fully 58 percent of respondents placed themselves on the side of the midpoint that endorsed thinking about the world as a struggle between good and evil. In fact, the modal category, occupied by 30 percent of respondents, was to most strongly agree with the statement. This rarely happens when respondents are asked to place themselves on a 7-point scale. Instead, the modal responses are usually found in the middle of the distribution. We see a similar pattern on the other side of the midpoint. Although only about 25 percent of Americans place themselves on the side of the midpoint that disagrees that the world is fundamentally a struggle between good and evil, by far the most highly populated cell at this end of the distribution is the most strongly disagree option. Even the distribution of responses suggests how strongly felt (perhaps polarized) sentiments are.

As we expected, the good versus evil item's correlation with authoritarianism is very strong (r = .35) for survey data such as these. We should add that this relationship is not simply a function of partisanship. Since President Bush has sometimes cast U.S. foreign policy in these terms and since we have shown that authoritarianism is now an important ingredient of party identification, the correlation between the good versus evil worldview and authoritarianism could be spurious. When we take the partial correlation between the items controlling for the 7-point party identification scale, however, the correlation is still .35. While it is true that Republicans are more inclined than Democrats to agree that the world is best understood as a struggle between good and evil, it has no bearing on the latter's relationship with authoritarianism. Importantly, these results also make clear the segment with whom Bush's language most likely resonated.

To provide a clearer sense of what a correlation of this size suggests, we can examine a cross-tabulation of the two variables. For ease of presentation, we collapse authoritarianism into our now familiar three-category measure, with those providing zero or one authoritarian responses to the child-rearing battery classified as low authoritarian, those providing two authoritarian responses classified as middle authoritarian, and those providing three or four authoritarian responses classified as high authoritarian. The results appear in Table 10.1.

As the strong positive correlation suggests, those in the high authoritarian category are much more likely to fall in the strongly agree group that the world is a struggle between good and evil. Among those scoring high in authoritarianism, 40 percent fall into this cell. In contrast, only about 15 percent of those scoring high in authoritarianism placed themselves in any of the three categories on the disagree end of the distribution. Contrast that with those scoring low in authoritarianism. A quarter of them placed themselves in the most

TABLE 10.1. *Thinking about the World as a Struggle between Good and Evil by Authoritarianism,* 2008

Struggle between Good and Evil	Low Auth	Medium Auth	High Auth	Total
1 Strongly Disagree	25	13.0	6	12
2	12	6	3	6
3	10	8	7	8
4	18	20	14	17
5	10	15	15	14
6	9	16	16	14
7 Strongly Agree	17	23	40	30
TOTAL	24	27	49	100

Source: AmericasBarometer by LAPOP, 2008

strongly disagree category, significantly more than any other cell. Indeed nearly 50 percent of those scoring low in authoritarianism placed themselves on the disagree side of the midpoint.

We can also drill down further into the cross-tabulation. Although only 12 percent of respondents strongly disagreed with the good versus evil proposition and although low authoritarians make up only about one-quarter of the population, nearly half of the 182 people who said they strongly disagreed with the notion that the world today was characterized by a struggle between good and evil scored low in authoritarianism. The basic pattern holds for those who placed themselves at 2 on the 7-point scale as well. Conversely, even though nearly 50 percent of respondents score high in authoritarianism, they make up only about a fifth of responses in the two most extreme disagreement categories.

We find the opposite pattern at the other end of the "good versus evil" distribution. Those scoring low in authoritarianism are much less likely to place themselves at 6 or 7, suggesting strong agreement with the proposition. Although those scoring low in authoritarianism make up about a quarter of the population, they make up less than 15 percent of the cases in the two most strongly agree categories. Those scoring high in authoritarianism are much more likely to see the world in good versus evil terms relative to their numbers in the population. Although they make up a shade less than half the population, high authoritarians make up fully two-thirds of the cases in the most "strongly agree" category.

It is also possible that those scoring at opposite ends of the authoritarianism distribution tend to engage in different, and often incompatible, forms of moral reasoning. By moral reasoning, we mean answering fundamental questions about right and wrong. Piaget's (1932/1965) seminal work on cognitive development suggested that children go through a period early in life when respect for adult authority and rules is centrally important in organizing their emerging moral code. This period, however, ultimately gives way to more mature understandings of rules, in which children rely less on parental authority and more on the norms of reciprocity and fairness that develop among peers (for an outstanding review of this literature, see Haidt 2008). Kohlberg (1969) extended Piaget's work in a direction that might be helpful in understanding the polarization that we argue exists. Specifically, he suggested that children evolve through several different stages of moral development, but, of central import, not all people achieve all of the stages of development. The most basic stage is preconventional morality where children perceive the rightness or wrongness of their actions in terms of anticipated punishments. This is followed by the conventional stage. Here perceptions of right and wrong are driven by what the rules of society are. These two stages, particularly the second, seem to mesh with the portrait of authoritarianism we have sketched throughout the book.

According to Kohlberg (1969), many adolescents fail to reach the later postconventional stages of moral development. For those who do, rules about right and wrong are no longer just set by society but are rather justified and understood in terms of more abstract and universal principals. Given their apparent emphasis on abstractions like civil liberties and nondiscrimination, those who score low in authoritarianism likely make up a disproportionate share of those who progress to these more advanced stages of moral reasoning. Hence, whereas someone who has achieved only the conventional stage of moral development might not understand why gay people could possibly be allowed to marry since societal rules dictate that they should not, someone in the postconventional stage might feel the reverse just as strongly, believing that all people, no matter their orientation, ought to able to marry if that is what they desire. Happiness, even if it bucked societal norms, might be viewed as a universal principle that is more valuable than a societal rule.

The treatment of morality by a number of evolutionary psychologists challenges Kohlberg's understanding, but the implications of this research is the same as it relates to understanding polarization in our work. Evolutionary psychologists make a distinction between opinions and behaviors that are driven by automatic processes in the brain, which humans developed long ago in the evolutionary cycle, and processes that humans can control better with their cognitive tools because such processes developed more recently. Bargh et al. (1996) find that a range of morally relevant behaviors, including things like altruism and racism, result from automatic processes that people have little to no control over. As for understanding polarization, their work suggests that when politics divides people along the cleavage that we have described, people with the opposing worldviews we have sketched may not be able to comprehend how their political adversaries understand what is right and wrong. Moreover, since automatic processes in the brain likely govern these opinions and behaviors, it might not be possible for people to understand the moral code that their adversaries are living by. To us, this is the final piece of the polarization puzzle. The differences between Republicans and Democrats have come to *feel* irreconcilable.

In sum, those who score high and low in authoritarianism apparently see the world in fundamentally different ways. We suspect that this has a profound effect on how people make sense of political stimuli. We turn next to two examples from contemporary American politics that we think illustrate the point well.

HOW DIFFERENT WORLDVIEWS MATTER
TO POLARIZATION CLAIMS

The first example we draw on to illustrate our understanding of the basis for polarization is the response to Barack Obama's speech on race, delivered in Philadelphia, Pennsylvania, on March 18, 2008. Obama was pressed to give this speech because of the controversy involving his pastor and spiritual advisor, the Reverend Jeremiah Wright, after several of Wright's controversial sermons entered the public domain. The most incendiary comment was Wright's suggestion that the United States bore much of the responsibility for the September 11 terrorist attacks, an example of, in Wright's words, "the chickens coming home to roost." In addition, he expressed the belief that the U.S. government might be behind the spread of the AIDS virus in the African American community. Seen as anti-American by most observers, these statements put Obama in a box. He needed to repudiate the views, but he was reluctant to repudiate the Reverend himself because of their close relationship and the possible risk of alienating many black churchgoers. The compromise was Obama's race speech delivered in Philadelphia about a month before the Pennsylvania primary.

To some, perhaps even most, in the chattering class, the speech was a remarkable triumph. For example, on MSNBC, contributor Eugene Robinson termed the speech "amazing," Rachel Maddow "historic," and anchor Chris Matthews that it was "worthy of Abraham Lincoln." On CNN, anchor Campbell Brown termed it a "remarkable exploration of race," and contributor David Gergen described it as the "best political speech during this campaign." Brown also referenced the fact that Charles Murray, co-author of *The Bell Curve* – a controversial book that suggested blacks had, on average, lower native intelligence than whites, called the speech "flat out brilliant." Quality aside, there is no doubt that it was a subtle and complex speech. It did not present race in concrete terms but rather as full of different hues.

Yet one particular passage in the speech caused significant controversy for several days and is illustrative of how possessing an authoritarian or nonauthoritarian worldview might have an important effect on the interpretation of new information. Obama allowed that Wright had said controversial things in his presence, but that, at his core, he was a good man who had never said anything derogatory about any ethnic or racial group. Moreover, Obama noted, Wright's church embodied views that traversed the entire range of the black community. To Obama, the issue of Wright himself and race in general was complicated. He went on to say:

I can no more disown him than I can disown the black community. I can no more dis-own him than I can my white grandmother – a woman who helped raise me, a woman who sacrificed again and again for me, a woman who loves me as much as she loves anything in this world, but a woman who once confessed her fear of black men who passed by her on the street, and who on more than one occasion has uttered racial or ethnic stereotypes that made me cringe.

Obama apparently hoped to use his grandmother's experience as an illustration that he believed anyone could relate to – a person of a certain generation who said some things about race that she might not be proud of. But in Obama's view, those words or those views did not necessarily render a person defective. Certainly this was the way that Keith Olbermann, host of MSNBC's *Countdown*, interpreted the passage. Olbermann is perhaps the most unabash-edly liberal voice on cable television and, based on the opinions he expresses on the show regarding gays and lesbians, immigration, torture, and Bill O'Reilly, someone who likely scores very low in authoritarianism. Drawing on his own personal experience with the explosive issue of race, he related the following personal anecdote and analysis the day after the Philadelphia race speech.

My father, a firefighter, put himself in danger to save people, didn't care who they were. His parents were immigrants to this country, and they came to New York, you know, in the late 1800s. They're still naive, they told him, don't touch a black person, the color will come off on your hands. And one night, I was nine years old, my parents were out to dinner, he was baby sitting me, television's on, and, you know, the middle of *Hawaii Five-O* or ... whatever the show was, on comes the news bulletin from Memphis, Martin Luther King assassinated. And my grandfather who was a good man says, why did they interrupt my show to tell me about some "N" word getting shot?

And it went right through me because I know who Martin Luther King was, you know, I was like nine, and now, I knew about my grandfather. I can't talk to him about race relations and if we start talking who is the best ball player, Willie Mays or Mickey Mantle? I can't trust his answer. But I didn't love him any less and I couldn't throw him under a bus somewhere. *I'm just wondering, as complicated as this whole story is, did Obama bringing his own grandmother's prejudices into this thing suddenly make the whole issue amazingly simple?* (emphasis added)

The nonauthoritarian exemplar Olbermann sees Obama's use of his own grandmother's unattractive racial stereotyping as an effective way of advanc-ing the complicated dialogue on race.

That is not the way Ann Coulter, likely an exemplar of those scoring high in authoritarianism, interpreted the same passage. Although Coulter expressed concerns about the entire speech, she saved her strongest words for Obama's treatment of his grandmother, in her syndicated column titled, "Throwing Grandmother under the Bus." Coulter wrote,

Discrimination has become so openly accepted that – in a speech meant to tamp down his association with a black racist – Obama felt perfectly comfortable throwing his white grandmother under the bus. He used her as the white racist counterpart to his black racist "old uncle"; Rev. Wright.

First of all, Wright is not Obama's uncle. The only reason we indulge crazy uncles is that everyone understands that people don't choose their relatives the way they choose, for example, their pastors and mentors. No one quarrels with the idea that you can't be expected to publicly denounce your blood relatives.

But Wright is not a relative of Obama's at all. Yet Obama cravenly compared Wright's racist invective to his actual grandmother, who "once confessed her fear of black men who passed by her on the street, and who on more than one occasion has uttered racial or ethnic stereotypes that made me cringe."

Rev. Wright accuses white people of inventing AIDS to kill black men, but Obama's grandmother – who raised him, cooked his food, tucked him in at night, and paid for his clothes and books and private school – has expressed the same feelings about passing black men on the street that Jesse Jackson has.

Unlike his "uncle" – who is not his uncle – Obama had no excuses for his grandmother. Obama's grandmother never felt the lash of discrimination! Crazy grandma doesn't get the same pass as the crazy uncle; she's white. Denounce the racist!

The view is fundamentally different, and our sense is that it is not just the usual hyper-partisanship Coulter routinely engages in to sell books. Rather than seeing Obama's admission about his grandmother as something that might cause racial healing, Coulter interpreted it as treasonous. We should add that Coulter's view on the matter was not isolated, although it was much more pointed than the opinions expressed by others. A search of the Vanderbilt Television News archive revealed that all the major networks devoted time to this passage of the race speech between March 18, the date of the speech, and March 20.

March 20 is significant because a secondary racial controversy sprang up after Obama attempted to quell the firestorm about his grandmother. Again, it is revealing how different people process the same information differently. That morning, Obama appeared on 610 WIP, a Philadelphia radio station. In attempting to explain why he made the reference in the speech, he suggested that racial stereotypes exist even among good people like his grandmother. He said his "point was not that she harbors any racial animosity; she doesn't." But in reacting cautiously toward people of color she does not know, Obama described his grandmother as "a typical white person." On his Friday radio show, Rush Limbaugh summed up his take on Obama's treatment of his grandmother as follows: "Obama threw his grandmother under the bus in his speech on Tuesday, and yesterday he put the bus in reverse and ran over her."

People we suspect score high in authoritarianism apparently failed to appreciate the nuance that a person, especially one of a certain age, could think and talk in racial and ethnic stereotypes and still, in Obama's mind, not be a racist. Instead, a controversy erupted because those with this view believed that Obama meant to suggest that all white people were racists because "typical white people" sometimes think stereotypically about blacks. This controversy illustrates how difficult it is to find common ground when people approach an issue using such different lenses. Add to it that the issue is race, one that is deeply felt and potentially explosive, and it makes finding common ground all the more difficult, even when, apparently, common ground is what a politician is trying to find.

The same understanding, or perhaps misunderstanding, is evident in how to deal with terrorism and world affairs. Two companion op-ed pieces that appeared in the *Wall Street Journal* in May 2008 illustrate the point. The first, written by former Democrat and now independent senator Joe Lieberman is titled "Democrats and Our Enemies." The second, written two days later by soon to be Democratic vice presidential nominee, Senator Joe Biden (D-Del.), is titled "Republicans and Our Enemies." Senator Lieberman argues that the Democratic Party (with which he still caucuses) has lost its way. The party of FDR and Truman was once "unhesitatingly and proudly pro-American, a party that was unafraid to make moral judgments about the world beyond our borders." That party, which through the time of JFK pledged to unhesitatingly "pay any price, bear any burden" to support our friends and oppose our foes, no longer exists.

"This worldview," as Lieberman himself calls it, began to come apart in the late 1960s, when a view of America took root in the Democratic Party that saw our country as "morally bankrupt" and an "imperialist power whose militarism and 'inordinate fear of communism' represented the real threat to world peace." After a return to a more courageous foreign policy under Bill Clinton, everything changed after 9/11. Democratic leaders adopted a peace-at-any-price posture, failing to understand the true nature of the threat that President Bush saw clearly that fateful day: "a direct ideological and military attack on us and our way of life." In his failure to understand his own party's proud tradition, Obama stands in stark contrast to John McCain, who understands the "difference between America's friends and America's enemies." For Lieberman, the blindness of Obama and the Democratic Party to this basic distinction is nothing less than a matter of our survival as a people.

Biden's response argued that Lieberman had it backward – that the great tradition of FDR, Truman, and JFK is divorced not from Obama but from the course of President Bush, John McCain, and Senator Lieberman. Like Lieberman, Biden sees 9/11 as a pivotal moment. But it represents something far different for Biden than for Lieberman. For Biden, 9/11 represented an opportunity to "unite Americans and the world in common cause." Bush failed to embrace that opportunity – instead "exploiting the politics of fear," while choosing an "optional war" in Iraq, instituting policies on torture that contradict American values, and dividing Americans from each other and the world.

For Biden, the "heart of this failure is an obsession with the 'war on terrorism' that ignores larger forces shaping the world," including the emergence of new great powers like China, the "spread of lethal weapons and dangerous diseases," and a host of other issues: from uncertain energy supplies to the persistence of poverty, ethnic conflict, state failure, climate change, and more. In short, Lieberman believes that the problems facing America are simple and straightforward – we live in a world divided into our friends and enemies. Our failure to act in a tough and decisive manner in the face of that clear, incontrovertible reality spells our doom. The left's constant harping on our own shortcomings only prevents it from confronting the true nature of the threats that we face.

By contrast, Biden, who voted for the 2002 resolution authorizing force in Iraq and has long been considered a national security Democrat, sees the challenges facing America as multilayered and complex. For him, failure to see the world in its complexity and insistence on "saber-rattling" is the "most self-defeating policy imaginable." Senator Lieberman's journey from liberal Democrat in the early 1970s to moderate in the 1980s to a cast-off in 2006, to an outsider looking in at his own former party in 2008 is just a single example. But it powerfully encapsulates the worldview-based differences that provide contemporary American politics its unique nature.

A FINAL WORD

Considering our story up to now, we believe we have adduced powerful evidence for the increasingly central role that authoritarianism has come to play in structuring party competition, mass preferences, and the relevant issue agenda of the past forty years. Never since at least the dawning of the survey era has there been such fundamental clarity and distinction between the two parties on such a wide range of issues organized around a particular worldview. Beginning in the late 1960s, our political system began a transformation that, in fits and starts but inexorably, produced a picture in increasingly sharp resolution – one in which the division between people's fundamental outlooks became refracted onto a landscape of increasingly irreconcilable political differences.

We do not mean to suggest that all of American politics can be understood through this lens now or that this cleavage line will continue to divide mass partisans long into the future. As Layman and Carsey (2002) have persuasively argued, American politics is experiencing an era characterized by conflict extension, in which multiple and seemingly cross-cutting dimensions all divide Republicans from Democrats, rather than one issue cleavage completely displacing another. And, as is always the case, different contexts tend to make different considerations more important. The ingredients of party identification and vote choice, for example, were surely much different in 1992 and 2004. Specifically, the economy, in large measure because of the efforts of Bill Clinton's campaign, made it centrally important to voting behavior in 1992. But with the war on terrorism three years old and the war in Iraq 20 months along, the economy did much less to affect politics in 2004. In 2016, something altogether different may have arisen to reorient politics in ways that we could not hope to forecast now.

In understanding the nature and intensity of political conflict in early twenty-first century America, however, the concept of authoritarianism is indispensable. No single issue could have accomplished such clarity and sorting on its own. Instead, a series of issues, beginning with the extraordinarily powerful and disruptive racial transformation of the 1960s, through to the catastrophic attacks of September 11, and including the rise of gay rights and immigration as issues of significant import, have filled in the political landscape, giving it its current incandescent colors and clear lines of demarcation.

Epilogue

THE 2008 GENERAL ELECTION

Barack Obama's victory in 2008 was historic as he became the first African American to be elected president. Moreover, his triumph over John McCain was substantial both in terms of the popular vote, which he won by more than 7 percentage points, and the electoral college vote, which he carried by 364 to 174. We think that authoritarianism likely played an important role in this outcome, although data are not available at the time of this writing to test our hypotheses rigorously. Certainly the themes raised in the fall campaign often mirrored those from the primary campaign between Obama and Hillary Clinton. And, as we showed in Chapter 9, that intraparty Democratic campaign made authoritarianism a significant dividing line. Moreover, the electoral map and the pattern of support for the candidates further suggest its importance.

As for the party standard-bearers, John McCain, at first glance, would not seem the best vessel for a campaign organized around issues structured by authoritarianism. Although his voting record is conservative, he has often bucked the party line. He was long associated with moderate positions on immigration, gay rights, and the use of torture. In fact, McCain's credentials among the most conservative elements of his party were suspect enough to have raised serious doubts among elite opinion makers, like Rush Limbaugh and Ann Coulter, about his fitness to be the candidate. But given the apparent importance of the party's base in shaping electoral strategy, it appears that his campaign's decision to highlight Obama's "otherness" and to question his ability to protect America was, if not inevitable, certainly the most likely outcome.

As we argued in Chapter 9 with regard to the primary, Democrat Barack Obama exuded a temperament consistent with a nonauthoritarian world-view – a tendency to see issues as complex, an aversion to dividing the universe into black and white categories, and a message of inclusiveness that celebrated America's growing diversity. To be clear, Obama's intensely passionate supporters certainly viewed the presidential election as a life and death matter, and many did not refrain from vitriol in characterizing Republicans. The point is, however, that what was most notable about Obama – both his complicated racial and ethnic background and his temperamental inclination toward nuance and complexity – would have been manna for nonauthoritarians as much as it was anathema to his more authoritarian detractors.

CAMPAIGN THEMES

In our necessarily brief analysis of the 2008 campaign, we do not attempt to assess the tone of the McCain campaign relative to Obama's or others in recent memory. At least one analysis of the 2008 campaign actually suggests that it was Obama who ran more and a higher percentage of negative campaign ads than McCain (Geer and Vavreck 2009). That commentators in 2008 tended to see McCain as the more negative probably suggests that the media really did favor Obama in some respects and that the issues that McCain attacked Obama on were of a different quality – more visceral, perhaps polarizing. Moreover, in assessing the McCain campaign's decisions, it is important to bear in mind just how desperate its situation was in 2008, with the party having presided over an increasingly unpopular war in Iraq for more than five years and a looming financial crisis with no obvious solutions. Political campaigns are tasked with winning elections. In 2008, survey data suggested that the public thought the Bush administration had failed and was ready for a change. Hence, the best hope for the GOP was to increase people's fears about what such a change might mean.

Particularly after John McCain chose as his running mate Governor Sarah Palin (R-Alaska), an evangelical Christian whose main appeal was to the conservative base of the party, the kinds of messages consistent with an authoritarian worldview became central to his campaign. Picking up where Hillary Clinton left off in the primaries, perhaps the key question that the McCain campaign raised was "Who is Barack Obama?" – a question that spoke directly to concerns about Obama's "exotic" background. One controversial McCain advertisement dismissed Obama as a "celebrity" and linked him to various Hollywood icons, including two white female stars known for their sexual exploits, Britney Spears and Paris Hilton.

The contrast to Obama's exoticness as well as the racially diverse nature of his electoral coalition is what the campaign characterized as "real" citizens. This thrust took at least three forms. An example of the first occurred at a mid-October fund-raiser in Greensboro, North Carolina. Governor Palin said to the crowd, "We believe that the best of America is in the small towns that we get to visit, and in the wonderful little pockets of what I call the real America, being here with all of you hard-working, very patriotic, very pro-America areas of this great nation." The next day, top McCain aide, Nancy Pfotenhauer followed up the theme on MSNBC in describing the race in Virginia. "I can tell you that the Democrats have just come in from the District of Columbia and moved into northern Virginia. And that's really what you see there. But the rest of the state, real Virginia, if you will, I think will be very responsive to Sen. McCain's message." Of course, this tack suggests that Obama and his followers were less real, less patriotic, and hence a potential threat to the American way of life.

The second part of the case against Obama's "American-ness" played on his relationship with William Ayers. Ayers, a university professor, aided Obama's political rise in Chicago. In the late 1960s and early 1970s, however, Ayers was a member of an organization called the Weather Underground, a domestic terrorist organization that went as far as to detonate a bomb in the U.S. Capitol among its acts against the government. Although Ayers had not been linked to radicalism for several decades, his extreme anti-government views in the 1960s and 1970s and his association with Obama were brought into sharp relief on the stump. In the early weeks of October, for example, Palin accused Obama of "palling around with terrorists."

Finally, Republican operatives, particularly late in the campaign, accused Obama of being a socialist and reminded audiences at campaign events and fund-raisers that Obama's middle name was Hussein, indirectly suggesting as the Clinton campaign had done that he was a Muslim. Similar efforts went beyond the presidential campaigns themselves. Republican Party literature from California, New Mexico, and Virginia painted Obama alternatively as a terrorist and a food stamp recipient. In Missouri, Senator Kit Bond mocked Obama's preferences for Supreme Court justices in the following terms: "Just this past week, we saw what Barack Obama said about judges. He said, 'I'm tired of these judges who want to follow what the Founding Fathers said and the Constitution. I want judges who have a heart, have an empathy for the teenage mom, the minority, the gay, the disabled. We want them to show empathy. We want them to show compassion."

At least to a small sliver of people, this strategy appeared to bring emotions to a fevered pitch. On two occasions, first in Florida and next in Pennsylvania, newspaper reports suggested that a person at a Palin rally shouted "kill him" when Obama's name was uttered. According to a post-election report from *Newsweek*, the Secret Service had to alert the Obama family in October to a spike in threats against the candidate.

The thread that plausibly ties these strands together is that they all plausibly tap into authoritarianism. In fact, among the noteworthy elements of the 2008 campaign was the degree to which many of the most potent messages of the past four decades – terrorism, socialism, patriotism, sex education, liberalism – were introduced at one point or another, which we suspect was driven by an understandably desperate effort by the McCain campaign to compete as the economy deteriorated.[1]

---

[1] In a provocative *LA Times* op-ed shortly after the election, Neal Gabler suggested that the roots of the modern Republican Party were not, as so many have asserted, Goldwaterism. Rather, he argued, it was Joseph McCarthy and his related themes of anticommunism, intolerance, and even homophobia that laid the foundation for contemporary GOP political appeals.

THE OUTCOME

Although the economic collapse that began to take hold in late 2008 was surely the most important issue of the campaign, most of the changes in the electoral map square well with the story we have woven throughout the book. Obama held all the states that Kerry had won in 2004 while nine states that had backed George W. Bush moved to the Democratic column in 2008. As we highlighted in Chapter 8, the Republican position on illegal immigration, which was driven by a party base attracted by issues structured by authoritarianism, undermined its usual hegemony in states with large and growing Latino populations. Indeed, four of Obama's pickups occurred in Nevada, New Mexico, Colorado, and Florida, all states with Latino populations above the national average. According to exit poll data, Latinos gave Obama 67 percent of their vote compared with 31 percent for McCain. Recall that in 2004, Bush received at least 40 percent of the Latino vote and maybe more. Moreover, in places like Nevada and New Mexico, the Latino vote was decisive, with Obama doing particularly well with this group, winning 76 percent of the Latino vote in Nevada and 69 percent in New Mexico.

He also picked up two states in the former Confederacy, Virginia and North Carolina. Importantly, both have experienced marked demographic changes over the last two decades leading to much higher levels of education and income. Heavy turnout and big Obama margins in Northern Virginia and the Research Triangle in North Carolina – areas that Judis and Teixeira (2002) refer to as "ideopolises" because of their emphasis on education and high-tech industries – were part of a larger trend. Since those who score low in authoritarianism score high in education and income, we should see as part of the worldview evolution we have described a marked increase in Democratic voting among upper income and education groups. In fact, we do in 2008.

Although those with graduate educations have disproportionately supported Democratic candidates for decades, George W. Bush continued a trend in 2004 among those who reported either graduating from college or having attended some college, winning by better than 5 percentage points. In 2008, however, Obama actually won a narrow victory among those groups, and his edge among those with a graduate education increased from 11 to 18 points. We find an even more striking change with income. Those with high incomes supported Bush in big numbers in 2004 as he won by greater than 15 percentage points in 2004 among those earning more than $100,000 a year. In 2008, Obama and McCain ran to a statistical dead heat among those earning over $100,000, and Obama actually won a narrow plurality among those earning over $200,000. We suspect that these voters, who are usually attracted to the Republicans on redistribution, came to weigh more heavily the incompatibility of their positions with the Republicans' on the issues we have described throughout, as the party's management of economic matters came into question. Indeed, conservative *New York Times* columnist, David Brooks, repeatedly criticized the "anti-intellectualism" of the Republican

Party during the campaign, referring to Palin, whose qualifications to serve as vice president came into question after a series of gaffe-filled interviews, as a "fatal cancer."

With the exception of the states affected by Latino migration, the electoral map bears a remarkable resemblance to those produced in elections around the turn of the twentieth century except that the Democrats now dominate the population centers (what scholars of American political development called the Metropole) and the Republicans dominate the more rural areas (the periphery). Of course, the beginning of this electoral era was dominated by the response to the Civil War and Reconstruction as well as U.S. involvement in the Spanish-American war, obviously issues that might be organized by the same kind of worldview as issues like immigration, gay rights, the proper response to terrorism, and the war in Iraq in early twenty-first-century America.

Given what we have described as the potency of such appeals, it begs the question: why didn't those scoring high in authoritarianism offset the apparent gains Democrats made with those who score low despite their emphasis on such appeals? Chapter 6 explains why such appeals are often successful, yet they could not prevent an impressive Democratic victory. We suspect that several things short-circuited the effect of authoritarianism-structured appeals that have traditionally been successful in peeling away lower middle-class white Democrats from their party's candidate.

First, perceived threat is important in determining whether people's preferences on these issues move to the right. Those who score high in authoritarianism will tend to have conservative preferences on issues structured by authoritarianism regardless. But those who score in the middle of the distribution or lower might have more liberal preferences when they feel less threat and more conservative ones when they feel more. As a result, the potency of issues like terrorism was likely on the wane by 2008. On terrorism, arguably one of the great successes of the Bush administration was the fact that it had kept the American homeland safe from foreign terror attacks after September 11, 2001. It is natural that Americans, as a consequence, might have felt much less threatened by world terrorism than they had four years earlier. Hence, they might have been more inclined to find the Republicans' position on related issues less attractive.

Second, we argued in Chapter 10 that people will not always make decisions based on authoritarian-structured issues if other factors become more pressing. While the kinds of appeals that have helped Republicans succeed over the past forty years represent a significant development in American political history, they emerged at a time of relative prosperity. To be sure, economic inequality has been growing since the 1970s. But, particularly as discount stores like Wal-Mart came to dominate the marketplace and credit became much easier to secure, even those toward the bottom of the income ladder could own giant televisions, drive spiffy cars, and generally have access to the accoutrements of mainstream consumerism. We believe such changes allowed appeals on issues for which preferences are structured by authoritarianism to provide a compelling basis for voting behavior much further down the income ladder than might otherwise be expected.

September 2008, however, witnessed a major financial meltdown described by many analysts as the most serious since the Great Depression. People, particularly those of moderate means, perhaps no longer felt the luxury of making political decisions on noneconomic grounds. In that sense, it might be useful to think of authoritarianism as a post-materialism of the right for those who score high in the worldview. Amidst a bursting housing bubble, a collapsing financial system, high gas prices, and the looming prospect of a sea change in Americans' living standards, the issues we have described throughout this book simply packed less punch. Exit poll data seem to bear out our contention. In 2008, voters earning under $50,000 a year, a group that would disproportionately feel economic anxiety from the downturn, gave McCain only 38 percent of their votes compared with 44 percent in both the Bush victories. We believe these voters no longer felt they could vote against what in many cases was probably their economic self-interest. Doubts about whether Obama was a true American likely mattered less than if people thought he would have more success fixing the economy.

Third, Obama received some high-profile support from sources well positioned to thwart such attacks, perhaps most notably Colin Powell. Powell, both a former chairman of the Joint Chiefs of Staff and former secretary of state in the administration of President George W. Bush, spoke with deep emotion about the attacks on Obama as an "Arab." On the morning he announced that he would be voting for Obama, just over two weeks before election day, Powell told Tom Brokaw on *Meet the Press*:

I'm also troubled by, not what Senator McCain says, but what members of the party say. And it is permitted to be said such things as, "Well, you know that Mr. Obama is a Muslim." Well, the correct answer is, he is not a Muslim, he's a Christian. He's always been a Christian. But the really right answer is, what if he is? Is there something wrong with being a Muslim in this country? The answer's no, that's not America. Is there something wrong with some seven-year-old Muslim-American kid believing that he or she could be president? Yet, I have heard senior members of my own party drop the suggestion, "He's a Muslim and he might be associated with terrorists." This is not the way we should be doing it in America.

Did John McCain fight the last war, then, in his decision to pick Palin and adopt a play-to-the-base strategy? Perhaps. But an ideological and political infrastructure constructed over many years, particularly one that had yielded great success, is likely not amenable to dramatic change overnight. That is why the worldview evolution we have described here proved so politically relevant in 2008. Even when a different approach might have been warranted – for example, taking advantage of McCain's reputation for relative moderation and demonstrated ability to compromise with Democrats during a time when the public craved moderation and bipartisanship – such alternatives were hard to pursue.

Bibliography

Abrajano, Marisa A., Jonathan Nagler, and R. Michael Alvarez. 2005. "A Natural Experiment of Race-Based and Issue Voting: The 2001 City of Los Angeles Elections." *Political Research Quarterly* 58: 203–218.

Abramowitz, Alan. 2007. "Disconnected or Joined at the Hip?" In Pietro S. Nivola and David W. Brady, eds., *Red and Blue Nation? Characteristics and Causes of America's Polarized Politics, Vol. 1*. Washington, DC: Brookings Institution Press, pp. 72–84.

2008. "Rejoinder." In Pietro S. Nivola and David W. Brady, eds., *Red and Blue Nation? Characteristics and Causes of America's Polarized Politics, Vol. 2*. Washington, DC: Brookings Institution Press.

Abramowitz, Alan I. and Kyle L. Saunders. 1998. "Ideological Realignment in the U.S. Electorate." *Journal of Politics* 60: 634–652.

Abramowitz, Alan and Kyle L. Saunders. 2008. "Is Polarization a Myth?" *Journal of Politics* 70: 542–555.

Abramowitz, Alan I. and Walter J. Stone. 2006. "The Bush Effect: Polarization, Turnout, and Activism in the 2004 Presidential Election." *Presidential Studies Quarterly* 36: 141–154.

Adams, Greg. 1997. "Abortion: Evidence of an Issue Evolution." *American Journal of Political Science* 41 (3): 718–737.

Adorno, Theodor, E. Frenkel-Brunswick, D. Levinson, and N. Sanford. 1950. *The Authoritarian Personality*. New York: Harper and Row.

Aldrich, John H. 1995. *Why Parties? The Origin and Transformation of Party Politics in America*. Chicago: University of Chicago Press.

Aldrich, John H. and David W. Rohde. 2000. "The Republican Revolution and the House Appropriations Committee." *Journal of Politics* 62: 1–33.

Altemeyer, Robert. 2006. *The Authoritarians*. Online: theauthoritarians.com.

2007. *The Authoritarians*. Self-published manuscript, available at http://members. shaw.ca/jeanaltemeyer/drbob/TheAuthoritarians.pdf.

1996. *The Authoritarian Specter*. Cambridge: Harvard University Press.

2001. "Changes in Attitudes toward Homosexuals." *Journal of Homosexuality* 42: 63–75.

1988. *Enemies of Freedom: Understanding Right-Wing Authoritarianism*. San Francisco: Jossey-Bass.

1981. *Right-Wing Authoritarianism*. Winnipeg: University of Manitoba Press.

Ansolabehere, Steven, Jonathan Rodden, and James M. Snyder Jr. 2006. "Purple America." *Journal of Economic Perspectives* 20: 97–118.

Bacevich, Andrew J. 2002. *American Empire: The Realities and Consequences of American Diplomacy*. Cambridge, MA: Harvard University Press.

Bargh, John A., Mark Chen, and Lara Burrows. 1996. "Automaticity of Social Behavior: Direct Effects of Trait Construct and Stereotype Activation on Action." *Journal of Personality and Social Psychology* 71: 230–244.

Barker, David and James D. Tinnick. 2006. "Competing Visions of Parental Roles and Ideological Constraint'" *American Political Science Review* 100: 249–263.

Barone, Michael. 2001. "49 Percent Nation." *National Journal* 33: 1710–1716.

Bartels, Larry M. 2002. "Beyond the Running Tally: Partisan Bias in Political Perceptions." *Political Behavior* 24: 117–150.

2006. "What's the Matter with What's the Matter with Kansas." *Quantitative Journal of Political Science* 1: 201–226.

Beinart, Peter. 2007. "When Politics No Longer Stops at the Water's Edge: Partisanship and Foreign Policy." In Pietro Nivola and David Brady, eds., *Red and Blue Nation: Characteristics and Causes of America's Polarized Politics, Vol. 2*. Washington DC: Brookings Institution Press.

Biden, Joseph. 2008. "Republicans and Our Enemies." *Wall Street Journal*, May 23, p. A19.

Bishop, Bill. 2008. *The Big Sort: Why the Clustering of Like-Minded America Is Tearing Us Apart*. Boston: Houghton Mifflin.

Bolce, Louis and Gerald De Maio. 1999. "Religious Outlook, Culture War Politics, and Antipathy toward Christian Fundamentalists." *Public Opinion Quarterly* 63: 29–61.

Bowman, Karlyn and Adam Foster. 2006. "Attitudes about Homosexuality and Gay Marriage." *AEI Studies in Public Opinion*. Available online at www.aei.org.

Brewer, Paul R. 2003. "The Shifting Foundations of Public Opinion about Gay Rights." *Journal of Politics* 65: 1208–1220.

Value War: Public Opinion and the Politics of Gay Rights. Lanham, MD: Rowman and Littlefield.

Broder, John S. 1999. "Gay and Lesbian Group Offers Thanks to Clinton." *New York Times*. October 4, 1999.

Bullock, Charles S. 1975. "The Election of Blacks in the South: Preconditions and Consequences." *American Journal of Political Science* 19: 727–739.

1984. "Racial Crossover Voting and the Election of Black Officials." *Journal of Politics* 46: 238–251.

Burnham, Walter Dean. 1970. *Critical Elections and the Mainsprings of American Politics*. New York: W.W. Norton.

Burns, Peter F. and James G. Gimpel. 2000. "Prejudice, Economic Insecurity, and Immigration Policy." *Political Studies Quarterly* 115: 201–225.

Campbell, Angus, Philip E. Converse, Warren E. Miller, and Donald E. Stokes. 1960. *American Voter*. New York: Wiley.

Campbell, David and J. Quin Monson. 2007. "The Case of Bush's Reelection: Did Gay Marriage Do It?" In David E. Campbell, ed., *A Matter of Faith: Religion in the 2004 Presidential Election*. Washington, DC: Brookings Institution Press.

Carmines, Edward G. and James A. Stimson. 1981. "Issue Evolution, Population Replacement, and Normal Partisan Change." *American Political Science Review* 75: 107–118.

  1989. *Issue Evolution: Race and the Transformation of American Politics*. Princeton, NJ: Princeton University Press.

  1986. "The Structure and Sequence of Issue Evolution." *American Political Science Review* 80: 901–920.

  1980. "The Two Faces of Issue Voting." *American Political Science Review* 74: 78–91.

Carsey, Thomas M. and Geoffrey C. Layman. 2006. "Changing Sides or Changing Minds? Party Identification and Policy Preferences in the U.S. Electorate." *American Journal of Political Science*. 50: 464–477.

Carter, Dan T. 1996. *From George Wallace to Newt Gingrich: Race in the Conservative Counterrevolution, 1963–1994*. Baton Rouge: Louisiana State University Press.

Citrin, Jack, Donald P. Green, Christopher Muste, and Cara Wong. 1997. "Public Opinion toward Immigration Reform: The Role of Economic Motivations." *Journal of Politics* 59: 858–881.

Clinton, Hillary. 2007. "Comments before the United States Senate Committee on Armed Services." April 27. Transcript.

Converse, Philip. 1964. "The Nature of Belief Systems in Mass Publics." In David E. Apter, ed., *Ideology and Discontent*. London: Free Press of Glencoe, pp. 206–261.

Cooper, Marc. 2006. "The Minutemen Hit the Wall." *The Nation*, October 23, 2006.

Coulter, Ann. 2008. "Throwing Grandmother under the Bus." *New Republic*, March 18, 2008.

Council on Foreign Relations. 2007. "Republican Debate, South Carolina." May 15. Transcript. Available online at http://www.cfr.org/publication/13338/ Accessed: June 25, 2008.

Dahl, Robert A. 1976. *Democracy in the United States: Promise and Performance*, 3rd ed. Chicago: Rand McNally.

Dean, John. 2006. *Conservatives without Conscience*. New York: Penguin Group.

Delli Carpini, Michael X. and Scott Keeter. 1996. *What Americans Know about Politics and Why It Matters*. New Haven, CT: Yale University Press.

Democratic National Committee. 1992. *Democratic Party Platform of 1992: A New Covenant with the American People*. Available online at http://www.presidency.ucsb.edu/ws/index.php?pid=29610. Accessed: July 1, 2008.

  1996. "*Democratic Party Platform of 1996: Today's Democratic Party: Meeting America's Challenges, Protecting America's Values*. Available online at http://www.presidency.ucsb.edu/ws/index.php?pid=29611. Accessed: July 1, 2008.

DiMaggio, Paul, John Evans, and Bethany Bryson. 1996. "Have Americans' Social Attitudes Become More Polarized?" *American Journal of Sociology*, 102: 690–755.

Dionne, E.J. 1991. *Why Americans Hate Politics*. New York: Simon and Schuster.

Dorris, John. 1999. "Antidiscrimination Laws in local Government: Analysis of Municipal Lesbian and Gay Public Employment." In Ellen Riggle and Barry Tadlock, eds., *Gays and Lesbians in the Democratic Process*. New York: Columbia University Press.

Doty, Richard, Bill Peterson, and David Winter. 1991. "Threat and Authoritarianism in the United States, 1978–1987," *Journal of Personality and Social Psychology* 61 (4): 629–640.

Dow, Jay K. 1999. "Voter Choice in the 1995 French Presidential Election." *Political Behavior* 21: 305–324.

Downs, Anthony. 1957. *An Economic Theory of Voting*. New York: Harper and Row.

Duckitt, J. 2001. "A Cognitive-Motivational Theory of Ideology and Prejudice." In M. P. Zanna ed. *Advances in Experimental Social Psychology*. San Diego: Academic Press, 33: 41–113.

Duckitt, John. 1989. "Authoritarianism and Group Identification: A New View of an Old Construct." *Political Psychology* 10: 63–84.

    2003. "Prejudice and Iintergroup Hostility." In D. Sears, L. Huddy, and R. Jervis, eds., *Oxford Handbook of Political Psychology*. Oxford: Oxford University Press.

    1992. *The Social Psychology of Prejudice*. New York: Praeger Press.

Eckhardt, William and Allen G. Newcombe. 1969. "Militarism, Personality, and Other Social Attitudes." *Journal of Conflict Resolution* 13: 210–219.

Edsall, Thomas Byrne and Mary D. Edsall. 1991. *Chain Reaction: The Impact of Race, Rights, and Taxes on American Politics*. New York: Norton.

Ellis, Christopher and James Stimson. 2007. "On Symbolic Conservatism in America." Paper presented at the American Political Science Association Meeting, Chicago, Illinois, September 1.

Erikson, Robert S., Michael B. MacKuen, and James A. Stimson. 2002. *Macro Polity*. Cambridge: Cambridge University Press.

Espenshade, Thomas J. and Charles A. Calhoun. 1993. "An Analysis of Public Opinion toward Undocumented Immigration." *Population Research and Policy Review* 12: 189–224.

Evans, John H. 2003. "Have Americans' Attitudes Become More Polarized? – An Update," *Social Science Quarterly*, 84: 71–90.

Feldman, Stanley. 2003. "Values, Ideology, and the Structure of Political Attitudes." In D. O. Sears, L. Huddy, and R. Jervis eds. *Oxford Handbook of Political Psychology*. New York: Oxford University Press.

Feldman, Stanley and Karen Stenner. 1997. "Perceived Threat and Authoritarianism." *Political Psychology* 18: 741–70.

Ferguson, Thomas. 1994. *Golden Rule: The Investment Theory of Party Competition and the Logic of Money-Driven Political Systems*. Chicago: University of Chicago Press.

Finckenauer, James. 1978. "Crime as a National Political Issue: 1964–76," *Crime and Delinquency* 24 (1): 13–27.

Fiorina, Morris, Samuel J. Abrams, and Jeremy C. Pope. 2004. *Culture War? The Myth of Polarized America*. New York: Pearson Longman.

    2006. *Culture War? The Myth of Polarized America, 2nd ed.* New York: Pearson Longman.

Fiorina, Morris P. and Matthew S. Levendusky. 2006. "Disconnected: The Political Class versus the People." In Pietro S. Nivola and David W. Brady, eds., *Red and Blue Nation? Characteristics and Causes of America's Polarized Politics, Vol. 1*. Washington, DC: Brookings Institution Press, pp. 49–57.

First Amendment Center. 2004. *State of the First Amendment, 2004*. Nashville: First Amendment Center.

Frankovic, Kathy. 2007. "Immigration a Top Issue – For GOP Only." *CBS News*. Available online at http://www.cbsnews.com/stories/2007/05/30/opinion/pollpositions/main2866834.shtml. Accessed May 15, 2008.

Gabennesch, Howard. 1972. "Authoritarianism as World View." *American Journal of Sociology* 77: 857–875.

Geer, John G. 2006. *In Defense of Negativity: Attack Ads in Presidential Campaigns.* Chicago: University of Chicago Press.

Gibson, James L. 1986. "Pluralistic Intolerance and Political Repression during the McCarthy Red Scare." *American Politics Quarterly* 14: 267–293.

1992. "The Political Consequences of Intolerance: Cultural Conformity and Political Freedom." *American Political Science Review* 86: 338–356.

1988. "Political Intolerance and Political Repression during the McCarthy Red Scare." *American Political Science Review* 82: 511–529.

Gibson, James L. and Richard D. Bingham. 1982. "On the Conceptualization and Measurement of Political Tolerance." *American Political Science Review* 76: 603–620.

Gibson, James L. 1989. "The Structure of Attitudinal Tolerance." *British Journal of Political Science* 19: 562–570.

Gilens, Martin. 1999. *Why Americans Hate Welfare: Race, Media, and the Politics of Antipoverty Policy.* Chicago: University of Chicago Press.

Gimpel, James G. and James R. EdwardsJr. 1999. *The Congressional Politics of Immigration Reform.* Boston: Allyn and Bacon.

Goren, Paul. 2002. "Character Weakness, Partisan Bias, and Presidential Evaluation." *American Journal of Political Science* 46: 627–641.

Graham, Fred. 1972. "The Supreme Court, 5–4, Bars Death Penalty as It Currently Exists under Present Statutes." *New York Times*, June 30, p. 1.

Green, Donald, Bradley Palmquist, and Eric Schickler. 2002. *Partisan Hearts and Minds: Political Parties and the Social Identities of Voters.* New Haven, CT: Yale University Press.

Green, John C., Mark Rozell, and Clyde Wilcox, eds. 2006. *The Values Campaign? The Christian Right and the 2004 Elections.* Washington, DC: Georgetown University Press.

Greenhouse, Linda. 2008. "Over Guantanamo, Justices Come under Election-Year Spotlight." *New York Times*, June 14, p. A10.

Greenstein, Fred I. 1965. "Personality and Political Socialization: The Theories of Authoritarian and Democratic Character." *Annals of the American Academy of Political and Social Science* 361: 81–95.

Greenwald, Glenn. 2008. *Great American Hypocrites: Toppling the Big Myths of Republican Politics.* New York: Crown Publishing Group.

Greider, William. 1992. *Who Will Tell the People – The Breakdown of American Democracy.* New York: Simon and Schuster.

Haider-Markel, Donald P. and Kenneth J. Meier. 1996. "The Politics of Gay and Lesbian Rights: Expanding the Scope of Conflict." *Journal of Politics* 58: 332–349.

Haidt, Jonathan. 2008. "Morality." *Perspectives on Psychological Science* 3: 65–72.

Hetherington, Marc J. Forthcoming. "Putting Polarization in Perspective." *British Journal of Political Science.*

2001. "Resurgent Mass Partisanship: The Role of Elite Polarization." *American Political Science Review* 95: 619–631.

2008. "Turned Off or Turned On? The Effects of Polarization on Political Participation, Engagement, and Representation." In Pietro S. Nivola and David W. Brady, eds., *Red and Blue Nation? Characteristics and Causes of America's Polarized Politics,* Vol. 2. Washington, DC: Brookings Institution Press.

2005. *Why Trust Matters: Declining Political Trust and the Demise of American Liberalism.* Princeton, NJ: Princeton University Press.

Hetherington, Marc J. and William J. Keefe. 2007. *Parties, Politics, and Public Policy in America*, 10th ed. Washington: CQ Press.

Hetherington, Marc J. and Thomas Nelson. 2003. "Anatomy of a Rally Effect: George W. Bush and the War on Terrorism." *PS: Political Science and Politics* 36: 37–42.

Hetherington, Marc J. and Jonathan Weiler. 2005. "Authoritarianism and Political Choice." Paper presented at the Annual Meeting of the Midwest Political Science Association. April 7–10.

Hillygus, D. Sunshine and Todd Shields. 2008. *The Persuadable Voter: Wedge Issues in Presidential Campaigns*. Princeton, NJ: Princeton University Press.

Hofstadter, Richard. 1955. *Anti-Intellectualism in American Life*. New York: Knopf.

  1964. "The Paranoid Style in American Politics." *Harper's Magazine*, November, 77–86.

Huckfeldt, Robert R. and Carol Kohfeld. 1989. *Race and the Decline of Class in American Politics*. Urbana: University of Illinois Press.

Huddy, Leonie, Stanley Feldman, Charles Taber, and Gallya Lahav. 2005. "Threat, Anxiety, and Support of Anti-Terrorism Policies." *American Journal of Political Science* 49: 610–625.

Hunter, James Davison. 1994. *Before the Shooting Begins: Searching for Democracy in America's Culture War, Dialogue on Values and American Public Life*. New York: Free Press.

  1991. *Culture Wars: The Struggle to Define America*. New York: Basic Books.

Hunter, James Davidson and Alan Wolfe. 2006. *Is There a Culture War? A Dialogue on Values and American Public Life*. Washington, DC: Brookings Institution Press.

Hurwitz, Jon and Mark Peffley. 1997. "Public Perceptions of Race and Crime: The Role of Racial Stereotypes." *American Journal of Political Science* 41: 375–401.

Hyman, Herbert and Paul B. Sheatsley. 1954. "The Authoritarian Personality – A Methodological Critique." In R. Christie and M. Jahoda eds. *Studies in the Scope and Method of "The Authoritarian Personality."* Glencoe, IL: Free Press, 1954.

Jackman, Simon and Lynn Vavreck. 2008. "Survey Analysis in Real Time." Paper presented at the Center for the Study of Democratic Politics Conference on the American Electoral Process, Princeton University, May 1.

Jacobson, Gary. 2006. "Disconnected or Joined at the Hip? Part II." In Pietro S. Nivola and David W. Brady, eds., *Red and Blue Nation?: Characteristics and Causes of America's Polarized Politics*, Vol. 1. Washington, DC: Brookings Institution Press, pp. 85–94.

  2007. *Divider, Not a Uniter: George W. Bush and the American People*. New York: Longman.

Jamieson, Kathleen Hall. 1992. *Dirty Politics: Deception, Distraction, and Democracy*. New York: Oxford University Press.

Johnson, David K. 2004. *The Lavender Scare: The Cold War Persecution of Gays and Lesbians in the Federal Government*. Chicago: University of Chicago Press.

Jost, John T., Jack Glaser, Arie W. Kruglanski, and Frank J. Sulloway. 2003. "Political Conservatism as Motivated Social Cognition." *Psychological Bulletin* 129: 339–375.

Judis, John B. 2008. "The Next McGovern?" *The New Republic*. April 23. Available online at http://www.tnr.com/politics/story.html?id=ec466d61-a900-414c-8daf-16ff27ccf85c.

Judis, John B. and Ruy Teixeira. 2002. *The Emerging Democratic Majority*. New York: Scribner.

Kellstedt, Lyman A., John C. Green, James L. Guth, and Corwin E. Smidt. 1994. "Religious Voting Blocs in the 1992 Election: The Year of the Evangelical?" *Sociology of Religion* 55: 307–326.

Key, V.O. 1966. *The Responsible Electorate: Rationality in Presidential Voting, 1936–1960.* Cambridge, MA: Harvard University Press.

Kinder, Donald R. and Lynn M. Sanders. 1996. *Divided by Color: Racial Politics and Democratic Ideals.* Chicago: University of Chicago Press.

Kinder, Donald R. and David O. Sears. 1981. "Prejudice and Politics: Symbolic Racism versus Racial Threats to the Good Life." *Journal of Personality and Social Psychology* 40: 414–431.

Klinkner, Philip A. 2006. "Mr. Bush's War: Foreign Policy in the 2004 Election." *Presidential Studies Quarterly* 36: 281–296.

Kohlberg, Lawrence. 1969. "Stage and Sequence: The Cognitive-Developmental Approach to Socialization." In D.A. Goslin, ed., *Handbook of Socialization Theory and Research.* Chicago: Rand McNally.

Kohn, Melvin and Carmi Schooler. 1983. *Work and Personality: An Enquiry into the Impact of Social Stratification.* New York: Ablex.

Kolbert, Elizabeth. 2005. "Firebrand." *New Yorker Magazine*, November 7. Available online at http://www.newyorker.com/archive/2005/11/07/051107crbo_books?currentPage=all. Accessed July 14, 2008.

Krehbiel, Keith. 1998. *Pivotal Politics: A Theory of U.S. Lawmaking.* Chicago: University of Chicago Press.

Krosnick, Jonathan A. 1991. "The Stability of Political Preferences: Comparisons of Symbolic and Non-Symbolic Attitudes." *American Journal of Political Science* 35: 547–576.

Kruglanski, Arie W., Antonio Pierro, Lucia Mannetti, and Eraldo De Grada. 2006. "Groups as Epistemic Providers: Need for Closure and the Unfolding of Group-Centrism." *Psychological Review* 113: 84–100.

Kuklinski, James H. and Norman L. Hurley. 1994. "On Hearing and Interpreting Political Messages: A Cautionary Tale of Citizen Cue-Taking." *Journal of Politics* 56: 729–751.

Lakoff, George. 1996. *Moral Politics: How Liberals and Conservatives Think.* Chicago: University of Chicago Press.

Lane, Robert E. 1962. *Political Ideology: Why the Political Common Man Believes What He Does.* New York: Free Press.

Lasch, Christopher. 1977. *Haven in a Heartless World: The Family Besieged.* New York: Basic Books.

Lassiter, Matthew. 2007. *The Silent Majority: Suburban Politics in the Sunbelt South.* Princeton, NJ: Princeton University Press.

Lavine, H., Diana Burgess, Mark Snyder, John Transue, John L. Sullivan, Beth Haney, and Stephen H. Wagner. (1999). "Threat, Authoritarianism, and Voting: An Investigation of Personality and Persuasion." *Personality and Social Psychology Bulletin* 25: 337–347.

Lavine, Howard, Milton Lodge, and Kate Freitas. 2005. "Threat, Authoritarianism, and Selective Exposure to Information." *Political Psychology* 26: 219–244.

Layman, Geoffrey C. 1999. "Culture Wars in the American Party System: Religious and Cultural Change among Partisan Activists since 1972." *American Politics Quarterly* 27: 89–121.

Layman, Geoffrey. 2001. *The Great Divide: Religious and Cultural Conflict in American Party Politics*. New York: Columbia University Press.

Layman, Geoffrey C. and Thomas M. Carsey. 2002. "Party Polarization and 'Conflict Extension' in the American Electorate." *American Journal of Political Science* 46: 786–802.

1998. "Why Do Party Activists Convert?: An Analysis of Individual Change on the Abortion Issue." *Political Research Quarterly* 51: 723–749.

Leal, David L., Matt A. Barreto, Jongho Lee, and Rodolfo O. de la Garza. "The Latino Vote in the 2004 Election." *PS: Political Science and Politics* 38: 41–49.

Leege, David C., Kenneth D. Wald, Brian S. Krueger, and Paul D. Mueller. 2002. *The Politics of Cultural Differences: Social Change and Voter Mobilization Strategies in the Post-New Deal Period*. Princeton, NJ: Princeton University Press.

Levendusky, Matthew. Forthcoming. *Choosing Sides: The Rise of Liberal Democrats and Conservative Republicans*. Chicago: University of Chicago Press.

Lieberman, Joseph I. 2008. "Democrats and Our Enemies." *Wall Street Journal*, May 21, 2008, p. A19.

Limbaugh, Rush. 2008. *The Rush Limbaugh Show*. March 21. Transcript.

Lindaman, Kara and Donald Haider-Markel. 2002. "Issue Evolution, Political Parties and the Culture Wars." *Political Research Quarterly* 55 (1): 91–110.

Lipset, Seymour Martin. 1959. "Democracy and Working-Class Authoritarianism." *American Sociological Review* 24: 482–501.

1964. "Religion and Politics in the American Past and Present." In Robert lee and Martin E. Marty, eds., *Religion and Social Conflict*. New York: Oxford University Press, pp. 69–126.

Loftus, Jeni. 2001. "America's Liberalization in Attitudes towards Homosexuality, 1973–1998." *American Sociological Review* 66: 762–782.

Luskin, Robert C. 1987. "Measuring Political Sophistication." *American Journal of Political Science* 31: 856–899.

Mansbridge, Jane. 1986. *Why We Lost the ERA*. Chicago: University of Chicago Press.

Martin, James G. 1964. *The Tolerant Personality*. Detroit: Wayne State University Press.

McCann, Stewart. 1997. "Threatening Times, Strong Presidential Popular Vote Winners, and the Victory Margin, 1824–1964." *Journal of Personality and Social Psychology* 73: 160–170.

McCarty, Nolan, Keith T. Poole, and Howard Rosenthal. 2006. *Polarized America: The Dance of Ideology and Unequal Riches*. Cambridge, MA: MIT Press.

McClosky, Herbert. 1964. "Consensus and Ideology in American Politics." *American Political Science Review* 58: 316–382.

McClosky, Herbert and Alida Brill. 1983. *Dimensions of Tolerance: What Americans Think about Civil Liberties*. New York: Russell Sage.

McClosky, Herbert and John D. Zaller. 1984. *The American Ethos: Public Attitudes toward Democracy and Capitalism*. Cambridge, MA: Harvard University Press.

McGirr, Lisa. 2002. *Suburban Warriors: The Origins of the New American Right*. Princeton, NJ: Princeton University Press.

McIntyre, Thomas J. 1979. *The Fear Brokers*. New York: Pilgrim Press.

Mendelberg, Tali. 2001. *The Race Card: Campaign Strategy, Implicit Messages, and the Norm of Equality*. Princeton, NJ: Princeton University Press.

Miga, Andrew. 2008. "Lieberman Irks Democrats by Criticizing Obama." *Washington Post*, June 15.

Miller, Arthur H., Christopher Wlezien, and Anne Hildreth. 1991. "A Reference Group Theory of Partisan Coalitions." *Journal of Politics* 53: 1134–1149.

Miller, Gary and Norman Schofield. 2003. "Activists and Party Realignment in the United States." *American Political Science Review* 97: 245–260.

Miller, James. 2001. *Democracy Is in the Streets: From Port Huron to the Siege of Chicago*. Cambridge, MA: Harvard University Press.

Monogan, James. 2007. "Issue Evolution and Public Opinion on Immigration." Paper Presented at the Annual Meeting of the Midwest Political Science Association, April 12.

Morolla, Jennifer and Elizabeth Zechmeister. Forthcoming. *Democracy under Stress: Crises, Evaluations and Behavior*.

Mudde, Cas. 2007. *Populist Radical Right Parties in Europe*. Cambridge: Cambridge University Press.

Mueller, John. 1988. "Trends in Political Tolerance." *Public Opinion Quarterly* 52: 1–25.

Murray, Shailagh. 2005. "Conservatives Split in Debate on Curbing Illegal Immigration." *Washington Pos*, March 25, 2005, p. A2.

Mutz, Diana C. and Bryon Reeves. 2005. "The New Videomalaise: Effects of Televised Incivility on Political Trust." *American Political Science Review* 99: 1–15.

Nelson, Michael. 2005. "How the GOP Conquered the South." *Chronicle of Higher Education*, October 21. Available online at http://chronicle.com/free/v52/i09/09b01401.htm. Accessed: April 15, 2008.

Nicholson, Stephen P. 2005. *Voting the Agenda: Candidates, Elections, and Ballot Propositions*. Princeton, NJ: Princeton University Press.

Obama, Barack. 2007. "Comments to the Council on Global Affairs." April 23. Transcript.

Olbermann, Keith. 2008. *Countdown with Keith Olberman*. MSNBC. March 18. Transcript.

Oppenheimer, Bruce I. and Marc J. Hetherington. 2006. "Running on Empty: Coalition Building Constraints in the U.S. Senate 1970s and 2000s." Paper presented at the Conference on Party Effects in the United States Senate, Duke University, April 7–9.

Overby, L. Marvin and Jay Barth. 2006. "Radio Advertising in American Political Campaigns: The Persistence, Importance and Effects of Narrowcasting." *American Political Research* 34: 451–478.

Oxley, Douglas R., Kevin B. Smith, John R. Alford, Matthew V. Hibbing, Jennifer L. Miller, Mario Scalora, Peter K. Hatemi, and John R. Hibbing. 2008. "Political Attitudes Vary with Physiological Traits." *Science* 321 (5896): 1667–1670.

Packer, George. 2008. "The Fall of Conservatism – Have Republicans Run Out of Ideas?" *New Yorker Magazine*. May 26.

Page, Benjamin I. and Robert Y. Shapiro. 1983. "Effects of Public Opinion on Policy." *American Political Science Review* 77: 175–190.

Page, Benjamin I., Robert Y. Shapiro, and Glenn R. Dempsey. 1987. "What Moves Public Opinion." *American Political Science Review* 81: 23–43.

Patterson, Thomas P. 1993. *Out of Order*. New York: Knopf.

Peffley, Mark and Jon Hurwitz. 2002. "The Racial Components of 'Race-Neutral' Crime Policy Attitudes." *Political Psychology* 23: 59–75.

Peffley, Mark, Jon Hurwitz, and Paul Sniderman. 1997. "Racial Stereotypes and Whites' Political Views of Blacks in the Context of Welfare and Crime." *American Journal of Political Science* 41: 30–60.

Perlstein, Rick. 2001. *Barry Goldwater and the Unmaking of the American Consensus.* New York: Hill and Wang.

    2008. *Nixonland: The Rise of a President and the Fracturing of America.* New York: Scribner.

Perrin, Andrew J. 2005. "National Threat and Political Culture: Authoritarianism, Antiauthoritarianism, and the September 11 Attacks." *Political Psychology* 26: 167–194.

Peterson, Bill, Richard Doty, and David Winter. 1993. "Authoritarianism and Attitudes toward Contemporary Social Issues." *Personality and Social Psychology Bulletin* 19 (2): 174–184.

Pew Hispanic Center. 2005. "A Statistical Portrait of Hispanics at Mid-Decade." Pew Research Center. Available online at http://pewhispanic.org/reports/middecade/.

Piaget, Jean. 1965. *The Moral Judgment of the Child.* New York: Free Press. (Original work published in 1932)

Poole, Keith, Howard Rosenthal, and Nolan McCarty. 2006. *Polarized America: The Dance of Ideology and Unequal Riches.* Cambridge MA: MIT Press.

Powell, Colin. 2007. Interview. *Meet the Press with Tim Russert.* June 10. Transcript.

Price, Vincent and Mei-Ling Hsu. 1992. "Public Opinion about AIDS Policies: The Role of Misinformation and Attitudes toward Homosexuals." *Public Opinion Quarterly* 56: 29–52.

Prior, Markus. 2003. "Any Good News in Soft News? The Impact of Soft News Preference on Political Knowledge." *Political Communication* 20: 149–171.

Putnam, Robert. 2000. *Bowling Alone: The Collapse and Revival of American Community.* New York: Simon and Schuster.

Putz, David W. 2002. "Partisan Conversion in the 1990s: Ideological Realignment Meets Measurement Theory." *Journal of Politics* 64: 1199–1209.

Rabinowitz, George and Stuart McDonald. 1989. "A Directional Theory of Issue Voting." *American Political Science Review* 83: 93–122.

Raden, David. 1999. "Is Anti-Semitism Currently Part of an Authoritarian Attitude Syndrome?" *Political Psychology* 20: 323–343.

Ray, John J. 1976. "Do Authoritarians Hold Authoritarian Attitudes?" *Human Relations* 29: 307–325.

    1983. "Reviving the Problem of Acquiescent Response Set." *Journal of Social Psychology* 121: 81–96.

Republican National Committee. 1976. *Republican Party Platform of 1976.* Available online at http://www.presidency.ucsb.edu/ws/index.php?pid=25843. Accessed June 24, 2008.

    1980. *Republican Party Platform of 1980.* Available online at http://www.presidency.ucsb.edu/showplatforms.php?platindex=R1980. Accessed June 24, 2008.

    1984. *Republican Party Platform of 1984..* Available online at http://www.presidency.ucsb.edu/ws/index.php?pid=25845. Accessed June 24, 2008.

    2004. *2004 Republican Party Platform: A Safer World and a More Hopeful America.* Available online at http://www.presidency.ucsb.edu/ws/index.php?pid=25850. Accessed June 24, 2008.

Rohde, David W. 1991. *Parties and Leaders in Postreform House*. Chicago: University of Chicago Press.

Rokeach, Milton. 1960. *The Open and Closed Mind*. New York: Basic Books.

Sales, Stephen M. 1972. "Economic Threat as a Determinant of Conversion Rates to Authoritarian and Nonauthoritarian Churches." *Journal of Personality and Social Psychology* 23: 420–428.

1973. "Threat as a Factor in Authoritarianism: An Analysis of Archival Data." *Journal of Personality and Social Psychology* 28: 44–57.

Sanbonmatsu, Kira. 2006. *Where Women Run: Gender and Party in the American States.*, Ann Arbor: University of Michigan Press.

Sanchez, Gabriel. 2006. "The Role of Group Consciousness in Latino Public Opinion." *Political Research Quarterly* 59: 435–446.

Schaller, Thomas F. 2006. *Whistling Past Dixie: How Democrats Can Win without the South*. New York: Simon and Schuster.

Schuman, Howard, Lawrence D. Bobo, and Maria Krysan. 1992. "Authoritarianism in the General Population: The Education Interaction Hypothesis." *Social Psychology Quarterly* 55: 379–387.

Seelye, Katherine. 1995. "Anti-Crime Bill as Political Dispute: President and G.O. P. Define the Issue." *New York Times*, February 21, p. A16.

Shaw, Daron R. 1999. "The Effect of TV Ads and Candidate Appearances on Statewide Presidential Votes, 1988–1996." *American Political Science Review* 93: 345–361.

Shils, Edward A. 1954. "Authoritarianism: Right and Left." In R. Christie and M. Jahoda eds. *Studies in the Scope and Method of "The Authoritarian Personality"* Glencoe: Free Press, pp. 24–29.

Shilts, Randy. 1987. *And the Band Played On: Politics, People and the AIDS Epidemic*. New York: St. Martin's Press.

Sniderman, Paul M., Joseph F. Fletcher, Peter H. Russell, and Philip E. Tetlock. 1996. *The Clash of Civil Rights: Liberty, Equality, and Legitimacy in Pluralist Democracy*. New Haven, CT: Yale University Press.

Sniderman, Paul M., Joseph F. Fletcher, Peter H. Russell, Philip E. Tetlock, and Brian J. Gaines. 1991. "The Fallacy of Democratic Elitism: Elite Competition and Commitment to Civil Liberties." *British Journal of Political Science* 21: 349–370.

Sniderman, Paul M., Louk Hagendoorn, and Markus Prior. 2004. "Predispositional Factors and Situational Triggers: Exclusionary Reactions to Immigrant Minorities." *American Political Science Review* 98: 35–50.

Sniderman, Paul and Thomas Piazza. 1993. *The Scar of Race*. Cambridge, MA: Harvard University Press.

Stanley Harold W. and Richard G. Niemi. 2006. "Partisanship, Party Coalitions, and Group Support, 1952–2004." *Presidential Studies Quarterly* 36: 172–188.

Stellmacher, Jost and Thomas Petzel. 2005. "Authoritarianism as Group Phenomenon." *Political Psychology* 26: 245–274.

Stenner, Karen. 2005. *The Authoritarian Dynamic*. Cambridge: Cambridge University Press.

Stipp, Horst and Dennis Kerr. 1989. "Determinants of Public Opinion about AIDS." *Public Opinion Quarterly* 53: 98–106.

Stonecash, Jeffrey M. 2000. *Class and Party in American Politics* Boulder, CO: Westview Press.

Stouffer, Samuel A. 1955. *Communism, Conformity, and Civil Liberties*. Garden City, NJ: Doubleday.

Strassell, Kimberly A. 2003. "Messing with Texas: A Dixie Chick Regrets Anti-Bush Remark." *Wall Street Journal*, March 20. Online edition. Available at http://www.opinionjournal.com/columnists/kstrassel/?id=110003223.

Sullivan, John L., George E. Marcus, Stanley Feldman, and James E. Piereson. 1981. "The Sources of Political Tolerance." *American Political Science Review* 75: 92–106.

Sullivan, John L., James E. Piereson, and George E. Marcus. 1979. "An Alternative Conceptualization of Political Tolerance: Illusory Increases 1950s–1970s." *American Political Science Review* 73: 781–794.

Sullivan, John L., James Piereson, and George E. Marcus. 1982 *Political Tolerance and American Democracy*. Chicago: University of Chicago Press.

Sullivan, John L. and John E. Transue. 1999. "The Psychological Underpinnings of Democracy: A Selective Review of Research on Political Tolerance, Interpersonal Trust, and Social Capital." *Annual Review of Psychology* 50: 625–650.

Sullivan, John L., Pat Walsh, Michal Shamir, David G. Barnum, and James L. Gibson. 1993. "Why Politicians Are More Tolerant: Selective Recruitment and Socialization among Political Elites in Britain, Israel, New Zealand, and the United States." *British Journal of Political Science* 23: 51–76.

Sundquist, James L. 1983. *The Dynamics of the Party System: Alignment and Realignment of Political Parties in the United States*. Washington, DC: Brookings Institution Press.

Thompson, Erik, Robert J. Roman, Gordon B. Moskowitz, Shelly Chaiken, and John A. Bargh. 1994. "Accuracy Motivation Attenuates Covert Priming: The Systematic Reprocessing of Social Information." *Journal of Personality and Social Psychology* 66: 474–489.

Tichenor, Daniel J. 1994. "The Politics of Immigration Reform in the United States, 1981–1990." *Polity* 26: 333–362.

Tomasky, Michael. 2004. "The Pathetic Truth." *The American Prospect*, September 13. Available online at http://www.prospect.org/cs/articles?articleId=8490 Accessed: November 10, 2007.

Toobin, Jeffrey. 2007. *The Nine: Inside the Secret World of the Supreme Court*. New York: Doubleday.

Wald, Kenneth D. 1987. *Religion and Politics in the United States*. New York: St. Martin's Press.

Waldman, Paul. 2008. "Fear and Loathing in Prime Time." Report prepared for Media Matters. Available online at http://mediamattersaction.org/reports/fearandloathing/online_version.

Walker, Samuel. 1978. "Reexaming the President's Crime Commission," *Crime and Delinquency*, 24 (1): 1–12.

Wilcox, Clyde. 2000. *Onward Christian Soldiers: The Religious Right in American Politics*, 2nd ed. Boulder, CO: Westview.

Wilcox, Clyde and Ted Jelen. 1990. "Evangelicals and Political Tolerance." *American Politics Quarterly* 18: 25–46.

Wilcox, Clyde and Carin Larson. 2006. *Onward Christian Soldiers? The Religious Right in American Politics*, 3rd ed. Boulder, CO: Westview Press.

Wolbrecht, Christina. 2000. *The Politics of Women's Rights*. Princeton, NJ: Princeton University Press.

Wolfe, Alan. 2005. "'The Authoritarian Personality' Revisited." *Chronicle of Higher Education.* October 7, p. B12.

Wuthnow, Robert. 1988. *The Restructuring of American Religion: Society and Faith since World War II.* Princeton, NJ: Princeton University Press.

Yang, Alan S. 1997. "Attitudes toward Homosexuality." *Public Opinion Quarterly* 61: 477–507.

Zaller, John R. 1992. *The Nature and Origins of Mass Opinion.* Cambridge, England: Cambridge University Press.

Index